GRATUITOUS SUFFERING AND THE PROBLEM OF EVIL

Suffering that is not coupled with any redeeming good is one of our world's more troubling, apparent glitches. It is particularly vexing for any theist who believes that the world was created by a supremely morally good, knowledgeable, and powerful god. *Gratuitous Suffering and the Problem of Evil: A Comprehensive Introduction* is among the first book-length discussions of theistic approaches to this issue. Bryan Frances' lucid and jargon-free analyses of a variety of possible responses to the problem of gratuitous suffering will provide serious students or general readers much material with which to begin an extended contemplation of this ancient and contemporary concern.

The perfect size and scope for an introductory philosophy class' discussion of the problem of evil and suffering, and deliberately crafted to be approachable by all interested readers, *Gratuitous Suffering and the Problem of Evil* is philosophy doing what it does best: serious, engaged, rigorous explorations of even the darkest truths.

The book offers many useful pedagogical features, including chapter overviews and summaries, and annotated suggested readings.

Bryan Frances is Associate Professor of Philosophy at Fordham University.

GRATUITOUS SUFFERING AND THE PROBLEM OF EVIL

A Comprehensive Introduction

Bryan Frances

Routledge
Taylor & Francis Group

NEW YORK AND LONDON

First published 2013
by Routledge
711 Third Avenue, New York, NY 10017

Simultaneously published in the UK
by Routledge
2 Park Square, Milton Park, Abingdon, Oxon OX14 4RN

Routledge is an imprint of the Taylor & Francis Group, an informa business

© 2013 Taylor & Francis

Library of Congress Cataloging in Publication Data
Frances, Bryan.
Gratuitous suffering and the problem of evil : a comprehensive
introduction / by Bryan Frances.
    pages cm
Includes bibliographical references and index.
1. Suffering. 2. Suffering—Philosophy. 3. Suffering—Religious aspects.
4. Good and evil—Philosophy. 5. Good and evil—Religious aspects.
6. Suffering of God. I. Title.
B105.S79F73 2013
214—dc23   2012049923

ISBN: 978-0-415-66295-6 (hbk)
ISBN: 978-0-415-66296-3 (pbk)
ISBN: 978-0-203-07177-9 (ebk)

Typeset in Bembo
by Cenveo Publisher Services

For my father Ronald Gordon Stewart

CONTENTS

1

INTRODUCTION

The Need for Trustworthiness and Competence

When I was all but finished writing this book I went on vacation with my wife to the White Mountains of New Hampshire. After returning from a hike up (and down) Mount Whiteface, my wife and I stopped in a small strip mall. She needed to get something from a knitting shop there. In order to pass the time, I strolled into a small bookshop a couple stores away. I came across a book I had never heard of: Timothy Keller's *The Reason for God*. I learned that Keller's book spent a considerable time on the *New York Times* best seller list, which is nothing to sneeze at. I also saw that in the second chapter of his book he takes on the "Problem of Evil," which can be introduced with the question "Why does the supremely good, knowledgeable, and powerful God permit such horrific suffering, especially that experienced by, and ruinous of, so many innocent creatures?" Keller thinks this is a pretty easy topic to tackle. He goes so far as to say this, which I initially found to be an extraordinary claim:

> [T]he effort to demonstrate that evil disproves the existence of God "is now acknowledged on (almost) all sides to be completely bankrupt." Why?

The section immediately following this passage is titled "Evil and Suffering Isn't Evidence *Against* God." What the hell? Here I had just about finished writing a book discussing these issues, and I had definitely concluded that certain classes of suffering do indeed amount to significant evidence against God, even though I also thought the evidence in question is not conclusive. More importantly, I also knew perfectly well that a great many people who have thoroughly investigated the topic believe that the evidence *is* conclusive.

Notice that Keller is quoting someone in that passage. So, I looked at Keller's footnote that identifies the author of the quote. It's William Alston, the rightfully distinguished philosopher, and the quote is from an article of his from 1991.[1] Then I looked up the Alston passage that Keller was quoting. That's when things got interesting.

First off, Keller misquotes Alston in a telling way, which is a sign that things might not be as they seem. Where Keller has

> [T]he effort to demonstrate that evil disproves the existence of God "is now acknowledged on (almost) all sides to be *completely* bankrupt" [my italics]

Alston has

> It is now acknowledged on (almost) all sides that the logical argument is bankrupt ...

What Alston means by "the logical argument" I'll get to in a moment. For now, notice that Keller has inserted "completely" into Alston's sentence. Did he *intentionally* alter Alston's statement because the original was not extreme enough to suit Keller's purposes? That would be rank deception. Or did Keller make a slightly more honest mistake in the sense that Keller believes the logical argument—which says that any suffering at all is logically incompatible with God's existence—is completely bankrupt, and so just unconsciously projected that view on to Alston? That's not as bad as intentional deception, but pretty bad. Either way, Keller doesn't look too trustworthy.[2] It doesn't strike me as at all likely that Keller *just happened* to insert a word that would suit his purposes perfectly. It wasn't a boo boo, as unintentionally altering an "is" to an "it" might be.

But matters are much worse than that slip by Keller; you certainly would not be reading about Keller here if that were the only problem with his chapter on the relation of God to suffering. Here is the full, unedited, paragraph from Alston (the first paragraph of his article):

> The recent outpouring of literature on the problem of evil has materially advanced the subject in several ways. In particular, a clear distinction has been made between the "logical" *argument against the existence of God* ("atheological argument") from evil, which attempts to show that evil is logically incompatible with the existence of God, and the "inductive" ("empirical," "probabilistic") argument, which contents itself with the claim that evil constitutes (sufficient) empirical evidence against the existence of God. It is now acknowledged on (almost) all sides that the logical argument is bankrupt, but the inductive argument is still very much alive and kicking.
>
> *(Alston 1991, 29; his emphasis)*

Alston is getting at the following very reasonable and usually acknowledged thoughts, which we will set out more fully in chapter 2. There are two "problems of evil" (actually, as we will see in chapter 2 there are three main ones, each with multiple variants, but that doesn't matter here). One, the "logical" one in Alston's terminology, is almost universally thought to be not at all convincing—precisely as Alston asserted. That argument sets out to show that the mere existence of suffering is logically incompatible with the existence of God—almost like how being naked is logically incompatible with having a dress on. The logical argument says that it's just plain impossible for God to create a world with any suffering in it: God's goodness, knowledge, and power are strictly incompatible with his creating a world with any suffering at all; hence, given the existence of suffering, such a God does not exist. But the second problem of evil, the "inductive" one, doesn't assert any such incompatibility or impossibility. It doesn't say that it's literally incompatible with God's goodness, knowledge, and power that he creates a universe with suffering. All it says is that the existence of suffering—in particular, certain instances of apparently pointless suffering—is powerful if not conclusive *evidence* against the existence of God. (These distinctions will become clear in chapter 2 below.) Furthermore, this second problem of evil, the inductive one, is very often thought to be quite good—and among the people who endorse it are a great many very intelligent, serious, fair-minded people who have studied the problem with a high degree of competence and care over a long period of time (years, sometimes decades). Not that you would learn that from Keller.

Instead, Keller presents his altered version of the Alston quote immediately before a discussion of the inductive problem (the section title of that discussion is "Evil and Suffering Isn't Evidence *Against* God," which is an explicit statement that the inductive problem of evil supplies no evidence against the existence of God). It is clear that Keller is attempting to persuade the reader that *the inductive problem* is "acknowledged on (almost) all sides" to be completely bankrupt—even though Alston's remark was about *the logical problem* alone. That is, he uses the Alston quote to get the reader to conclude "Wow! Philosophers and other intellectuals who have thought a lot about the Problem of Evil think that it's no good at all," which is utterly inaccurate with regard to the inductive problem, as anyone with the vaguest familiarity with philosophy would know full well. Indeed, the entirety of the Alston paragraph says exactly that. But Keller neglects to include that part of Alston's paragraph; we wouldn't want the reader to get the wrong (i.e., accurate) impression.

Further, in his "Evil and Suffering Isn't Evidence *Against* God" section, Keller attributes plainly fallacious reasoning to the many experts, including distinguished philosophers, who take suffering to be powerful evidence against the existence of God. The line of reasoning Keller attributes to others runs as follows: "We have been unable to find God's reasons for allowing extreme suffering; so he has no such reasons." But such a line of reasoning, contrary to Keller's claim, is in fact not put forward by those intelligent folks. Once again, we have the question of fraud, incompetence, or self-deception. The actual arguments used by philosophers who endorse the inductive argument will be presented in this book.

There are several possibilities for Keller's psychological state when writing this chapter of his book. For one, he may be "completely" uninformed: he may not understand the differences between the logical and inductive arguments (which I'll describe further in chapter 2); and he may be unaware of the highly respected status of the inductive argument *despite reading all this in the Alston paragraph he cites*. When it comes to the Problem of Evil, knowing the differences between the two arguments is like knowing arithmetic: it's pretty basic material. Alternatively, Keller may be intentionally deceiving his readers, if he knows how the two problems differ but deliberately uses the Alston remark about the logical problem alone to cleverly but dishonestly suggest that anyone who has examined the relevant matters thinks the Problem of Evil—including the inductive one discussed by Keller—is "completely" bankrupt. If this were true, then Keller would be just a fraud, plain and simple. However, a third possibility is that he may know, at least dimly, that the inductive and logical arguments are distinct and that the former is highly respected as providing excellent if inconclusive evidence that God doesn't exist, but he is deceiving *himself* about these facts, so desperate is he to reassure himself and his readers that the attacks on theism are baseless. Regardless of which characterization is right—clueless, fraudulent, or self-deceived—Keller is "completely" untrustworthy when it comes to the Problem of Evil.

If forced to guess, I would say very tentatively that Keller is mostly clueless with a touch of self-deception mixed in, and not a fraud (although the fact that he altered the Alston passage and then used it as a misleading segue to fit his own agenda makes me suspicious). I base this guess on two things: the discussion in the "Evil and Suffering Isn't Evidence *Against* God" section goes back and forth between the logical and inductive problems without any sign that Keller is aware that he is continually shifting gears; and his arguments *for* the existence of God, in his chapter 8, are so bad that if they were put in a freshman college essay they would be granted no more than a C+ grade, even in these days of grade inflation. Don't get me wrong: at least some of his chapter 8 arguments are *hints* at decent arguments for the existence of God, ones well worth taking seriously even if they are inconclusive. (We'll take a look at some of the worthy ones in chapter 4 of this book.) Now, perhaps Keller knows that his arguments for the existence of God, by themselves, are weak. That's perfectly fine: maybe all he wanted to do was offer a very brief introduction to those respectable arguments. Given space restrictions, there is nothing wrong with presenting crude versions of respectable arguments; it's all but unavoidable when working under certain space constraints. But then it's highly deceptive to not go on to state, unequivocally, that most experts who have examined those respectable arguments for many years have concluded that they are seriously flawed (again, we will see some of their reasons in chapter 4). Keller makes no such admission. So, as before, we have the question of cluelessness, fraud, or self-deception. In any case, Keller can't be trusted to present an informative, relatively unbiased, and accurate picture of what is currently known about the Problem of Evil. Regardless of his intentions or degree of competence, his presentation and discussion of the Problem of Evil is grossly inaccurate.

Despite all that, Keller's book was on the *New York Times* best seller list, as I mentioned earlier. It has also received a substantial number of awards and other accolades. Life is funny that way.

Keller's book is meant, in part, to be a response to some recent popular works by Sam Harris, Christopher Hitchens, Daniel Dennett, and Richard Dawkins that are highly critical of religion. By criticizing Keller I am not endorsing anything by those authors. In particular, the esteemed scientist Dawkins suffers from a malady that afflicts a surprisingly large percentage of outstanding scientists: the idea that he can succeed at philosophy because he has succeeded at science. It is easy to see how training in philosophy but not science would leave one utterly unprepared to do competent science—even if one is excellent at philosophy. What Dawkins misses is that the reverse is true as well: training in science but not philosophy leaves one utterly unprepared to do competent philosophy—regardless of how good one is at science. For instance, Dawkins thinks that "it has not escaped the notice of logicians that omniscience [roughly: knowing everything] and omnipotence [having all power] are mutually incompatible."[3] See how easy that was? We can prove that God doesn't exist in one long sentence: if God exists as traditionally conceived, with omnipotence and omniscience, then it's possible that a single thing has both characteristics; but that's impossible (as the logicians have noted); so, God doesn't exist as traditionally conceived. I studied logic for several years as a PhD student and yet know of no prominent logicians who have "noticed" this alleged incompatibility. I conclude that Dawkins is lying, grossly exaggerating, or more plausibly *simply making stuff up*. Do we really need to point out to Dawkins the many great logicians of the last century, for example, who are or were devout theists in spite of thinking quite hard about theism and logic? How about the contemporary philosopher and logician Saul Kripke, who is a committed theist and who started publishing groundbreaking papers in logic while attending high school in the 1950s?

Dawkins' overconfidence in his philosophical abilities doesn't end there. Many people are convinced of God's existence because they know that some intelligent and sincere people claim to have *perceived* God, actually experienced his presence. When addressing this topic Dawkins chooses to focus on the clearly mistaken and deluded of the folks who claim to have had such perceptions.

> One of the cleverer and more mature of my undergraduate contemporaries, who was deeply religious, went camping in the Scottish isles. In the middle of the night he and his girlfriend were woken in their tent by the voice of the devil – Satan himself; there could be no possible doubt: the voice was in every sense diabolical. My friend would never forget this horrifying experience, and it was one of the factors that later drove him to be ordained.

My youthful self was impressed by his story, and I recounted it to a gathering of zoologists relaxing in the Rose and Crown Inn, Oxford. Two of them happened to be experienced ornithologists, and they roared with laughter. "Manx Shearwater!" they shouted in delighted chorus. One of them added that the diabolical shrieks and cackles of this species have earned it, in various parts of the world and various languages, the local nickname "Devil Bird".

Many people believe in God because they believe they have seen a vision of him – or of an angel or a virgin in blue – with their own eyes. Or he speaks to them inside their heads. This argument from personal experience is the one that is most convincing to those who claim to have had one. But it is the least convincing to anyone else, and anyone knowledgeable about psychology.

You say you have experienced God directly? Well, some people have experienced a pink elephant, but that probably doesn't impress you. Peter Sutcliffe, the Yorkshire Ripper, distinctly heard the voice of Jesus telling him to kill women, and he was locked up for life … Religious experiences are different only in that the people who claim them are numerous.

(Dawkins, The God Delusion, London: Bantam Press, 2006, 87–88)

Depending on the right interpretation of the passage, I'm with Dawkins 100 percent here, at least up to the last sentence. I think the brain is an awesome device not merely for getting accurate information about the world but for generating the most convincing illusions. I am somewhat confident that of the people who claim to have perceived God, the percentage who are right in that particular judgment is close to zero (if not equal to zero). When it comes to perceiving God almost everyone is deluded; to that extent I *suspect* Dawkins is right (although this suspicion of mine plays no role in this book). But this is to focus on the wrong group of individuals. When it comes to the question "Has anyone actually perceived God?" we need to look at the people with the best case for providing an affirmative answer: intelligent people who have devoted their lives to some rigorous training in a form of meditation. Dawkins probably doesn't know it, but these people tend to be highly skeptical of their ability to perceive God. The person who meditates is often told that he or she has, once again, failed to understand what she is experiencing; she is like a blind person who is struggling to see for the first time. And this is usually held to be true for people at all stages of meditation, even the so-called experts.

I'm not saying that the meditators have really experienced God. In fact, I will argue that the publicly available evidence that they have experienced him is poor (chapter 4). My point *here* is that when it comes to the question of the alleged perception of God, these are the right folks to focus on. They are a far cry from the teenager hearing scary sounds in the woods one night, or the certifiably insane murderers. It's a well-known fact that if you choose your opponents carefully, focusing on the ignorant or deluded, then you will have no trouble shooting them down. If I wanted to defend theism by attacking its opponents (which is not what I do in this book), it would be dialectically clever of me to focus on atheists like Dawkins, but this would do little to actually discredit atheism.

Despite all that, in my judgment Dawkins has done the world a tremendous favor by showing that atheism is a reasonable view to endorse—no matter how you spell out "reasonable." He's not the first to do this, of course, but he has done it in a very public and more or less capable manner. But competence in philosophy comes from a training regiment very different from that received in the sciences.[4] Dawkins is no more trustworthy than Keller when it comes to the fundamental philosophical issues about religion.

Folks like Keller and Dawkins think they know the answer to the Problem of Evil. I don't; it has surpassed my philosophical abilities, at least for now. However, I am confident I know the richness and subtlety of the problem. I think some substantive conclusions can be reached, but they aren't the wildly optimistic or pessimistic ones endorsed by Keller, Dawkins, or other authors who have recently tackled the topic in the public square. This book presents the twists and turns as well as the conclusions.

Foreshadowing

As an informal warm-up to our topic, and a quick guide to the book's chapters, pretend that you know some very, very old woman who is incredibly wise. Everyone calls her "Mother Abigail." She is wise in knowing about life in general as well as being incredibly, almost supernaturally perceptive: she has the uncanny ability to see right into your soul and know what kind of person you are, what your strengths, weaknesses, hopes, dreams, and fears are. Numerous reports say that she is unfailingly kind, fair, and loving to everyone. Mother Abigail has adopted many orphaned children as well. Then some of the orphans come to you with tales of woe: they have had to suffer on many occasions while living in Mother Abigail's fine large home. You find these stories puzzling: how could Mother Abigail permit such suffering in her home?

You can think of various possible explanations. One, maybe she doesn't know about the suffering, so even if she would find it unacceptable and would not permit it, because she doesn't even know it's happening she fails to put a stop to it. Two, she knows about it and wants to prevent it but for some reason it lies outside of her control, so she can't do anything about it. Three, she's secretly a horrible person who knows about the suffering, could put a stop to it, but lets it go on anyway. Four, she knows about it, thinks it's terrible, can put a halt to it, but she allows it to happen because she knows that there is some hidden benefit to the suffering (e.g., it "builds character"). But if she knows about the suffering, it's within her power to stop it, she's a morally excellent person, then she will put a stop to any suffering that *isn't* worth it by, for instance, leading to some benefit that outweighs the suffering. So we can understand why there is suffering in Mother Abigail's home: she permits it *when she knows that the suffering is worth it*.

However, what we don't have is an explanation of how there could be suffering in her home that is *not* worth it—call that kind of suffering "gratuitous." If we were presented with conclusive evidence that there was gratuitous suffering in her home, then we would probably reason this way:

a. If reports about Mother Abigail are accurate, then she knows about all the suffering in her house, she is powerful within her home (so she can put a stop to the suffering of children who live there), and she is a morally excellent person. That's what people *say* about her: she knows what's going on, she holds sway in her own home, and she's as morally upright as anyone is.

b. But if she has all that knowledge, power, and moral excellence, as people have said, then she will permit suffering in her house only when that suffering is worth it: no gratuitous suffering allowed.

c. Hence, if the reports about her are accurate, then if there is any suffering in her home, it won't be gratuitous.

d. But that's just false: some of the suffering in her home really is gratuitous.

e. Thus, the reports aren't accurate. So, either she doesn't know about all the suffering in her home, or she isn't all powerful in her home when it comes to suffering, or she's not as morally wonderful as people say.

Most theists think God is in a position a bit similar to Mother Abigail's: he knows all about the suffering in the universe, he is all powerful, and he is morally perfect. Those are the "reports" concerning God, analogous to those regarding Mother Abigail with respect to her home. Most theists don't want to give up any of those reports about God. When faced with the reasoning in (a)–(e) applied to God, they will usually decide that (d) is really false, contrary to appearances: God must know of some good reason to permit the suffering to occur, even if we have no idea what it might be. Whenever we encounter suffering that doesn't seem worth it, we are mistaken: it's always worth it. There is no gratuitous suffering.

My objective in this book is to spell out and then partially evaluate the ways theists might respond, in a potentially rational and informative manner, to the (a)–(e) reasoning applied to God. In chapter 2 I will present in detail the "Problem of Gratuitous Suffering," which is more or less captured by (a)–(e) and is a potent challenge to theistic belief. As noted immediately above, most theists will want to argue that all the instances of suffering are somehow worth it, that God has a plan which shows that all that suffering had some good purpose even if we don't and perhaps even can't know what it is. Such folks reject (d). However, not all theists will react that way. In chapter 3 I introduce the five potentially reasonable and informative ways theists can respond to the Problem of Gratuitous Suffering. Here is a brief and approximately accurate introduction to the first four ways:

1. ***The Confident Approach*** (chapter 4). According to this response, many theists have *certain* knowledge of God's existence—knowledge so secure that when faced with virtually any argument against his existence they can simply infer that there's a mistake somewhere in that argument even if they can't spot it. Upon encountering the application of (a)–(e) to God, they know there has to be a mistake in it, even if they can't put their finger on its exact location. They don't give up (a) though, the "reports" about God: they think that either (b) or (d) must be the culprit.
2. ***The Compatibilist Approach*** (chapter 5). The theist who takes up this response accepts that there is gratuitous suffering but holds that (b) is false. So this person says that God permits suffering he knows to not be worth it.
3. ***The Profoundly Hidden Outweighing Goods Approach*** (chapter 6). This time, the theist thinks that it's definitely (d) that's false: in reality, there is no gratuitous suffering because God only permits suffering that is worth it— where an instance of suffering is worth it when it is connected to some good thing whose goodness outweighs the badness of the suffering. This theist is ambitious because she thinks she knows what the outweighing goods actually are.
4. ***The Skeptical Approach*** (chapter 7). This theist is like the former one in holding that (d) is mistaken. But unlike the former theist, she admits that she doesn't know what the goods are that make all suffering worthwhile. So why is she so confident that there is no gratuitous suffering when she admits that she can't find the outweighing goods? Here is the main part of her answer: she holds we have excellent reason to think that we are actually awful at making judgments like "That bit of suffering wasn't worth it." She thinks our cognitive abilities are completely unreliable when making such judgments.

The fifth and final approach, addressed in chapter 8, is very different from the first four: it is endorsed by people who think God exists but not as he is usually advertised. Roughly put, they say that God is not as powerful as people have said; or, he's not as knowledgeable; or, he's not as good. Hence, they reject the "reports" about God as inaccurate. They accept the whole argument (a)–(e) when applied to God but retain their theism. For reasons that will become clear later, this is called ***The Non-4-Part Approach***.

Although I don't think I have solved the problem of God and suffering, I do think I have given good arguments for nine central conclusions, which are articulated in the final chapter, 9 (in addition, there are secondary conclusions listed at the ends of chapters 4, 6, and 7). Roughly put, I will end up arguing that given the evidence available to most of us, we should not endorse any of the first four theistic responses to the problem: for each one, the overall evidence most of us have regarding it is not sufficient for us to endorse it (I will also further clarify my uses of "overall evidence available to us" and "should not"). The fifth, non-standard, approach might be perfectly adequate as a response to the Problem of Gratuitous Suffering, but I will argue that endorsing it usually makes it a mystery why the theist should worship, love, trust, or admire God; and if that's the case, why be religious at all?

Although I myself do not believe in God (I've been agnostic my whole life), I do not take any comfort in those negative assessments. At the end of the book, in chapter 9, I will explain why these negative conclusions are less significant than they appear, as they offer no solid basis for endorsing atheism or any other anti-religious attitude. Such an upshot may seem disappointingly meager, but the Problem of Gratuitous Suffering is a tough philosophical problem. In this book I'm just trying to describe and fill out the ways to think carefully, honestly, and thoroughly about the problem.

One surprising feature of this little book is the fact that there is no name-dropping. In the coming pages I'm not going to tell you what Foucault or Nietzsche or Levinas or de Beauvoir or Spinoza or other famous philosophers said about suffering. Upon finishing this book you won't be able to hold forth at parties while elucidating and then criticizing the deep thoughts of Marx, Kant, Aristotle, or Augustine on these issues. I'm not here to impress you with my vast knowledge of the history of thought; and I'm not here to help you impress others in the same way. Are you looking for something clever and worldly to say about evil, or are you interested in delving into the heart of the matter? I'm here to take you on a personal journey in which you meditate on the most pressing problem there is for theism. This is a book for grownups—not necessarily adults, but people who have a deep appreciation of the evils of the world and want to get to the bottom of what they mean for religion. In my experience as a philosopher, I have found that focusing on what famous philosophers have said usually leads to excessive attention to exposition and fails to encourage independent thinking on the issues that those philosophers were concerned with. I omit discussion of what other philosophers have said on the topic not out of disrespect. Indeed, although I refrain from discussing what individual philosophers have written, I will often describe what the philosophical community as a whole has concluded about various ideas.

Suggested Readings

Some of what appears in this book is informed by what has already been written (e.g., the deer and Holocaust examples of chapter 2 are well known throughout the philosophical literature). But the vast majority of it represents my own thinking on the topic. Thus, it's an excellent idea for the reader to access some other views on the subject matter.

For discussion of what some other individual philosophers have said about the Problem of Gratuitous Suffering one can hardly do better than start with the freely available entries "evil, problem of" online at *The Stanford Encyclopedia of Philosophy* and "The Evidential Problem of Evil" online at *The Internet Encyclopedia of Philosophy*. These are quality pieces of philosophy, and this book is more than sufficient for understanding them. Of course, there is a great deal more written on the general topic, as it has been discussed for many centuries. The two online articles include extensive bibliographies.

If you want a single professional journal devoted to producing essays written not just for professional philosophers, the philosophy journal *Philosophy Compass* has several directly relevant articles:

Justin P. McBraye (2011). "Skeptical Theism," *Philosophy Compass* 6, 611–623.
Luke Gelinas (2010). "The Problem of Natural Evil I: General Theistic Replies," *Philosophy Compass* 5, 533–559.
Luke Gelinas (2010). "The Problem of Natural Evil II: Hybrid Replies," *Philosophy Compass* 5, 560–574.

In addition, chapter 4 of this book presents and evaluates several classic arguments for the existence of God, arguments that have been discussed extensively. The above sources also provide good introductions to those arguments. The *Stanford Encyclopedia of Philosophy* and *Internet Encyclopedia of Philosophy* have search engines one can use to find entries such as "cosmological argument" and "fine-tuning argument." *Philosophy Compass* has the following essays on those topics:

David Leech and Aku Visala (2012). "Naturalistic Explanation for Religious Belief," *Philosophy Compass* 7, 552–563.
Joshua Rasmussen (2011). "Cosmological Arguments from Contingency," *Philosophy Compass* 6, 806–819.
Michael Thune (2011). "Religious Belief and the Epistemology of Disagreement," *Philosophy Compass* 6, 712–724.
William Hasker (2010). "Intelligent Design," *Philosophy Compass* 5, 586–597.
Neil A. Manson (2010). "The Fine-Tuning Argument," *Philosophy Compass* 5, 271–286.
Nathan L. King (2008). "Religious Diversity and its Challenges to Religious Belief," *Philosophy Compass* 3, 830–853.
David Alexander (2008). "The Recent Revival of Cosmological Arguments," *Philosophy Compass* 3, 541–550.
Kai-man Kwan (2006). "Can Religious Experience Provide Justification for the Belief in God? The Debate in Contemporary Analytic Philosophy," *Philosophy Compass* 1, 640–661.

Finally, the Princeton philosopher Thomas Kelly has an article related to chapter 4's Social Argument for theism (as of 2012 it's also available on his Princeton website):

Thomas Kelly (2011). "*Consensus Gentium*: Reflections on the 'Common Consent' Argument for the Existence of God," in Kelly Clark and Raymond Van Arragon (eds) *Evidence and Religious Belief*, Oxford University Press, pp. 135–156.

2

THE QUESTION: IS THERE GRATUITOUS SUFFERING THAT RULES OUT GOD?

The Problem of Gratuitous Suffering

In the summer of 2011 in Norway right-wing lunatic Anders Behring Breivik slaughtered many people, including children. At one point, a group of children had found a good hiding place from the gunman. They stayed there a while, terribly afraid yet well hidden. Eventually, they saw a police officer, who told them it was safe to come out now. Thank goodness! Unfortunately, the man was no police officer. It was the gunman in disguise. After luring them from their hiding place, he murdered them.

Does that seem pretty awful? In one respect it is trivial. The attacks on the United States on September 11, 2001 killed around 3,000 people, which dwarfs Breivik's work. The USA spent the subsequent decade radically transforming itself, and much of the world, in response. But 9/11 was trivial as well: globally, around six million children die of hunger every year now, which amounts to the equivalent of a 9/11 massacre about every four hours, every damn day. Needless to say, the USA is doing nothing comparable in response to help those children.

But the story of our starving children is just one among many tragedies this world has seen. Consider the Black Death, which killed around 50 percent of Europe in the fourteenth century. That's around 75 million people dying horrible deaths, approximately a million times the number killed by Breivik and 25,000 times the 9/11 attacks. And why stop there, with humans? There are plenty of non-human animals that can suffer horribly. The Cretaceous-Paleogene extinction 65 million years ago (most likely caused in large part by a meteor impact) wiped out around 75 percent of the species on Earth according to recent estimates. Of course, a good portion of those species were not animals that could feel much pain or suffer, but given the staggering numbers involved surely a great many animals did suffer: untold billions of them starving to death or burned up from the meteor impact and volcanic explosions.

Closer to home, and vastly shrinking in size, in the midst of writing this book my mother became ill and died quite suddenly, over just three days, despite being quite healthy beforehand. This was both horrible and strangely appropriate for this book. The latter characteristic I can easily describe, and will do so below. But I can't really describe the horror of it. At least, there is no chance it can be adequately described to one who has not had a similar experience of someone in the immediate family dying. Oh, I can try to give a hint of what it is like. Inside my mind is a shiny, smooth, attractive black stone. It's the kind of stone that begs to be picked up and lovingly turned over and over in one's hands, the kind of stone that one might keep in one's pocket to take out again and again. It is the sum of my thoughts and feelings of my mother. However, just before one touches it, when one's fingers are less than a millimeter from the stone, one experiences a jolt of pain that makes one realize that touching the stone will bring utterly appalling pain: upon contact the bones in one's body will instantly turn to a raging fire. And the worst part is, the fire will not kill. One's soul will just continue to burn.

This sounds awful, as it should, but the sad fact is that it is wholly common-place. There is nothing remotely out of the ordinary about it. My reaction to her quick descent into illness and then death is as typical as can be. Worse yet, at any given moment on this planet there are many people living through the same experience, grasping their own stones of fire. And everyone will, at some point in his or her life, experience the same fierce psychological pain. This demonstrates the ubiquity of suffering. If you have yet to experience it, just wait: it's coming for you too.

Our world contains enormous amounts of suffering. Virtually all the higher animals, humans included, experience fear, terror, agony, sorrow, misery, anguish, and torment. In fact, these horrors are not exceptions but the rule, since for untold eons nearly all higher mammals, again including humans, have experi-enced each of these at various points in their lives. What happens to the vast majority of animals in the perfectly normal course of nature would without a second thought be labeled as the worse types of torture if done by a person. Such a tormentor would be confidently pronounced a moral monster who deserves the harshest punishment justice allows. Of course, there are great amounts of love and happiness in the world. But there is agony and torment as well, and they touch all but the exceedingly fortunate.

And yet a great many people, including some of the world's great geniuses today as well as many throughout history, believe that our universe was created by a being who knows exactly what he is doing, who loves us, who is perfectly good, and who is powerful without limit. This is paradoxical. If he knows exactly what is going on, he loves us, he's perfectly good, and he is powerful enough to create just about any universe he wanted, then why on earth did he create one with such stunning quantities and kinds of torment, misery, and terror? Maybe there are certain good things he wants us to achieve and the path to those goods is lined with suffering, but with all his knowledge and power surely he'd be able to achieve those goods without such a colossal amount of horrific suffering. Our universe hardly looks anything like what you would expect such a loving, good, knowledgeable, and powerful being to make. At least, it sure doesn't look that way to people who actually know a thing or two about suffering.

When faced with this paradox most people who believe in God suppose that there must be some good reason God allows vast amounts of horrific suffering. He must have a plan of some kind, even if we cannot discern it. All that suffering must be worth it in some fashion; otherwise, he wouldn't have permitted it. Every single instance of suffering, regardless of whether it is minor or appalling, must have some good if unfathomable purpose attached to it, even if that attachment is obscure. God knows what he's doing, even if we don't know what he's doing. Many theologians and other believers in God will give a response along this line when challenged with the existence of horrific suffering. In fact, there are many books devoted to the question "Why does God permit so much horrific suffering?" and most of them are written by devout theists who defend some version of that idea.

One of the burdens of this book is to explain why the clear majority of philosophers, me included, find this theistic response to the question of suffering so unsatisfactory. I will also explain what is meant by "unsatisfactory" in this context. The reason this is so important is that the problem of suffering is frequently thought to be the primary issue in the philosophy of religion, and it generates the most potent evidence against theism.

Of course, philosophers who are doubtful of the idea that all suffering is somehow worth it admit that it is easy to see that many instances of suffering are definitely attached to good things that justify them. The theistic response sketched in the previous paragraphs is by no means silly or unreasonable; it is based in part on some accurate reflections on suffering and goodness. For instance, when I donated blood one Sunday my small dose of suffering was outweighed by the benefit the donation led to when someone in a hospital got that blood of mine. In this case there is an instance of suffering and then, later, there is an instance of goodness that is the result of the suffering. In other cases an instance of suffering leads not to an obvious case of a good thing but to the prevention of a really bad thing. For instance, I take some truly awful medicine for a major illness. It tastes so hideous that I suffer a bit because I drank it. But it was worth it because it stopped a bad thing from happening (the illness worsening perhaps). These are the simple cases, but it's good to have some simple ones in mind before we tackle the complicated cases.

Sometimes the order is reversed: a good thing inevitably leads to a bit of suffering. For instance, on Saturday evening I have three glasses of superb champagne. This is a delightful experience. But I know that the champagne will cause me to have a headache in the middle of the night that will wake me up. Happens every time. Even so, it's worth it to me to endure the headache because the badness of the headache is amply outweighed by the goodness of the champagne. A better example: I give my children a large amount of freedom in their lives. My children, Julia and Alec, often (not always!) get to do whatever they want. My wife Margaret and I decided long ago to adopt this practice, as we both know how incredibly valuable autonomy is to children (especially teenagers). Even so, I know that this freedom is going to lead to them screwing things up in huge ways. A minor example: I know that over time Alec's roughhousing has a good chance of leading to injury. Even so, I think it's worth it, even if he breaks a bone. This is a case of a good thing (autonomy) almost inevitably leading to some bad things.

So, we are well aware that many instances of suffering are perfectly acceptable or morally justified because they are **coupled with** or linked to (or however one wants to put it) some good whose goodness **outweighs** the badness of suffering, where the good might come before or after the suffering (or simultaneous with it, for that matter) and might be either a positive good thing or the prevention of a worse bad thing.

But are *all* instances of suffering throughout history offset by good things? In order to profitably explore that question let's define an instance of suffering as **gratuitous** if it is not coupled with any combination of goods whose goodness outweighs the badness of the suffering. I will also use the somewhat awkward but convenient phrase "a suffering" to talk of a particular *instance* or occasion of suffering (and the word "sufferings" will indicate multiple instances of suffering). Be careful: a gratuitous suffering does *not* have to lead to or be otherwise coupled with *no* good at all. As I'm using the term, a "gratuitous suffering" *may* be coupled with *plenty* of goods but such goods would not *outweigh* the suffering. For instance, suppose I split my head open on the pavement but then see some pretty colors hallucinatorily race across my field of vision as a result. Here, the suffering is coupled with a good thing (the interesting vision), but the goodness of the good isn't anywhere near sufficient to outweigh the badness of the suffering. Thus, just because an instance of suffering is coupled with some good doesn't mean that it fails to be gratuitous.

Most philosophers who write on this general topic use the phrase "gratuitous *evil*" in order to talk about instances of suffering (as well as other bad things that might not involve suffering) that don't have outweighing goods. Indeed, the challenge to theism that we will be investigating in this book might be called "The Problem of Gratuitous Evil," whereas I'm using the word "suffering" instead of "evil." I will focus on suffering alone, as it presents a serious challenge to theism even when we ignore other kinds of "evil" (e.g., some people would say that the destruction of great art is a bad thing even if humanity has gone extinct so no one is around to suffer as a consequence). By the way, one should not give those philosophers a hard time over their use of the term "evil." In order to avoid getting bogged down in purely semantic quibbling you should ignore whether "evil" is the right word in this discussion. Obviously, "evil" isn't quite the right word for a bad headache or even a broken arm! By "evil" in books like this one all that authors mean to indicate are bad things of various kinds, so they do not have to be *extremely* bad or the horrible product of folks like Adolph Hitler or Lord Voldemort.

I will offer some more clarifications regarding the notion of gratuitous suffering later in this chapter. For the next few pages it will suffice to (i) stick with familiar examples of how instances of suffering are often coupled with outweighing goods and (ii) keep an open mind regarding what further examples might be like. For (i), we already have a good intuitive understanding of such coupling: think of the cases given earlier—champagne, blood donation, medicine, autonomy—as well as many other cases you can think of yourself. For (ii), consider the fact that some people think that there are "moral laws" that should *never* be broken even if the circumstances are so extreme that the breaking of the moral law will actually produce much more good than evil (e.g., torturing someone in order to get information that prevents a bomb going off and killing millions of people). This opens the possibility that God allows suffering in many cases because there are absolute moral rules that have to be followed even though they bring about great amounts of suffering and don't seem to lead to any tangible good that adequately compensates for that suffering. I'm not saying that any of this is true; I'm just saying that the outweighing goods might be quite a bit different from the familiar cases I have already listed. So we have to keep an open mind when considering potential goods that might be tied with instances of suffering.

All I just did was partially *define* the phrase "gratuitous suffering" (although as I said I will further clarify the notion below). Now we need to ask whether there *actually are* any gratuitous sufferings—that is, whether there are any cases of suffering that actually fit the definition. And we also need to determine how the existence of such sufferings (if there are any) bears on the question of the existence of God.

Here are two important claims to consider when pondering the relation of God to suffering:

> **Consequence Premise:** If the universe has been created by a supremely morally good, knowledgeable, and powerful being, then that being arranged things so that there is no gratuitous suffering.[5]
>
> **Gratuitous Premise:** But there is gratuitous suffering.

The *Problem of Gratuitous Suffering* is simply this:

> There is good reason to think that the Consequence Premise is true, there is good reason to think the Gratuitous Premise is true, and yet if both are

true then there is no supremely morally good, knowledgeable, and powerful creator of the universe.[6]

Obviously, if the Consequence Premise and the Gratuitous Premise are true then God doesn't exist. Of course, this last statement assumes that the word "God" is supposed to pick out the supremely morally good, knowledgeable, and powerful creator of the universe. And one could be a relatively traditional or mainstream theist and reject that conception of God. We'll look at some of those views near the end of this book, in chapter 8. For now, we should think of the Problem of Gratuitous Suffering as focusing on a particular conception of God: let's call that conception the ***4-Part conception***, since it says that God is the unique (1) supremely moral, (2) supremely knowledgeable, (3) supremely powerful, (4) creator of the universe. Many contemporary philosophers would call this the "traditional" conception of God, but since there are mainstream traditional versions of theism that reject the 4-Part conception (as we'll see later), this word choice looks like a mistake. I'll stick with the neutral "4-Part conception" in order to not prejudge the matter.

I will clarify the "supreme" power, knowledge, and moral goodness ideas as they come up in the book. For the most part, the lack of specificity of "supremely knowing and powerful" will not matter, as we will consider the whole spectrum of possible ways of filling it out. In chapters 4–7 we look at the idea that whatever the limits are on God's knowledge and power, these limits do not figure in the correct response to the Problem of Gratuitous Suffering; in chapter 8 we examine the idea that the limitations are severe enough to figure in the response.

Although we are focused on the 4-Part conception, this does not at all mean that the theists who reject that conception are off the hook when it comes to responding to the Problem of Gratuitous Suffering. As we will see in chapter 8, they may have as much difficulty dealing with the problem as the theists who do accept the 4-Part conception.

Other theists don't exactly *reject* the 4-Part conception but insist that God is such a mystery that we can know almost nothing about him—in fact, we know so little about him that we should not be confident that he fits the 4-Part conception. So they neither accept nor reject the 4-Part conception. In conversations I have heard them say that the Problem of Gratuitous Suffering doesn't apply to them because they don't embrace the 4-Part conception; they say they don't have to deal with the Problem of Gratuitous Suffering. Some professors of philosophy have insisted on this idea to my face. But in response I usually ask them this (without the insulting manner):

So, what part of the 4-Part conception are you willing to give up? Are you saying that God's strength is significantly limited, so he can't do anything about the horrific suffering all around us? Or is it his knowledge that is significantly lacking, so he doesn't do anything about suffering because he's clueless about what's going on? Or is he so morally flawed that he knows about our suffering, can relieve or prevent it, but just doesn't give a shit—and doesn't that make him the ultimate evil tyrant? Or what? Stop smiling and gimme some details.

After struggling with these questions for a while, many (not all) theists who emphasize God's mystery start to think the 4-Part conception actually looks pretty good! Again, these questions, and several alternative conceptions of God, will be examined in chapter 8.

Depending on your educational and cultural background, it may come as a surprise to you to learn that a great many philosophers think there is no 4-Part God. In fact, *most* of today's philosophy professors think there is no God at all: they are atheists or at least strongly "lean" toward atheism. The same is true of scientists. I realize that atheism strikes some readers as about as reasonable as the idea that the Easter Bunny really exists, is responsible for all the yummy chocolate we devour around Easter, and hangs out with Spiderman at the local pool hall. If that is how you view atheism, as something only borderline crazy or silly or clueless people endorse, then I'm sorry to inform you that you have led a sheltered life when it comes to intellectual culture. Although there are some reasons for thinking God exists, there are also reasons for thinking that he doesn't exist—ones that extremely intelligent, informed, and fair-minded people think, after much sober reflection, to be *very good* reasons.

Many philosophers reached their non-theistic opinion in the following way: they looked very hard at a good portion of the primary evidence theists point to when defending their views and upon evaluating it they conclude that in reality it provides little good reason to think there are any gods at all, let alone one that is the omniscient, omnipotent, morally perfect creator of the universe. Given the absence of significant decent evidence for God's existence, they conclude that most likely there is no God. This last step isn't any fancy inference: virtually all of us do the very same thing when we conclude that there probably are no ghosts on the basis of our judgment that there is no decent evidence for the existence of ghosts. So this is a case in which philosophers go from "There is little good evidence *for* theism" to "Most likely, there is no God. "But in addition some philosophers go from "There is good evidence *against* theism" to "Most likely, there is no God." Many professional philosophers take the Problem of Gratuitous Suffering (as well as other philosophical lines of argument) to mount a strong argument for atheism. But the vast majority of philosophers who are atheists take a *combined* view: they go from "There is little good evidence for theism and there is good evidence against theism" to "Most likely, there is no God." And they say that the Problem of Gratuitous Suffering supplies some (but certainly not all) of the good evidence against theism, or at least 4-Part theism. I'm not saying that they are *right* about any of this; I'm just reporting some sociological facts about philosophers who have looked at a good portion of the evidence for the existence of God.

Why should we *care* what philosophers have thought about the Problem of Gratuitous Suffering? Why not consider the opinions of scientists or theologians or poets, for instance? The short reason is this: of all groups of people, philosophers have spent the most amount of time probing the issue in a thorough and an as unbiased a manner as possible. Regardless of their areas of specialization, a great many philosophers regularly investigate topics in the philosophy of religion as parts of their teaching, and most of those topics concern the evidence, pro and con, regarding the key claims of theism. This is not to say that philosophers are totally unbiased when it comes to religious matters; philosophers are usually human beings. But it's part of our training, over many years, to look at the evidence in as unbiased as a way as possible.

In the rest of this chapter we will take a preliminary look at the two premises, in order to better understand what they are saying and why one might think that they are true. I'll start with the Gratuitous Premise and then move on to the Consequence Premise. Later in the book we will encounter careful, step-by-step arguments for both premises.

The Gratuitous Premise

At first glance, before one thinks really hard about the matter, there certainly *seem* to be gratuitous sufferings, right? Suppose an exceedingly cute deer (adorable enough for a Disney movie) is slowly burned to death in a forest fire. She experiences much excruciating pain before death. This is definitely a case of horrific suffering (indeed, it is a low percentage of people nowadays who have even the slightest idea of what such pain is like—such as having a limb blown off or burned away or chewed off; I'll return to this point a couple times in this book). A key question is this: is the deer's suffering coupled with an outweighing good or combination of goods?

It is easy to *imagine* goods that could be linked to the deer's suffering:

⟿ in respect to humans. Selfish? 1, 3

1. If she hadn't died she was going to accidently spread a disease that led to the extinction of humanity. So by her dying a really bad thing was prevented.
2. Her dying led some people to see how awful the consequences of forest fires are. This in turn led a great many people to be much more ethical in their treatment of non-human animals for many years.
3. A lion ate her carcass. And a hunter who was about to die of starvation killed the lion and ate some of it, thereby cheating death. Then the hunter went on to save the universe from the Dark Lord (either Voldemort or Sauron).

But just because it's easy to imagine these things doesn't mean that any of them are really true. When we are confronted with the question "Is this instance of suffering coupled with an outweighing good?" we can't justify an affirmative answer just because we can easily *imagine* that the suffering is linked with an outweighing good. We need good reason to think the suffering really, as a matter of fact, is coupled with an outweighing good. We're not engaged in fantasy here; we are concerned with reality.

The deer example illustrates another important point about the linkage between suffering and goods. Even if her death was a good thing overall, why did it have to involve such extreme suffering—or any suffering at all? Just because she had to die in order for certain great things to happen—which would be the case if any of (1)–(3) were true—gives no reason why she had to suffer while dying. In reality, (1)–(3) would do nothing whatsoever to justify her suffering even if one of them were true! At most, they justify her *dying*, not her *suffering*. The modest lesson is this: seeing how suffering and goods are related is a tricky matter, requiring careful thought.

Q1: What's the worse suffering you have ever experienced in your life? You can think of either purely physical or emotional suffering, either long-term or short-term. Do you think that that instance of suffering was worth it?

In order to fruitfully think about the Gratuitous Premise we should consider the *extent* of suffering (in addition to its intensity in many particular instances, an issue I will address in chapters 5 and 6). There were animals on earth capable of feeling horrific pain for many millions of years before humans showed up. Thus, there have been trillions (that's millions of millions) of animals who have felt pain. And almost all of them have, at some point in their lives, felt truly horrific pain; such is the life of an animal in the wild. So that's *many, many trillions of instances of horrific pain*. All the Gratuitous Premise says is that *some* of those cases of horrific pain were not morally justified by some outweighing goods. To put it mildly, it's not easy to think of justifications for *all* those trillions of instances of suffering. Indeed, most people find it hard to think of justifications for even a tiny percentage of that suffering.

I need to say something right away to prevent a common misunderstanding of the Gratuitous Premise. I assume that most of you could write at length about how some really bad things actually led to outweighing goods—even though when the bad things were happening there were *no* signs that everything would turn out all right. Your argument might even come from your own personal experiences: you may recall enduring some painful suffering in your past but you now think that all that suffering was definitely worth it, even though the suffering was intense and at the time you were suffering there was no way you could have known that it was going to end up worth it. (I tend to think this way too: when I was a child and teenager my family was near poverty for several years, and I resented it during some of that time, but now I am glad that I've grown up in such a way that I don't need many material things to make me happy.) Ministers tend to make such appeals. They often note that many people come to them with tales of woe but go on to say that long afterwards they came to firmly think their own suffering was worth it. You might get excited at this point and think that you've shown that there is no good reason to think that there are any gratuitous sufferings, as there is always a real chance that a good thing will come about that justifies the suffering. Who knows what the future may bring? So, you conclude that there is no good reason to accept the Gratuitous Premise.

That argument has the significant merit of showing that on *many interesting real-life occasions* there are hidden goods (often located in the future) that justify significant amounts of suffering. I think this is one of life's lessons, one that wise people heed. (We will see in chapter 7 a particular way that truth may be philosophically significant.) It has the merit of reminding us to be open-minded about whether the future will contain goods that outweigh present suffering. But unfortunately the argument of the preceding paragraph doesn't even come close to showing that the Gratuitous Premise is doubtful. The minister, of all people, should know better! After all, he's in New York City, say, at some fancy church. Naturally, the people who come to him will tend to be the ones who have "made it through" their suffering to the other side. After all, they are healthy enough to see him and communicate with him. In order to have a more intelligent view the minister should contemplate or actually witness battlefields, or concentration camps, or starving communities, or animals being killed in the wild: that way he will shift his attention to the billions of cases in which things don't seem to turn out on balance okay—the cases where it seems that much suffering is gratuitous. The person who thinks there are gratuitous sufferings is saying that in addition to all the fantastically wonderful things in life there are *some* really awful things that are not coupled with outweighing goods (and as a result, some of those awful things are gratuitous sufferings). In order to cast doubt on that idea you can't just note that *in lots of interesting cases that come to our attention* human suffering is justified by some hidden good, as that does next to nothing to show that it happens *absolutely every time*, for humans and non-human animals. That is, in order to cast doubt on the Gratuitous Premise you have to argue that it's plausible that *absolutely all* suffering has outweighing goods. The argument of the previous paragraph would be a good one to present to someone who thought that on balance the world was a simply horrible place in which suffering is almost never justified. But we aren't considering such a depressing idea. The person who presents the Problem of Gratuitous Suffering as a challenge to theism need not be someone who thinks that the universe or human existence is doomed or hideous or depressing, that life is not worth living. At least, there is nothing in her argument that requires such a view.

Many people will say that it's just about the most obvious thing in the world that there are gratuitous sufferings, so it's abundantly clear that the Gratuitous Premise is true. For them, the idea that one would need to provide *evidence or argument* in favor of that premise is almost ridiculous. After all, what about the Holocaust?! It's easy to admit that the Holocaust probably led to *some* good here and there (e.g., some friendships among concentration camp prisoners that would not have occurred otherwise), but the idea that it's coupled with some goods that are so stupendous that they *justify the suffering of the Holocaust* may well strike an intelligent and reflective person as profoundly insulting if not positively insane or malicious. Some people with that view go on to assert that it's an affront to those who suffered in the Holocaust to even attempt to discuss, in a logical, dispassionate way, the possibility that some outweighing goods justified the Holocaust's enormous evil. It's just plain stupid and insensitive, they say, to think that the Holocaust was morally justified due to its being coupled with goods that were so amazingly good that their goodness outweighed the badness of the Holocaust. Only the grossly insensitive or ignorant person could entertain such thoughts.

At the very least, we can all agree that it's *hard* to discover the goods that justify the Holocaust, assuming for the moment that there are any such goods. Nevertheless, though it may strike you as incredible, most theists who accept the 4-Part God think there is an adequate justification for horrors like the Holocaust; and some of them even think they have a plausible idea what the justification is. We'll get to those views below. One thing advocates of these views do is suggest that the goods associated with suffering are often unfamiliar, hard to understand, or difficult to detect; and that the connections between the goods and the suffering are often hard to see or are indirect. They claim that these difficulties explain why it certainly *seems* as obvious as anything ever gets that there are many gratuitous sufferings, even though in reality there are none.

Q2: Give three very different examples of suffering that seem to be coupled with some goods but not goods that are sufficient to justify the suffering. (I'm including the word "seem" in order to allow that ultimately speaking the instances of suffering really are coupled with goods.)

However, many other people who have thought deeply about the nature of evil think that the idea of outweighing goods for all suffering is based on either delusion or an understanding of suffering that is almost comic in its naiveté. In order to even begin to look for outweighing goods one has to have a real grasp of the intensity of suffering; otherwise one would have no chance of judging when a good is *good enough* to outweigh the badness of the suffering. But very few people who read this little book have suffered incredible pain, either physical or psychological; neither are they significantly aware of it through other means. Sure, many of us have broken some bones or burned a hand or had a family member die after a long and hideous fight with cancer. Some of us have read detailed first-person accounts of such things as well. But who has actually witnessed one of their parents or children tortured to death? How many of us who have the luxury of reading philosophy have suffered unbearable pain not just for an hour or two or three until the pain medications kicked in but have suffered the pain for *years upon years* until our minds were warped beyond repair? Who has had to sit idly by while that happened to his or her child? How many of us have realized that our own faults have directly led to the agonizing, torturous deaths of our loved ones? Worse yet, how many of us know this but also know that we could have *done* something to prevent all that suffering and death?

The answer is the same every time: very few people reading these words have much understanding of the *intensity* or *depth* of extreme suffering, either physical or emotional. The intensity of suffering goes up to level 100; the vast majority of people who read books like this one have experienced nothing beyond the teens. If you have the opportunity to read this book, then you're probably one of the lucky ones who have avoided suffering so intense that it ruins your ability to think straight or have the time to read philosophy books. I recall the main character Winston Smith in George Orwell's masterpiece *1984* and how he was stunned upon feeling the first "real" pain of his life when the officers of Big Brother beat him for the first time after his capture. It immediately became plain to him that up until then he had had no idea of what pain can be—and keep in mind that this was a very short-term pain: still relatively weak compared to the truly horrific kinds of suffering noted above. I suspect the same is true of almost all of us (who read this book). Earlier I mentioned my reaction to my mother's death, which was awful for me. But compared to what many others have suffered, I am complaining about a nasty hangnail while they have burns over 75 percent of their bodies. I got off easy with my mother's death.

Q3: Give three very different examples of suffering that don't seem to be coupled with any goods at all. (I'm including the word "seem" in order to allow that ultimately speaking the instances of suffering really are coupled with goods.)

These people who emphasize the prevalence of ignorance regarding the intensity of suffering insist that some things are so utterly horrendous and soul-destroying that nothing conceivable could justify them; and philosophers who think otherwise are like innocent preteens arrogantly pontificating about the intricate emotions of couples who have been married for decades. (Some more analogies: it's like people from the fourteenth century trying to think about the Big Bang, twenty-first-century mathematics, or evolutionary theory: in each case the people don't even come close to having the background necessary to think competently about the topic.) According to this line of thought, the approach that says "God has some plan that makes every bit of suffering worthwhile" is doomed from the beginning. Even if all the goodness in the universe hung on one particular evil, if the evil is horrendous enough—keep in mind the cases described above—this hardly means that the evil is outweighed by all the goodness. The evil of the suffering has *gone off the scale* and no goodness can justify it.

People with this opinion sometimes have an illustration and an argument backing up their view. First the illustration, then the argument.

There are the finite numbers: -2, -1, 0, +1, +2, etc. These are numbers on the number line we learn about in elementary school:

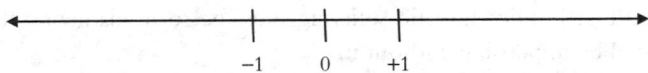

$$-1 \qquad 0 \qquad +1$$

And then there is infinity, which isn't on that line at all. Infinity is a characteristic of the line of finite numbers; it's *not* another entry on the line. Normal, everyday instances of suffering are like the finite numbers on the number line. It makes sense to ask whether they are paired with outweighing goods. But some cases of suffering are so horrendous that they are utterly unlike the ordinary cases of suffering: they are like infinity in being off the scale. They are in a different category altogether. For them, there can be no justification, no outweighing good. That's the illustration. It has its limits, but it is suggestive anyway.

For the argument, they start by pointing out the extreme horrors of the world and then say to the folks who continue to insist that there is no gratuitous suffering

> How on earth do you reconcile your view with the horrors we already know about? What would it take to show you that some suffering is gratuitous? If every one of the billions of creatures on earth died a horrible death through extreme suffering and you were the last one standing, would that, finally, be enough to convince you? Suppose further that you died and ended up in an afterlife of utter misery for trillions of people and animals. You would recant *then*? Probably not! You would say "Well, there simply must be some good reason for all this suffering, even if we can't see it; maybe there is an after-after life of bliss and justice." You are so wedded to your view that no matter what horrors are visited on the world, either natural or supernatural, you will continue to insist that there must be some outweighing good of some kind, even if we can never discover it. It must be oddly comforting to be so irrationally devoted to an idea that one will never give it up, no matter what the circumstances or evidence before one's eyes.

Speeches like that one are pretty common on this topic. They are typically intended to make several points.[7] The one I want to focus on is this: most of us have a strong tendency to vastly underestimate the badness of suffering. And that means we have a strong tendency to vastly underestimate how wonderful something has to be in order to outweigh the horrendous sufferings so many people and animals experience. As a consequence of all this, we end up taking seriously the possibility that there are outweighing goods in all cases when what we *should* be doing is laughing at that possibility—or so many people think (the people who tend to give speeches like the one above). Some philosophers who are vividly aware of this problem have concluded that only some kind of *supernatural* good lying far beyond our understanding and experience could possibly be good enough to outweigh the horrors that people and animals experience. Others have said that any good that justifies horrific suffering must be so fundamental that consciousness would be impossible without it.

> Q4: Brainstorm a bit to think of possible outweighing goods for the Holocaust. In order for a collection of goods to justify the Holocaust three conditions have to be satisfied: the goods have to really exist, they have to be appropriately coupled with the Holocaust, and their collective goodness has to be greater than the collective badness of the Holocaust.

I respect both the view and its supporting argument for the thesis that horrific suffering is much worse than most of us think and the goods people think of as justifying that suffering are laughably inadequate. Like many people, I *sometimes* think it's the nail in the coffin for the idea that the 4-Part God exists, and thus all the careful argumentation in books like this one is based on ignorance of its topic. Fortunately, I can't evaluate the argument for the simple reason that I have not experienced any evil of that character. It would probably be prudent of us to withhold judgment on it until that sad day when, God forbid, we experience such evil. This issue of our lack of personal understanding of the intensity and depths of suffering will come up when we examine particular possible outweighing goods in chapter 6.

> Q5: Give three very different examples of suffering that are both very bad and that do *not* appear to be gratuitous. Have at least one of them be the kind of suffering that's outweighed by a positive good thing; and have at least one of them be the kind of suffering that's outweighed not by a positive good thing but the prevention of a worse bad thing.

I would like to make a couple more clarifications regarding "gratuitous suffering." First, some contemporary philosophers use the phrase "gratuitous suffering" in a way importantly yet subtly different from how I'm using it. We need to be aware of the differences in the two conceptions, as they will matter to my arguments in this book. I will use some stories to illustrate the difference (this book will contain *many* little stories).

Suppose you have been bitten on the hand by a stray cat and need to get a tetanus shot. The shot is going to be painful but we usually say that it's worth it, as it will prevent a nasty infection. So in this case there is an outweighing good; that's why we willingly go and get the shot even though we know it will be painful. As far as we're concerned in *this* book, that settles the matter: the suffering you endure because of the shot is not gratuitous because there is an outweighing good. However, most philosophers think that this is letting God off far too easy. After all, he could have arranged things so that we didn't have to endure painful shots in order to prevent infections. God is awfully powerful; he isn't limited by the state of medical knowledge like we are. He is supposed to be able to do just about anything one can coherently imagine—and much that we are too cognitively weak to imagine.

There is a lot to be said for this idea! After all, suppose you are faced with two courses of action and you have to choose just one of them. Let's pretend that you are a parent and you are choosing medical procedures for one of your children who is ill. Each procedure gets you the same good outcome, G. For instance, G might be a mended arm, as your child has fractured her forearm. Both action-procedures have a downside in the sense that your child will have to suffer a bit in order to get G: if you choose action (medical treatment) A1 she will suffer pain P1 in order to secure G, and if you choose action A2 she will suffer pain P2 in order to secure G. Pretend that otherwise the two medical procedures A1 and A2 are identical when it comes to pain, cost, discomfort, annoyance, etc. Since G is so great compared to either P1 or P2, either course of action is worth it overall. Thus, according to the definition of "gratuitous suffering" used in this book, neither action involves any gratuitous suffering. As far as this book is concerned, that's the end of the story.

But now suppose you learn that P1 is much worse than P2: if you go with procedure A1 your child will suffer much more than if you go with A2. And you are fully able to choose to do either A1 or A2. And you know what's going to happen as a result of choosing between A1 and A2. Well, if those are the circumstances, then it sure seems that you should go with A2 instead of A1. If you go with A1 instead of A2—so you're choosing the more painful one knowing full well that it's more painful!—then even though you are not responsible for producing any gratuitous suffering in the sense of that phrase used in this book—as there was an outweighing good—you're still a jerk, or you're not jerk but you forgot what was going on, or you lost your mind, or something similar—all because you really should have gone with the less painful option, A2 instead of A1.

Q6: Often we can make judgments of the form "That was painful for me but it was worth it, as the benefits outweighed the cost." For instance, I once had a cat attack me and bite me several times on my hand. Naturally, my hand swelled up pretty bad. So, I went to the doctor and got some shots to make the infection go away. The shots hurt a bit (apparently you need a big needle for some injections) but it was easily worth it because if I hadn't got the shot the infection would have gone haywire quickly. But can we always make judgments like that? Think of three cases in which a bit of suffering is coupled with a good but it seems very hard to make any comparison judgment such as "The goodness of the good outweighed/failed to outweigh the badness of the suffering."

But according to many philosophers that is precisely the position God is in for many situations that involve suffering (after all, God is often compared to a parent, and we are his children). In order to cure your wound you needed to get a tetanus shot; given your knowledge, ability, and culture in which you live you had no better alternative. But God is not off the hook because he had many alternative and superior ways to get rid of your infection. For many cases of suffering that have outweighing goods, God could have secured those goods without all that suffering: he had *better* ways to go that he knew were fully available to him. The lesson: many instances of suffering that this book is *not* about, as they fail to fit our definition of "gratuitous," are nonetheless often thought to constitute a serious challenge to theism. *This means that many philosophers would criticize me as letting God (or theists) off too easy*, as I am completely ignoring all sorts of instances of suffering that pose a serious challenge to theism! (Other philosophers, theists, occasionally tell me that I'm being too biased against theism because I'm letting the atheists off too easily; no one can win that game.) Still, I choose to stick with my way of doing things because the instances of suffering that I focus on, although smaller in number than under the alternative conception of "gratuitous suffering," are more than sufficient to pose a very serious challenge to theism and they also make the arguments significantly less convoluted. From time to time I'll have to focus on the larger groups of alleged gratuitous sufferings, for reasons that come up in chapter 6.

The medical examples are probably not the best ones to choose here because it's easy to object that if God intervened in cases like those then he would be taking away our freedom to make decisions, which would make us all into something like robots, which is a very bad thing. God has to let us make our own way in the world, and that means not intervening every second in order to cure our infections and other difficulties. I brought up those examples and this criticism here just to let you know early on that I'm aware of them and will be addressing them and related cases later in the book, in chapter 6. But if you want a better example that illustrates the difference between the two kinds of "gratuitous suffering" perhaps this story will help: imagine a deer who survives a raging forest fire but in her escape suffers severe burns, which were incredibly painful both at the time of the fire and off and on for many years afterward. Furthermore, pretend that the experience teaches her some valuable lessons in danger avoidance that enable her and her children and some further generations to thrive for many years. So according to our definition of "gratuitous suffering" the suffering she experienced while escaping the fire (from the severe burns) was not gratuitous because the badness of the suffering was outweighed by the goodness of the knowledge and subsequent goods gained through the suffering. Even so, God could have imparted that knowledge in any of several considerably less painful ways—and *he knew it the whole time* while he was allowing her to suffer severe burns (in fact, he probably knew it long beforehand). Again, many philosophers would say that the deer's suffering sure looks unjustified even if non-gratuitous given that God could easily have arranged things so that she got the knowledge without the severe suffering.

[margin handwriting: depends on whether people consider knowledge an outweighing good]

So, many philosophers would say that my conception of gratuitous suffering is too narrow. I am certainly not saying that any of those philosophers are wrong. I'm saying that there is a somewhat *simpler* challenge to theism based on the apparent existence of instances of suffering that are not in fact coupled with outweighing goods.[8] We can focus on this simpler challenge instead of the *further* philosophical challenge that even if there is no gratuitous suffering (in my sense of "gratuitous") God isn't off the hook since he knowingly allows much more suffering than he needs to in order to secure goods such as happiness.

> Q7: Suppose you thought that God is just a 3-Part God, so he's missing one of the four standard parts. Does this make the Problem of Gratuitous Suffering easier to respond to? If so, how? Answer those questions for each of the four parts of the 4-Part conception: creator, omnipotence, omniscience, and perfect goodness. That is, imagine that God fits the first three parts but not the last one (for instance; you need to do all four possible combinations), and then figure out if that makes it easier to respond to the Problem of Gratuitous Suffering.

Now I'll give my second clarification regarding "gratuitous suffering," one I implicitly started expressing above. A religious person might well respond to my tetanus shot story as follows.

> Sure, God could easily alleviate your pain and cure your infection without any painful shot. And he knows all about it. And he knows it would be better, in a sense, if you didn't have that infection. Even so, he is wise in not getting rid of either the infection or the pain associated with it. After all, if

he's going to take care of your infection he won't be able to stop there! He will have to take care of virtually every infection (maybe he wouldn't have to take care of Hitler's infections, but let's not try to figure that out). Fairness demands it. And if he's going to take care of infections, then he will have to take care of stomach aches, skinned knees, broken arms, broken hearts, etc. There is no fair stopping point. But now look where we end up: God has undermined our ability to make our own way in the world. He has taken away our autonomy or freedom or whatever you want to call it. But no one wants that! So when you look at the big picture you can see why he permits all sorts of suffering: in order to secure some really important goods—like freedom—he is bound, by fairness, to allow a great deal of suffering.

This is an insightful line of reasoning. It is saying that the pain associated with the infection is coupled with an outweighing good, but the connection—the "coupling"—is subtle and is governed by fairness considerations. It's *subtle* because the outweighing good isn't some easily identifiable thing closely connected to the suffering; it is *governed by fairness* because God's eliminating the infection would require him, by principles of fairness, to eliminate many other, similar, cases of suffering, which in turn would result in the loss of some truly important goods. Note that parents engage in very similar reasoning when figuring out how to raise their children. I will examine these and similar ideas in chapter 6. This is the end of my second clarification of "gratuitous suffering."

Q8: Here is one intelligent idea we encounter a lot when talking about suffering and God; give several reasons why it's inadequate as a response to the Problem of Gratuitous Suffering: "Lots of suffering, even the extreme cases, is justified because we need it in order to improve ourselves. If we didn't suffer we wouldn't understand what goodness is, we wouldn't be motivated to do anything, and we wouldn't seek God. So, suffering is integral to a just world."

Q9: We are using a certain conception of "gratuitous suffering." Explain how it's different from or identical with these conceptions:

a. An instance of suffering is gratuitous = it isn't coupled with any goods.
b. An instance of suffering is gratuitous = it isn't coupled with outweighing goods.
c. An instance of suffering is gratuitous = although it may be coupled with outweighing goods, God could have prevented that suffering from happening without introducing some new bad thing at least as bad as the old suffering.

Thus far we have some decent reason to think the Gratuitous Premise is true, although please keep in mind that we certainly haven't come remotely close to *proving* that it's true! All we're doing at this early point in the book is warming up to the topic by seeing what the two premises really say and why there is at least some good reason to think they are true.

Q10: Isn't it just plain obvious that there are zillions of cases of gratuitous suffering? Think of the deer in the forest fire case, from the book. Sure, we can suppose that in many forest fires the pain suffered by deer is linked with some goods (e.g., forests are often rejuvenated through fires). But it's clear that there is no good that justifies the deer's pain, as she *died*. Why isn't that enough, all by itself, to prove that the Gratuitous Premise is true—contrary to a great many theists?

The Consequence Premise

The idea behind the Consequence Premise is that a creator of the universe as powerful, morally good, and knowledgeable as God is supposed to be would (a) try to eliminate as many gratuitous sufferings as possible (even if he would allow some non-gratuitous sufferings), and (b) have the power to eliminate all gratuitous sufferings even while creating a universe with conscious beings living lives like ours. After all, if *you* knew for certain that the action you were contemplating performing would lead to trillions of truly terrible bouts of suffering (e.g., the torture of a young child, the slow burning to death of a deer), and you knew perfectly well that many of those awful things wouldn't be paired with any out-weighing goods (neither "positive" goods like pleasure or enlightenment nor "negative" goods like the prevention of something even worse), and you knew that you had the power to chose a similar but alternative action that didn't result in gratuitous suffering, then wouldn't you change your plan if you were being morally good? It seems so: *if* you had all that foreknowledge, and *if* you had all that power, and *if* you were being morally upstanding, then you would prevent all the gratuitous suffering you had the ability to prevent. Since the 4-Part God is supposed to be one for which all those "ifs" are true, he must have prevented as much gratuitous suffering as he could. And if he's all powerful, then surely he has the power to prevent *all* gratuitous suffering even while creating a world with conscious beings living lives like ours: he just needs to arrange things so that all suffering is worth it (in the long run or the short run; we won't distinguish these). That's the general line of thought that typically leads people to accept the Consequence Premise (we'll look at it a bit more carefully in chapter 5).

I have two children. It's not rare for me to make my kids suffer. No, I don't beat them, but I make them do things that they find truly awful and I make them refrain from doing things they greatly enjoy and desire. Often I'm able to explain why I'm making them suffer—explain it in such a way that they can understand me and see that I have a point behind my decision ("No, you can't have a pony, and here's why …"). They might think that my explanation isn't good enough to justify the hardship they have to endure, but they can see that I've got my reasons for my decision and they also see that I truly believe that my reasons are good ones, ones that justify my actions. But on other occasions the situation is worse: although I've got (what I sincerely think is) a good reason for making or allowing them to suffer, the reason is so sophisticated relative to their ages that there's simply no way my kids can understand why I'm causing or allowing their suffering. In those cases my kids just have to trust that I've got a good reason (this sucks for them and me). What would be truly awful is if I made them suffer, on purpose, when *I knew there was no compensating reason at all*. The Consequence Premise is saying that the 4–Part God never does that: he always has (and knows he has) an adequate reason for causing or allowing our suffering.

Thus, there is decent reason to think the Consequence Premise is true: *if* God the creator really is as powerful, knowledgeable, and morally upstanding as many people say he is, *then* he would successfully prevent all gratuitous suffering. But be **very** careful in interpreting the premise! Unfortunately, it's easy to misunderstand it. Here are some vital things to keep in mind when trying to understand what it says:

- The Consequence Premise doesn't presume that God exists; neither does it presume that God doesn't exist. All it says is that *if* he exists *and* fits the 4–Part conception, *then* a certain result follows (viz., the result that there is no gratuitous suffering).
- The premise does *not* say that God would have had to create a world without suffering. In fact, the advocate of the Consequence Premise (by "advocate" I mean the person who thinks the premise is true) is happy saying that the 4–Part God might exist and allow there to be *many trillions of cases of truly horrendous suffering*. All she's saying is that if God allowed all that horrendous suffering then he must have had a good reason for it—*all* that suffering must be linked with some truly fantastic goods that outweigh *all* the badness of those trillions of cases of horrific suffering. The advocate of this premise can admit that for all we know God often has excellent and perfectly morally upstanding reasons for allowing huge earthquakes, crippling plagues that wipe out millions of people, unimaginable physical and emotional pain, tsunamis that level whole countries, volcanoes that wipe out hundreds of villages, etc. Sometimes one encounters a person who says that according to the problem of evil there should be no earthquakes, tsunamis, or other natural disasters that cause great suffering; this is not the view we're considering in this book. All the Consequence Premise says is that a supremely morally good God would not allow there to be *gratuitous* suffering; it says nothing

about non-gratuitous suffering. It says that there is a certain kind of *limit* to the suffering God can permit: no gratuitous suffering is allowed. In sum: by the lights of the Consequence Premise truly enormous amounts of horrific suffering are morally acceptable *provided* that they're linked with goods that justify them. Don't forget this point! (I will briefly return to it in a moment, just to hammer it home.)

- The premise doesn't demand that we are made *aware* of the moral justification for each bit of suffering (or even a large portion of the instances of suffering). All it's saying is that the justification has to exist. (The 4-Part God will have to be aware of it, as he is supposed to know everything, but we need not.)
- Finally, the premise says something *only* about the 4-Part God. If you think that that conception of God is inaccurate, then you might not care much about what this premise says, since it says nothing about your God. However, there are troubling consequences of rejecting the 4-Part conception while remaining a theist, depending on what the alternative conception says; we'll take a brief look at some of those interesting consequences near the end of this book.

We have now seen that there is good reason to believe both premises, which makes the Problem of Gratuitous Suffering a genuine problem for the theist. The theist's critic is articulating the two premises (Consequence and Gratuitous), claiming that both are well supported, and requesting a rational and preferably informative theistic response to them (informative in the sense of telling which if any is false and precisely why it's false).

It may surprise you to learn that *there is no agreed-upon theistic response to the Problem of Gratuitous Suffering*. The problem has been known to some degree for centuries, but theists have come to no consensus as to what the best response is (this is true for many philosophical problems). A person highly skeptical about religion would probably conclude "Well no kidding! The reason there is no agreed on rational and informative theistic response to the problem is that there is no such response! You can't find what ain't there to be found. The Problem of Gratuitous Suffering is a *refutation* of theism!" Whether she is right about that is something we are investigating in this book.

No one, atheist or agnostic, is claiming that this has to be an *enormously difficult* problem for the theist. It all depends on the details of her kind of theism. For instance, if she thinks that the notions of morality fail to apply to God at all (God is good in some ways—he's great in power for instance—but he is not *morally* good or bad or any place in between)—or if she has some other reason to reject the 4-Part conception of God—then she is free to be utterly unperturbed with just accepting both premises as well as their conclusion. There is more on that possibility near the end of the book, in chapter 8. It is a much more challenging problem for the person who endorses the 4-Part conception of God, thinking that it is an accurate conception.[9]

Q11: Suppose a theist says God knows *nothing* about the universe: he creates the universe and then sits back and knows nothing of what happens in it. The Problem of Gratuitous Suffering might not seem to get any traction with her kind of theism. But suppose she says we should *worship* or *trust* God. Isn't there a problem there? Should we worship or trust a creator who has no clue about what he's created?

Every reasonable theist will admit that there is *some* good reason to accept both the Gratuitous Premise and the Consequence Premise.[10] But just because there is a reason to endorse a claim (even a good reason!), there might be evidence *against* it that is much, much more powerful than the evidence *for* it, and in fact the claim might even be false. For example, although there is evidence in favor of the idea that the Earth is still and the Sun goes around it once a day—as that's precisely how it looks from a non-scientific standpoint—there is evidence against this idea that is much, much more impressive, which is why we gave up the Earth-is-stationary-and-at-the-center idea centuries ago.

The Logical Problem of Suffering

In the next chapter I will briefly describe the five potential reasonable and at least in some cases informative ways the theist might respond to the Problem of Gratuitous Suffering. But before we look at those responses, it is well worth our time to note that the phrase "Problem of Evil" in philosophical literature actually stands for *several* philosophical challenges to theism, while this book focuses on just one. By looking at two of these other challenges we will better understand the specific one this book is about.

Some philosophers have argued that if God is truly omnipotent, omniscient, and morally perfect, then he could have, and would have, created a world with *no pain or suffering at all* even though it contains many familiar kinds of goodness that creatures like us enjoy. After all, if he has all possible power, if he can do anything at all (short of making $2 + 2 = 57$, or creating a married bachelor, or anything else contradictory), then why couldn't he make a universe with lots of goodness but no suffering whatsoever? And wouldn't he *want* to do just that if he was perfectly good? And since he knows everything, he would be aware of all these matters. The problem can be set up this way, with a fictional dialogue:

FRED: I just don't see how God can exist. After all, there's all this suffering in the world!

GEORGE: I agree that there's a lot of suffering, but why is that incompatible with God's existence?

FRED: It's just that the concept of God and the concept of suffering are dia-
metrically opposed. They're just incompatible.

GEORGE: But couldn't God allow suffering to exist as long as it's always worth
it, in virtue of leading to some really good thing?

FRED: But if God is truly *all powerful*, then he could create the universe with
those good things without the suffering!

The last statement is the key one: God could create the universe with all sorts of
great things but without any of the suffering. That idea is the key to the *Logical
Problem of Suffering*:[11]

1. If the 4–Part God existed, then he could make any universe possible, since he
    is omnipotent.
2. It's possible for there to be a universe more or less like ours (with conscious
    beings and many sorts of goodness such as happiness, pleasure, knowledge,
    and love) even though there is no suffering at all.
3. So, if the 4–Part God existed, then he could make a universe more or less
    like ours (with conscious beings and many sorts of goodness) but with no
    suffering whatsoever.
4. And since the 4–Part God is supposed to be perfectly morally good and
    knowledgeable, if he existed and was able to make such a universe, then he
    would not have made a universe more or less like ours (with conscious beings
    and many sorts of goodness) but with lots of suffering.
5. Thus, by (3) and (4) if the 4–Part God existed then he would not have made
    a universe more or less like ours (with conscious beings and many sorts of
    goodness) but with lots of suffering.
6. But we do indeed have such a universe.
7. Thus, the 4–Part God doesn't exist.

Note that premise (2) is not merely saying that God could make a universe
without suffering. That's easy: God could make a universe with no consciousness
or life at all. Such a universe would have no suffering. Instead, (2) is saying that
God could make a universe *with conscious beings living lives much like ours*, with lots
of goods such as love and happiness, but no suffering at all.

In my judgment it is hard to know that (2) is true. In fact, I think there is little
evidence that such a universe is really possible, although I won't go into any of the
reasons here. Perhaps we can *imagine* a universe with conscious beings more or less
like us, enjoying many of the goods that we enjoy, but with no suffering. One can
certainly *say* all those words out loud and not feel any immediate contradiction,
like you can't do when you say "Jon is a married bachelor" or "Jill is naked with
a blue dress on." But this quick imaginative task hardly gives us impressive reason
to think it's really possible. Other areas of philosophy suggest that the connection
between imagination and possibility is not very tight, so just because you can

imagine something doesn't mean that it's really possible. For instance, it's easy to imagine a world with lots of water but no hydrogen or oxygen, but there is little reason to think such a world is really possible—especially once we've discovered that water requires a particular combination of hydrogen and oxygen.

It must be said that my view is out of the mainstream of philosophy. Most philosophers think that the 4-Part God, if he existed, would not be bound by the laws of nature that govern our universe. Our universe has $E = mc^2$, as Einstein said, but God could have created a universe with different laws of nature—ones more forgiving to the experiences of sentient creatures. Or so people say. For my part, I don't think we are in any position to be confident that the laws of nature could have been different.

Be careful: we're not saying that (2) is false. Maybe it is, maybe it isn't; I don't know the answer. Competent philosophers continue to debate it in highly intelligent ways. All I'm saying is that I see little good reason to think it's true. And unless I can find a good reason to think (2) is true, I lack good reason to accept the argument (1)–(7). In that sense, it seems to me that the Logical Problem of Suffering isn't a successful argument against theism, or at least it's not as troubling as other challenges to theism that focus on the existence of profound suffering that appears gratuitous.

The philosophical problem we are focused on, the Problem of Gratuitous Suffering, nowhere says that (2) has to be true. So the failure of the Logical Problem of Suffering, because of the questionable nature of (2), casts no doubt on the Problem of Gratuitous Suffering.

The Problem of the Inferior Universe

A much more interesting philosophical problem of suffering centers on the idea that God must have put forth his *best effort* in creating the universe—where his best effort is the one he'd make if he were trying to create the best universe that was within his power to make. That is surely an initially reasonable thing to think an omnipotent, omniscient, morally supreme creator would do! After all, why shouldn't he do his absolute best when creating the universe? Surely he didn't have anything distracting him! The whole notion of being distracted doesn't apply to God at all. In fact, the idea that God "tries" to make the universe is silly too: God isn't supposed to be a person who is huffing and puffing in order to do his best when creating the universe. God says "Let there be light" and there's light; all he has to do is *will* it and it's done. Even so, shouldn't God make the universe with the best balance of good over evil—if he's morally perfect and he knows exactly what he's doing? These rough thoughts motivate what we can call the **Problem of the Inferior Universe**, which can be aptly summarized as follows:

A. If the 4-Part God existed, then because he is perfectly morally good and knowledgeable he must have created the best universe within his power to make.

B. But if the 4-Part God existed, then he could have made a universe better than ours, as he is all powerful and our universe, for all its good aspects, has many truly awful features. This isn't to say he could make a perfect universe, or one with no suffering but loads of familiar goods. But it is to say that he could have done better than the actual universe.

C. Thus, the 4-Part God doesn't exist.

This argument is undeniably intriguing and a theist who has a strong philosophical bent and lots of time for reflection should probably have a response to it. But there is a serious problem with that argument. One reason to doubt (A) is that it isn't clear that there is any such a thing as "the best universe the 4-Part God could make." What if there is no best one—just like there is no greatest number? For any number you can think of, there is a greater number.[12] Analogously, maybe for any possible universe (or possible universe that the 4-Part God could make) there is a better one—say, one with some more good in it. All we have to do is keep imagining bigger or more populous or longer lasting universes. Alternatively, we can imagine that pleasure and other kinds of goods have no limit to their degree of goodness. If the universes go on forever in increasing quality, then there is no top one in quality. It doesn't take a lot of reflection on these issues before one gets tied up in knots thinking about the infinite number of universes God could make, and trying to figure out what it means for one universe to be better overall than another—especially when the universes end up infinite in space or time or number of creatures. That makes thinking about the Problem of the Inferior Universe quite challenging to put it mildly.

This might seem to be a minor and "merely technical" objection to (A), not a substantive one. You might think: even if the universes increase in goodness infinitely, surely the 4-Part God would have to choose to make an awfully fantastic one if he's being truly morally good and loving; but since he didn't do so—look at the trillions of cases of horrific suffering!—it follows that there simply is no 4-Part God. I admit that there's something insightful in that line of thought, but I'm not sure what it is. I agree that it's reasonable to think that there are certain *minimal standards* for a universe made by the 4-Part God, even if there is no limit to how good the universe could get. It's hard not to see the appeal in that idea! Just because the possible universes might go on forever in increasing goodness hardly means that God could, while being perfectly good, create just any of them. This book is devoted to one such minimal standard: he has to make a universe with no gratuitous suffering, since he has the power and knowledge and goodness to do so. That's exactly what the Consequence Premise says. But I'm not sure of any other minimal standards.

Moreover, I still think the "universes might go on forever in quality" objection is not so easy to shrug off. It makes sense to ask of a human "Did she do her best when trying to get to work on time?" Presumably, the question requires clarification (e.g., are we implicitly assuming that in order to "do her best" she would have to conform to her moral code, or do we mean that she would have the option of violating it by using her car to run over a bunch of sweet old grandmas and cute babies?). But even so, we can get a grip on a human person doing her best at some task. However, presumably God has no bodily limitations, as he has no body. It seems odd to think of him *striving* to do something, as putting in his best effort as if he had obstacles in his way that he needed to overcome through effort. The notions of "best effort" and "less than best effort" don't seem to apply straightforwardly to a being like God is supposed to be. For those reasons it seems as though the entire infinity of possible universes is within his power to make, and so if there is no best universe then it doesn't seem to make a lot of sense to claim that his perfect goodness requires him to make "the" best universe. These are confusing matters, and I will return to them briefly near the end of chapter 8.

We aren't investigating that tricky problem in this book. The two premises we are focusing on, which are the backbone of the Problem of Gratuitous Suffering, nowhere say that God was morally required to do his best when creating the universe. Neither do they say that there is a best overall possible universe. All they presume is that (i) God was morally required to not knowingly produce gratuitous suffering if he could avoid it while making a universe roughly like ours (containing conscious beings like us), and (ii) given his power he could have created a universe like ours but with no gratuitous suffering. Presumably, that leaves him with a lot of possible universes to choose from when deciding what to make (maybe infinitely many), and some of these possible universes are morally better than others in having less non-gratuitous suffering and/or more bliss, either in total or per person or higher animal.[13] All the Consequence Premise is saying is that the 4-Part God must have a moral justification for allowing each bit of suffering, where the justification comes in the form of an outweighing good. The advocate of the Gratuitous and Consequence premises is willing to set aside the question of whether God created the morally best world within his power; her concern is with the question of whether God made a world with morally unjustified evils in the sense of "gratuitous suffering" we are using.

Q12: Explain the difference between the Problem of Gratuitous Suffering and the Problem of the Inferior Universe.

Q13: The Gratuitous Premise says that there are instances of gratuitous suffering; the Consequence Premise says that if that's true, then there is no 4-Part God. Explain what's lacking or otherwise deficient in the following responses to those two premises:

(a) The future's uncertain. So, we can hardly make any confident judgments that such-and-such a case of suffering is gratuitous, for we would have to be certain that there will *never* be an outweighing good for that suffering.

(b) In truth, there is no suffering at all; it's just an illusion. Sure, there are times when things look bleak and painful, but when viewed from the standpoint of eternity, all things have a purpose in the grand plan of the universe.

(c) God allows gratuitous suffering in order to let us make our own choices in our lives. If he went around making sure there was no gratuitous suffering, then we'd be like sheltered children who never have to lift a finger for anything. We would be robbed of all ambition and motivation.

(d) If God exists, then of course there is gratuitous suffering. What else would you call the crucifixion of Jesus?

(e) There's lots of suffering, but it's all accounted for and justified by the fact that Jesus rose from the dead. His life absolves us of sin, provided we admit it.

(f) Atheists are assholes who molest children and have sex with animals. Fuck 'em.

(g) God has to exist or there would be no morality at all. So the conclusion of the argument is false.

(h) The argument assumes that we have to know about all the goods that justify suffering. But that's silly. God has his own reasons; we are not privy to them.

(i) How are we supposed to know that God could have made a universe with no suffering, or at least no gratuitous suffering? None of us has even the slightest idea what it takes to make a universe. The Consequence Premise says that if God exists, then he didn't create a universe with gratuitous suffering, but we are in no position to know what he could or could not make.

3

POSSIBLE THEISTIC RESPONSES TO THE QUESTION

The Logic of Responses

In the rest of this book I'm going to describe and then evaluate how the theist might respond to the Problem of Gratuitous Suffering in a *rational and informative* way. She could of course just shrug her shoulders, or wink in a knowing manner, or stare into space, or freeze like a deer in the headlights, or scream obscenities, but those aren't *informative* responses and I won't have much to say about them.[14] But before I do that I need to make some general points about the possible rational and usually informative ways to respond to a two-premise argument. Otherwise we will probably miss out on some possible ways the theist might reasonably respond to the Problem of Gratuitous Suffering.

Suppose you're faced with an *obviously valid* argument with just two premises P1 and P2. When used in philosophy the compound term "obviously valid" has a specific meaning: an obviously valid argument is one in which it's obvious that *if* the premises P1 and P2 are true, then the conclusion is guaranteed to be true too. That is, it's perfectly clear that there is no possible way the premises can be true while the conclusion is false. Here is one such argument:

> P1: Socrates is a banana.
> P2: All bananas are fish.
> C: Thus, Socrates is a fish.

It's plain to everyone that if the two premises P1 and P2 are true, then the conclusion C simply must be true too. All three statements in the argument are ridiculously false, but what matters to obvious validity is the *combination* of the premises and the conclusion: it's clearly impossible for the latter to be false while the former are true. If you imagine a world in which the two premises are true, then in that world the conclusion will have to be true too; you simply can't coherently conceive a world in which the premises are true and the conclusion is false. (Try to write a short story in which at one given time Socrates is a banana, all bananas are fish, and yet Socrates isn't a fish; no matter how ridiculous or clever you get, your story will be incoherent.) Thus, if your position is that the conclusion of an obviously valid argument is false, then you are forced to conclude that at least one of the premises P1 and P2 is false too. So if your position is that the conclusion of an obviously valid argument is false, where the premises are P1 and P2, then your official philosophical position is this: either P1 or P2 is false (or both are false).

In the case of the Problem of Gratuitous Suffering, P1 is the Consequence Premise, P2 is the Gratuitous Premise, and C is the conclusion "There is no 4-Part God." Now we can introduce the five potential ways that the theist could respond in a rational and informative way to our P1–P2–C argument.

Q14: What does "PHOG" stand for?
What's an "obviously valid" argument?

The Five Approaches

If you are a theist but reject the 4-Part conception of God, so you think the 4-Part God doesn't exist, then you are free to accept P1, P2, and C. Theists who take this line are endorsing what I call the **Non-4-Part Approach** to the Problem of Gratuitous Suffering. These theists try to give us good reasons for thinking that although God exists, at least one of "all knowing," "all powerful," "perfectly morally good," and "creator of the universe" is mistaken; so these theists are saying that 4-Part theists have misunderstood what God is. Some Non-4-Part theists reject "perfectly morally good." For instance, some Catholics tell me that for many centuries there has been a strong strain of thought in Christianity that says God is not a "moral agent," meaning that his actions are not the kind of thing that can be morally good or morally bad (so his actions are very unlike ours). Under this conception, God is not morally good (or bad); so this conception of God rejects the 4-Part conception. Be careful: the idea is *not* that while we humans are in no position to judge the morality of God's actions or decisions, his actions and decisions are morally good anyway. Instead, the idea is that God's actions and decisions have no moral status at all: none of them are good or bad or anything in between. Not many contemporary theistic philosophers endorse this idea, which I will examine in chapter 8 along with a few other ways of filling out the Non-4-Part Approach. One common criticism of the Non-4-Part Approach is that if God isn't morally good, or fails to meet one of the other parts of the

4-Part conception, then he hardly seems worthy of worship or devotion, which deprives religion of its meaning. As a result, a good number of theists have rejected the Non-4-Part Approach (many others have rejected it not because of that consequence but simply because they think God's actions do have moral status).

On the other hand, if you're a 4-Part theist, as most of today's theists are (at least implicitly: if you press them on whether they agree with all four parts of the 4-Part conception, many if not most of them will eventually agree to all four of them), then your philosophical position is that the conclusion C is false and thus at least one of the two premises P1 and P2 is false as well. As mentioned above, some 4-Part theists will have no *informative* response to the Problem of Gratuitous Suffering. From now on, though, we will almost always limit ourselves to considering the options available to 4-Part theists who want to offer a *reasonable and informative* response to the problem. Theists who accept the 4-Part conception need to present to us their reasonable and informative explanation of why they think at least one of the two premises is false. After all, *they have staked out a serious philosophical position ("Either P1 or P2 is false"), and people want to know what their reasons are for endorsing it.* The informative strategies that the 4-Part theist can employ are these:

a. She explains why she thinks the overall evidence shows that P1, the Consequence Premise, is false.
b. She explains why she thinks the overall evidence shows that P2, the Gratuitous Premise, is false.
c. She explains why she thinks that the overall evidence shows that the conjunction of the two premises must be false even though she fully admits that she doesn't know *which* of the premises is false.

In the rest of this chapter I will comment briefly on (a)–(c), showing how they lead to four additional theistic approaches to the Problem of Gratuitous Suffering (the first of our five total theistic approaches was the Non-4-Part Approach, mentioned above). Of these four additional approaches, one fits (c), one fits (a), and two fit (b). What these four approaches have in common is that they think the conclusion C is false and at least one of the two premises P1 and P2 is false. When I'm finished describing those approaches, I'll take on the question of faith as a response.

Q15: Suppose you had an obviously valid argument with *three* premises and one conclusion: P1, P2, P3, and C. Describe all the possible ways of responding to the argument in a rational and informative manner (analogous to the ways talked about in the book for responding to a two-premise obviously valid argument).

I start my introduction of the remaining four theistic approaches with what is probably the most unfamiliar one, (c). The theists who take this approach begin by admitting that for all they can show the evidence for each of the two premises is genuinely good and strong. But they go on to claim that they can show that the overall evidence *against* the conclusion is much, much stronger than the evidence *for* the two premises. So they're happy to admit that *when viewed in isolation* each premise really does look true, as each premise has some significant evidence in its favor and they can't show what's wrong with either of them. But then they proceed to explain that the evidence against the conclusion (that is, the evidence for the existence of the 4-Part God) isn't merely "significant" but is much, much stronger than that. In such a case, one should reject the conclusion *even if one can't find anything wrong with the premises*, and it's rational to react this way because one is justifiably supremely confident the conclusion is false and not nearly so confident both the premises are true.

I realize that the third strategy (c) looks peculiar, but you may have already encountered things that fit the pattern. For instance, one can construct a mathematical "proof" with the conclusion that $1 = 2$ in which each line in the proof really looks true (even though on more careful examination one can usually discover which step in the reasoning is mistaken). Here is one of those simple "proofs" that $1 = 2$ (you can see some of these "proofs" on youtube.com):

Step 1: if a and b be positive numbers and are equal to each other, then this is true:

$$b = a \tag{1}$$

Step 2: if (1) is true and you multiply each side of (1) by a, then this is true:

$$ab = a^2 \tag{2}$$

Step 3: if (2) is true and you now subtract b^2 from each side of (2), then this is true:

$$ab - b^2 = a^2 - b^2 \tag{3}$$

Step 4: if (3) is true and you now factor each side of (3), then this is true:

$$b(a - b) = (a - b)(a + b) \tag{4}$$

Step 5: if (4) is true and you now divide each side of (4) by the common factor $(a - b)$, then this is true:

$$b = a + b \tag{5}$$

Step 6: since $a = b$ (as we said in (1)), if (5) is true and you replace the occurrence of a in (5) with b, then this is true:

$$b = b + b \qquad (6)$$

Step 7: if (6) is true and you now simplify the right side of (6), then this is true:

$$b = 2b \qquad (7)$$

Step 8: if (7) is true and you now divide each side of (7) by b, then this is true:

$$1 = 2 \qquad (8)$$

Even if you can't put your finger on the precise point in the argument where a mistake was made (and no, I'm not going to tell you where it is), you still know that the statement on line (8) is false! The (1)–(8) argument is formulated in terms of eight if-then premises and is valid (in the strict sense of "valid" we are using). When you string the eight together you get this conclusion:

If a and b are positive numbers and equal to each other, then $1 = 2$.

But this is clearly false. Just let the letters "a" and "b" both pick out the number 11: the "if" part of the conclusion will be true but of course the "then" part is ridiculously false, as 1 certainly doesn't equal 2. This shows that one can be confronted with an obviously valid argument, not see *anything* wrong with the premises that lead to the conclusion, and yet *know* that the conclusion is false and thus know that at least one of the premises simply must be false. As you might expect, these cases are pretty rare. But they *open up the possibility* that a theist could be confronted with the P1-P2-C argument, not see anything wrong with the premises P1 and P2, and yet know that C is false and thus know that at least one of the premises P1 and P2 (Gratuitous and Consequence) simply must be false.

Now you might think that the math example is a little silly, as it takes only a little expertise to find the error in the premises, whereas it is very difficult to see where the error is in either the Gratuitous Premise or the Consequence Premise (assuming, with the 4-Part theist, that there is an error in those premises). But there are quite a few famous cases in logic and philosophy in which there is an apparently valid argument for a crazy conclusion and yet even after *many centuries of dedicated investigation by some of the world's great geniuses* there is nothing even approaching consensus among experts regarding where the mistaken premises lie (some amateurs think they have found the solution, but their proposals always turn up inadequate). Here are just three of the conclusions of the arguments I have in mind: "No one is poor," "Everyone is bald," and "There are no pumpkins anywhere in the universe." (If you're interested in learning more about these argument-paradoxes, just Google the phrases "Liar paradox" or "Sorites paradox" or "Problem of the Many" for starters.) Most people think that even though we can't put our finger on the mistaken premise in the respective arguments, it's reasonable to hold that at least one of the premises is false anyway, as the conclusions are truly crazy.

I will call approach (c) the **Confident Approach** to the Problem of Gratuitous Suffering, since the person who takes it starts out supremely confident that a certain conclusion is false (just like how we start out completely confident in the falsity of the conclusion that $1 = 2$) and then infers that since the two-premise argument leading to that conclusion is obviously valid, at least one of the premises is false—even though she admits up front that she has no idea which of the two premises is false or why it is false. Just because this response is uninformative in that it doesn't say where the mistake is in the two premises doesn't mean it fails to be completely rational and reasonable. Even if you were unable to find the error in the "proof" that $1 = 2$ there was nothing terribly irrational or unreasonable in your concluding that there has to be a mistake somewhere in that argument. Similarly, and more seriously, there are the philosophical "proofs" mentioned above for outrageous conclusions (e.g., "There are no pumpkins anywhere in the universe") and I don't think there is anything worryingly irrational or unreasonable in concluding that there must be something wrong with those "proofs" even though the experts have been utterly unable to agree on what's wrong with those "proofs." Of course, you might think that the Problem of Gratuitous Suffering argument is importantly different from these other arguments, that even though the Confident Approach to the argument that $1 = 2$ is rational, the Confident Approach to the Problem of Gratuitous Suffering is irrational. That's a reasonable thing to say. We'll examine the Confident Approach in chapter 4. As we will see, the primary objection to the approach is that even if a lucky portion of us are rational in being *supremely* confident the 4-Part God exists, a great many of us are not in that fortunate position. As a consequence, many philosophers, including many who are theists, would reject the Confident Approach as inappropriate for the vast majority of us even if it is completely appropriate for some of us who are privileged enough to have high-grade knowledge of the 4-Part God's existence.

Let's move on to introduce another response to the Problem of Gratuitous Suffering. Suppose that you are a 4-Part theist who is convinced that P2, the Gratuitous Premise, is true (hence, you are convinced that there is gratuitous suffering). Then of course you'll endorse option (a): you explain why you think the overall evidence shows that P1, the Consequence Premise, is false. Philosophers who take this approach try to give us good reasons for thinking that although gratuitous suffering exists it is completely compatible with God being the all knowing, all powerful, and perfectly morally good creator of the universe. We call this response to the Problem of Gratuitous Suffering the **Compatibilist Approach**. As we will see in chapter 5, a significant majority of

4-Part theists think the Consequence Premise is true. As a result, most philosophers, including philosophers who are theists, have rejected the Compatibilist Approach.

Now suppose that you are a 4-Part theist who is convinced that P1, the Consequence Premise, is true. Then of course you'll endorse option (b): you explain why you think the overall evidence shows that P2, the Gratuitous Premise, is false. Since the great majority of 4-Part theists think the Consequence Premise is true, option (b) is very popular among 4-Part theists. Assuming these theists want to offer an informative response to the Problem of Gratuitous Suffering, they have the task of showing that the overall evidence is definitely against the Gratuitous Premise. And that means this: they need to successfully argue that the overall evidence shows that *all instances of pain and suffering* (even the Holocaust!) are coupled with goods that made all that suffering worth it.

There are several ways to try to show this (i.e., to take option (b)), and it is surprising how different they are from one another. Probably the most satisfactory way, in terms of conveying useful and interesting information, would be this: reveal the goods that justify all sufferings *and* explain in detail how they do indeed justify all that suffering. Theists who embark on this ambitious road aren't just arguing that the outweighing goods exist somewhere or other; they go far beyond that to *actually tell us what the outweighing goods really are*. There is a big difference between arguing "The outweighing goods simply must exist, but unfortunately I don't know what they are" and arguing "The outweighing goods exist—and now I'm going to tell you what they are." I will call the latter response, the really ambitious one, the **PHOG Approach**, where "PHOG" stands for "profoundly hidden outweighing good." One of the ideas behind the PHOG Approach is that the goods that justify the many, many trillions of cases of horrific suffering are fairly well hidden from at least most of us, since it's so hard for most of us to think of the goods that actually justify that colossal amount of horrible suffering.[15] As we will see in chapter 6, the primary objection to this approach is that the goods the PHOG Approach advocates have listed over the centuries don't seem up to the task of justifying anything remotely close to all suffering. As a consequence, many philosophers have rejected the PHOG Approach— although the philosophers who are theists like the approach much more so than philosophers generally.

Many philosophers who are 4-Part theists and think the Gratuitous Premise is false (i.e., philosophers who endorse option (b)) take a kind of "middle ground" between the Confident Approach and the PHOG Approach—or at least they are inclined to take this middle ground approach even if they haven't articulated it explicitly. In order to understand even the basics of this middle ground approach we need to go over some basic *epistemology* (which is the study of a closely knit group of concepts including knowledge, evidence, reason, understanding, wisdom, and rationality), which I will present at the beginning of chapter 7. The rough idea is to take the virtues of both the Confident Approach and PHOG Approach and add some modest doubts about our ability to spot when an instance of suffering is coupled with an outweighing good. The result is the **Skeptical Approach**, which is the subject of chapter 7. I conjecture that most philosophers would think this is the *best* option for the 4-Part theist, although as we will see it has some significant weaknesses as well.

Q16: Explain how the PHOG and Skeptical approaches differ.

Now I'm finished introducing the five theistic responses to the Problem of Gratuitous Evil. The next five chapters treat the five approaches. You will be happy to learn that the chapters may be studied more or less independently of one another. The all-important final chapter interprets the results of those chapters.

Faith as a Response

I have been emphasizing that this book is devoted to examining *reasonable and informative* theistic responses to the Problem of Gratuitous Suffering. But what about faith as a response? Surely any examination of theistic responses to the problem will have to address the most common one: faith alone, with no useful or illuminating information as to why there is so much horrific suffering.

There is no point, and I really mean *no point whatsoever*, in thinking about this response to suffering until we appreciate the fact that there are multiple meanings to "faith," some quite different from one another. For instance, sometimes faith is just a *feeling of trust* in something; other times it's a *whole way of life* that is subsequent to the trust; yet other times it's intended to be the *belief*— or perhaps *knowledge*—that the trust is justified; occasionally it's thought of as a *practical commitment* expressly taken up in awareness that one has little *evidence* that the object of the commitment—God—even exists. And that list is not exhaustive. I am not going to separate these notions here.[16] Instead, I want to emphasize the intellectual challenge suffering poses to most notions of faith.

Suppose Howard lived in the sixteenth century and put a great deal of faith in Saint Luca. Howard heard about Saint Luca from a traveling preacher, who recounted various deeds and teachings of the Saint. Howard has "faith" in Saint Luca—where you get to choose what kind of faith is operative here. But then Howard starts to hear many rumors from many different sources—rumors not about Luca but about the traveling preacher. He learns that many people—in fact, most people—now think the "preacher" is no preacher at all but a con artist who makes up stories and then tells them to crowds in the hope of being paid with money and favors. That is, Howard learns of *powerful evidence that the object of his faith doesn't even exist*. At that point, Howard would be unreasonable to just continue as if nothing had happened. Instead, he's got to pause and figure out what's going on. No matter what kind of faith he has in Saint Luca, if he acquires excellent overall evidence that there is no Luca at all, then he is a fool if he takes no heed of it. In that respect, faith is tied to evidence whether we like it or not.

This is relevant to the Problem of Gratuitous Suffering because that problem provides *powerful evidence that the 4-Part God doesn't exist*. Now, when I make that claim about evidence I am *not* saying that there is no 4-Part God. Neither am I saying that belief in the 4-Part God is irrational. All I am saying is that there is some powerful evidence against that belief. This is consistent with there being powerful evidence *for* the belief—in fact, the evidence for the belief might completely overwhelm the evidence against it. So although there is powerful evidence against the existence of the 4-Part God, our *overall* evidence—for and against— might be strongly in favor of his existence. For comparison, think of a jury trial. Carlos has heard excellent evidence that the butler killed the maid: the butler's diary says he's going to kill the maid, the butler is on a store videotape a week before buying a gun that matches the one that was found at the crime scene, some witnesses report that they saw the butler near the crime scene the day of the crime, etc. But Carlos also has excellent evidence that the butler *didn't* kill the maid: three witnesses say he was on the Amtrak train they were also on at 8pm, which is when the investigators said the murder happened, the train was going from Philadelphia to New York whereas the murder took place in Washington DC, there is videotape from the train station in New York that he indeed arrived at Penn Station in Manhattan, etc. This is a case in which Carlos has excellent evidence *for* the claim that the butler killed the maid but he also has excellent evidence *against* it. It might turn out that Carlos can be completely reasonable in dismissing the evidence that suggests that the butler didn't kill the maid. After all, Carlos himself may have witnessed the maid's murder and may have knowledge of the butler's attempt to put together what appears to be a strong alibi.

Thus, when I say that the Problem of Gratuitous Suffering provides powerful evidence against the existence of the 4-Part God I am saying nothing whatsoever, pro or con, regarding the *overall* evidence our beliefs have regarding the 4-Part God. My point here is about *the tie between faith and evidence*: if you have faith in the 4-Part God, then as the Saint Luca story suggests, you are not immune to considerations about evidence. To continue with that faith in the absence of any response to powerful evidence against it is not terribly reasonable—provided, that is, you're acutely aware of the challenge that suffering presents to theism. More on that "provided" clause immediately below.

Q17: The book says that there are five potentially reasonable and informative ways for a theist to respond to the Problem of Gratuitous Suffering. Are there more than that? If so, what are they?

Ignorance

Consider again the story about the butler, the maid, and Carlos. Imagine that Roberta is aware of just one side of the story: the evidence that strongly suggests the butler is innocent. She has heard nothing at all, even indirectly, regarding the evidence the prosecution will put forward. In that case Roberta's belief that the butler is innocent is perfectly reasonable. Her belief is false, and there is excellent evidence against her belief, but given that she is completely unaware of that contrary evidence and has nothing but excellent evidence for her belief, she is without fault in coming to think the butler is guilty.

It's her ignorance that saves her rationality—her ignorance of the excellent evidence that the butler is guilty. This is ignorance that is utterly without blame. Now what would happen if Roberta got *just a hint* of the evidence against the butler? She has known the butler for many years, he's never exhibited anything remotely like murderous behavior around her or her friends, his alibi sounds perfectly reasonable and convincing, etc. And then she hears that some people claim to have witnessed him at the crime scene right before the murder— contrary to what she heard in the alibi. At this point, with just a hint of the powerful evidence of his guilt, Roberta is quite reasonable in thinking to herself "Well, there must be some explanation of what's going on with those people; they must have made a mistake of some kind."

Similarly, if one has always been in an environment in which belief in God was maintained by the most reasonable and educated people, and one was totally unaware of any contrary evidence, then one could easily be completely reasonable in sticking with one's belief in God—even if God doesn't exist and there is powerful evidence against his existence. More to the point, even if this theist became *dimly aware* of the Problem of Gratuitous Suffering—so she's not someone who has read books like this one, who has thought about the problem in a deep and sustained way—then she could reasonably think "Well, I'll bet there is a good theistic response to the problem of suffering, although I just don't know what it is." It's only after you've thought seriously hard about it that you see that there's actually *very good* evidence for both the Gratuitous Premise and the Consequence Premise and it's pretty hard to find a way to reject either of them. Only then, I think, is the challenge of suffering potent enough to require a defense beyond that supplied by ignorance.

4

THE CONFIDENT KNOWLEDGE OF GOD

What the Approach Says

On this approach the theist tries to give good reasons to show that the evidence against the conclusion that the 4-Part God doesn't exist is *much* better than the evidence for the combination of the Gratuitous Premise and the Consequence Premise—even though she is unable to demonstrate any significant weakness in the two premises. Here is what this theist might say:

> I really don't know which of the two premises is false. At least: I don't know for sure, although I may have some ideas on the matter. I confess: you've stumped me! But I do know that the conjunction of the two premises is false because I already know for a fact that there is a supremely morally good, knowledgeable, and powerful creator. I fully admit that you've succeeded in presenting me with a mysterious philosophical-theological puzzle regarding God and suffering, but I know that there's a mistake in the two premises *somewhere* because I already know that the conclusion of the premises is false. This is similar to the case of a "proof" that $1 = 2$ in which some of us can't spot the fallacy in the premises. Now, don't get me wrong: it would be going way too far to say we know of the existence of the 4-Part God *as well as* we know that $1 \neq 2$! But still, a good portion of us do already know very well that the 4-Part God exists, and so we are in a position to know that at least one of the premises has got to be false. Here's how I already know that the conclusion "The 4-Part God doesn't exist" is false …

Again, we call this the **Confident Approach** to the Problem of Gratuitous Suffering since the person who takes this approach starts out very confident that the 4-Part God exists.

This theist tries to give us good reasons for thinking that we—or at least a significant number of us—*already know for sure* that God exists as the supremely moral, powerful, and knowledgeable creator. But then she'll point out that that knowledge won't make us experts regarding his nature. So we know for certain that God exists as creator, is perfectly morally good, omnipotent, and omniscient, and yet there seem to be gratuitous sufferings. This is puzzling, for sure, but not so much as to make us think we've gone wrong in thinking that God exists as advertised in the 4-Part conception. The most important part of this approach is that she says that we already know full well that the conclusion of the two premises is false, so we can also know full well that at least one of the premises is false as well (since the premises lead to that false conclusion) even if we don't know *which* of the premises is false or *why* it's false.

The Confident Approach advocate has a curious mix of modesty and confidence. Clearly, she is very confident that the 4-Part God exists. But she is modest as well: although she will probably have ideas regarding the premises, all she wants to insist on is the position that at least one of the premises is false. You might wonder: if she is so confident that the 4-Part God exists, then surely she must take herself to know a fair amount about God. After all, she insists that she knows that he is creator, supremely good, supremely knowledgeable, and supremely powerful. Wouldn't all that knowledge of divine matters carry over to the Problem of Gratuitous Suffering? If she knows so much about God, then why doesn't she know about his relation to suffering? Well, she will just have to say in response to your questions that although there are some things about God that she has figured out, they don't always help her figure out other important things about God.

Q18: According to the advocate of the Confident Approach a certain group of theists have a response to the Problem of Gratuitous Suffering that allows them to rationally retain their theism when faced with the Problem of Gratuitous Suffering. Describe all the relevant characteristics of the theists in that group, according to the Confident Approach.

The Confident Approach advocate may or may not have something impressive to say in response to the question "But how can you be so sure the 4-Part God exists—so certain that you can reject the premises without even being able to spot a flaw in them?" She might or might not have anything to say in defense of her belief in the 4-Part God. In a few pages I will briefly consider some of the positive reasons she might have for being so confident that the 4-Part God exists. We can assume that she would have intelligent if not completely convincing things to say in response to "Why do you think the 4-Part God really and truly exists?" She need not be someone who is confident in the 4-Part God on faith alone.

> Q19: In what three ways is the Confident Approach uninformative?
> The Confident Approach is said to be a "curious mix" of confidence and
> modesty. Explain what each element is.

Criticisms of the Approach

The most serious problem people have with the Confident Approach is the most obvious one: it starts out being *too confident* that there is a creator *and*, what is much more, that the creator is supremely morally good, omnipotent, and omniscient. Naturally, many people are indeed *personally* confident in all those things: they feel as though they are definitely right about all those claims. But many other intelligent people—including theists!—judge such extreme confidence in the 4-Part conception to be pretty dubious and unjustified.

Let me elaborate the point a bit, as it ends up bifurcating into two separate criticisms. Keep in mind that the Confident Approach advocate would have to be very confident not merely in God's existence but in the additional and more controversial view that he's supremely knowledgeable, supremely powerful, supremely morally good, and the creator of the universe. That is, she would have to start out very confident that *the entire 4-Part conception is accurate*. This looks to some people to be quite overconfident—especially since some standard kinds of theism reject the 4-Part conception of God! This objection holds even if we don't offer precise explanations of what "all knowing" and "all powerful" come to. Furthermore, as I mentioned above theologians inform me that for many centuries there has been a strong strain of thought in Christianity that says God is not a "moral agent," meaning that his actions are not the kind of thing that can be morally good or morally bad (and so his actions are very unlike ours).

I suppose that if the 4-Part God exists, then a person might have some incredible, mind-blowing, private, internal experience—a kind of divine "light bulb over the head" experience—that proves to her that some kind of being is communicating with her with love and forgiveness that dwarf anything we experience in the ordinary world. But how on earth could such an experience prove, or even reasonably suggest, that that being knows everything, created the universe, and is perfectly good and all powerful? She might get the impression that the being she is experiencing loves her intensely and radiates great power and understanding. But that is a far cry from the 4-Part conception. I know of no reason to think experiences that prove the whole 4-Part conception is accurate are even possible, let alone real.

> Q20: What's the difference between these two, assuming both exist:
> having an experience that proves to the person having the experience that
> God exists, having an experience that proves to the person having the

experience that the 4-Part God exists? (By "proves" I mean that it *success-fully* shows that God/the 4-Part God exists; so it's not just that the person *thinks* the experience provides proof.)

The upshot of the common criticism of the Confident Approach is that although we can be extremely confident that $1 \neq 2$, which means we already know that any "proof" that $1 = 2$ is fatally flawed, the large majority of us can't be anywhere near as confident that the 4–Part God exists (even if we can be highly reasonably confident that some being at least vaguely God-like exists while remaining uncertain regarding what its characteristics are). This criticism might not be true, but many intelligent people will claim that it is true. Presumably, if you're in heaven and have been hanging out with God a lot (okay, I realize that lots of theists think this hypothesis is silly, but I'm just using it as an illustration to make a point), then you could say "Well, I sure as hell know that God is perfectly morally good and powerful and all that (as I have [somehow] seen it for myself), so he must have set things up so that all suffering is worth it, although he hasn't bothered to take the time to explain it all to me." This person, who of course is in a really bizarre situation compared to us, might be able to adopt the Confident Approach in a rational and reasonable way. But presumably we, or at least the vast majority of us, are in no position to be so highly confident that the universe has a perfectly morally good, powerful, and knowledgeable creator. Or so the critic says.

So we've seen that there is a major criticism of the Confident Approach. It's certainly not a refutation of the approach! But it is a significant criticism.

Actually, though, it's two separate criticisms. First, there is the criticism that goes "No one can have *certain* knowledge of the 4–Part God's existence—certain enough that one can rationally say that the premises must be false even if one can't find any significant flaws in them." Second, there is the objection that runs "Even if some people can have that super-duper knowledge of the existence of the 4–Part God, the vast majority of us don't have it; so it hardly even matters." The second one is probably the key, as it leaves open the possibility that some people have certain knowledge of the 4–Part God's existence. It says: even if there is such a thing, it's so rare that it's practically irrelevant because so few people are in a position to respond to the Problem of Gratuitous Suffering in the way described by the Confident Approach.

Some philosophers hold that there are relatively simple and easily accessible kinds of experiences one can have that supply enough evidence that one's belief in the 4–Part God becomes justified and amounts to knowledge. They say that one doesn't need any fancy argument, either scientific or philosophical, in order to know that God exists. Neither does one need to witness anything extraordinary, like a miracle. Neither does one have to have some mind–blowing revelation, as if

God hit you with an experiential lightning bolt so that you could see for yourself that he exists (as was discussed a few paragraphs back). Instead, if in the right circumstances you just look at a newborn baby, or the starry skies, or a beautiful meadow, you can thereby have a calm internal experience that shows, quite simply, that God exists. So the theist can say to the atheist and agnostic,

> Well, I hate to tell you this, but there's this special calm spiritual mental state or process or whatever that has allowed me and millions of others to come to know that God exists, and until you get it you may (just "may") never find any epistemic item—argument, miracle, experience, or whatnot—that provides any decent support for theism. I know that stinks, from your perspective, and I know it stinks from the perspective of philosophical discussion. In fact, if I were in your shoes I might well find theistic belief positively nuts! But those are the facts. I wish I had better news for you. My apologies!

It won't strike you as surprising that atheists and agnostics tend to scoff at this idea. For one thing, it just seems crazy, they say, to think that a look at a beautiful meadow, even if awe inspiring, could possibly come anywhere close to proving that there is a being who (a) created the universe, (b) knows everything, (c) has all possible power, and (d) is perfectly good. For another thing, atheists and agnostics have seen a heck of a lot of newborn babies, starry skies, and beautiful meadows and they haven't had any experiences that even faintly suggest that there is some being that is perfectly powerful, loving, good, knowing and who created the universe. The theistic philosophers discussed in the previous paragraph reply: well, you guys are just *screwed up somehow*, in your minds, so you don't experience what we experience (i.e., God himself). This reply typically doesn't go over well. In any case, the critic of the Confident Approach is saying that there is no such incredibly common experience that can generate high-grade knowledge that the universe was created by an all knowing, all powerful, all good being.

Q21: Articulate in your own words the primary objections to the Confident Approach. If you have an additional major objection to it, or perhaps two of them, articulate them.

Whether the Confident Approach is a reasonable response to the Problem of Gratuitous Suffering rests with the question of whether the theist who makes this response *already has truly excellent overall support* for her belief that God exists *and* fits the 4-Part conception.[17] To that extent, the proper theistic response to the Problem of Gratuitous Suffering depends on how good the available evidence for the 4-Part God is. Unfortunately, it would take too many pages to discuss that latter issue in a truly adequate way. To that extent my presentation and assessment of the Confident Approach will have to be incomplete. But in this chapter I will try to give a brief explanation why the clear majority of philosophers think the evidence for the 4-Part God is flimsy.

However, before I do that I need to make two more observations about the Confident Approach. First, most people who opt for it also admit that the Consequence Premise is true: if the 4-Part God exists, then there are no gratuitous sufferings. Obviously, they can then deduce that since they believe in the 4-Part God, they have to conclude that there are no gratuitous sufferings. So, they simply *must* think that there are no gratuitous sufferings; they *must* hold that the Gratuitous Premise is false. They don't claim to know of the goods that justify sufferings—they are modest in that respect—but they do claim that they know that such goods have to exist.

(These 4-Part theists reject the Gratuitous Premise because (i) they are supremely confident that the 4-Part God exists and (ii) they admit that the Consequence Premise is true. Technically, that means that *these* theists are advocating approach (b), not (c), from chapter 3 (recall that (b) is the idea that the Gratuitous Premise is false, whereas (c) is the idea that although we don't know which premise is false, the evidence for the 4-Part God is so great that we know that at least one of the premises must be false). But since the main criticism of their view is the same as that of (c)—the criticism being that the vast majority of us are in no position to be so confident that God exists and fits the 4-Part conception—I have elected to treat their view here.)

Thus, they can't rest content with "Well, I know that at least one of the two premises is false, but I don't know which one." Instead, they have to hold that it's definitely the Gratuitous Premise that's false—even though they might not have the foggiest idea what the goods are that justify all the trillions of cases of horrific suffering. Their speech is something like this:

> Well, I already know that the 4-Part God exists. So, one of the two premises has got to be false. And I really don't see any way to quarrel with the Consequence Premise. So, that means that the Gratuitous Premise is very probably the false one. That is, each of the many trillions of instances of suffering in the universe must be outweighed by some good coupled with it. Now I am perfectly willing to admit right off the bat that in zillions of cases I might have no good idea as to what the outweighing goods are; I'm a *humble* theist! But I know that they are there somewhere, since I know God wouldn't allow suffering unless he had a good reason.

These folks still have to confront the main criticisms of the Confident Approach, as they are still starting out supremely confident that God exists and fits the 4-Part conception.

Now for the second important observation concerning the Confident Approach. Earlier I said that what I'm exploring in this book are potentially rational *and informative* theistic responses to the Problem of Gratuitous Suffering. I also said that there might be theistic responses that are fully rational yet disappointingly uninformative. The Confident Approach is just one such response, at least in some cases: *if* you really do have high-grade knowledge that the 4-Part God exists, *then* it seems to me that you are rational and reasonable in concluding that at least one of the two premises—or, more likely, the Gratuitous Premise—is false even if it turns out you have nothing remotely informative to say regarding the alleged goods that justify all cases of suffering or even regarding the general story regarding God, suffering, and goodness. This would mean that your response to the Problem of Gratuitous Suffering is rational but uninformative; so it succeeds in one respect and fails in another.[18] Of course, this is all based on a really big "if": the assumption that you do indeed have high-grade knowledge that the 4-Part God exists. That's the issue I turn to below.

Q22: Suppose that the Confident Approach is successful in this sense: there are people who not only feel very confident that God exists but they *truly know for certain* that the 4-Part God exists. So these people have very high-grade knowledge of God's existence. In fact, they know of his existence about as well as they know that $1 \neq 2$. And from that knowledge they competently deduce that either the Gratuitous Premise is false or the Consequence Premise is false. So now they *know* that one of those two premises is false, although they admit that they aren't sure which one is false (so they make no claim about being maximally informative in their response to the Problem of Gratuitous Suffering). There is still a major criticism of the Confident Approach even after making all those assumptions; what is it? Is it a good one?

Evidence for the Existence of God

In my experience, people who believe in God (and who are not philosophers) typically, though not always, give at least one of the following intelligent responses to the question "What reasons are there for thinking that there is a god?"

> *The Design Argument*: Nature has an intricate structure that seems very carefully designed. Nature doesn't consist of just dust particles randomly zigzagging through space. There is all this marvelous, incredible order to it all. This order or structure or whatever you want to call it couldn't have come about randomly, without some designer. Something must have designed nature. Only God could do that.

The Cosmological Argument: Something must have created the universe. It can't just be a big random accident. It got here somehow. Even if the Big Bang theory is wrong and the universe goes back in time infinitely, still there's got to be something that creates or sustains it in existence. It can't create itself, so something separate from the universe did it. That's got to be God.

The Social Argument: Throughout history literally billions of people have believed in God. Obviously, some of them did so for little or no good reason, but the idea that *all* of them are wrong—even the large number of great geniuses of science and philosophy who were or are theists—strains credulity. In addition, throughout history many of these theists have claimed that they have actually *perceived* God, usually through meditation. People get trained in meditation, which often takes years, and eventually learn to experience God. Sure, some people who say they have experienced God are utterly delusional (e.g., preachers on television), but it seems highly unlikely that *all* of them, including so many gifted ones, could be so completely wrong.

It is incredible how much thought philosophers have put into these arguments, especially the first two. I estimate that there have been literally over a *million pages* of expert philosophical attention paid to *each* of the first two arguments, and the other has received much attention as well. What appear above are not so much arguments but slogans, or even mere bumper stickers, for long and complex arguments that have many sub-arguments as parts. Philosophers have worked extraordinarily hard to find good arguments along these lines. Part of the reason for this devotion is that the arguments have been around in one form or other for hundreds of years. Another reason is that there are many superficially similar but importantly different *versions* of those arguments. If you enter "Cosmological Argument," for instance, into an internet search engine and look at some of the results, it won't take too long to learn of this multiplicity: "the" Cosmological Argument isn't so much *one* argument but a unified bunch of closely related arguments. Yet another reason for the million pages of work on these arguments is that just about every philosopher, no matter what her specialties, scrutinizes these arguments as a part of her teaching undergraduates and/or graduate students.

But you're not going to get any of that staggering complexity from me in this little book. Instead, I will do three things. First, I'll comment on what conclusions the community of philosophers has reached concerning those arguments, as well as other philosophical arguments for God's existence that I'm not going to present even as bumper stickers. Second, I'll give a hint of the reasons for the consensus.[19] Third, I will indicate what the consensus means for the rationality of theistic beliefs that are partly based on those arguments.

The philosophical community has concluded that the arguments are failures. I mean: the clear majority of contemporary philosophers think that *every* version of the three arguments outlined above fails to provide much impressive reason for thinking that God exists (whether or not the argument is intended to show that he fits the 4-Part conception). So their view isn't merely that the arguments aren't airtight or that they have some flaws here and there; it's the view that they don't supply *any* significant evidence for thinking God exists. Moreover, the clear majority opinion is that the other arguments for God's existence, not summarized above, have failed as well. This consensus certainly isn't unanimous! Some philosophers of international distinction defend versions of some of these arguments, while many others of equal distinction insist that those versions are no good. But the considered opinion of the clear majority of philosophers is that the arguments fail to supply good reason for God's existence.

Let me elaborate a little. There are many subfields of philosophy, just like there are many subfields of psychology, biology, physics, economics, anthropology, etc. No philosopher is an expert in all these subfields, under any worthwhile way of spelling out "expert" I know of. Even so, a very high percentage of philosophers study a large amount of readings in the philosophy of religion (compared to the percentage of philosophers who study a large amount of the readings in a different subfield), as most of us teach topics belonging to that subfield, since people enjoy the topics. As part of our preparation for that teaching we read a significant portion of the primary contemporary readings in the philosophy of religion—including some but not all of the complicated versions of the above arguments for the existence of God. What usually happens—at least, this is my impression based on interacting with philosophers for many years—is that upon evaluation of this *limited* set of professional, contemporary theistic arguments philosophers come to think "These arguments are poor, significantly worse than what we encounter in other areas of philosophy; I'm not going to bother with further study." So these philosophers typically don't keep up with *every* new version of the Cosmological Argument, for instance, because they have already examined several versions and thought that they had almost no promise of being improved enough to take seriously. I'm not advocating their reasoning; I'm merely reporting it.

When I say that most philosophers judge the arguments to be "poor" I mean this: they think that expert investigation of the arguments reveals serious flaws in them. However, I think most of those philosophers would agree that when *initially* faced with the arguments, before the long philosophical training, the arguments often look quite good. In particular, the Design Argument is simply excellent—provided one is unfamiliar with contemporary science. Prior to the rise of sophisticated biology, I think that just about any informed intelligent person would have to be highly impressed with that argument. I'll return to this important point later in this chapter when I've finished discussing the Design, Cosmological, and Social arguments.

So, I'm saying that the philosophical consensus is that those theistic arguments are poor. Some philosophers tend to object to facts about consensus. They like to say "Well, sure, the clear majority of philosophers disagree with my position, but this isn't like science in which consensus usually implies really good evidence that the consensus is based on." But it's not so easy to dismiss the consequences of philosophical consensus. If a philosopher thinks that philosophical consensus doesn't count for much, that strongly suggests that she should think that she has a dim view of the ability of philosophers to gather strong evidence for various philosophical positions. But if she has *that* view, then she should have that view about herself, as she is just another philosopher. And if she has a dim view about her own philosophical abilities, then why does she trust her own philosophical judgment—especially those judgments regarding religion and God?

In any case, philosophers probe the traditional arguments for the existence of God even today because (a) it's not proven beyond doubt that the criticisms of the old versions of the arguments are airtight, and (b) people continue to come up with new and allegedly improved versions of the arguments all the time. I realize that it is easy to be cynical if not incredulous about these continuing efforts! Many philosophers think the (uncommon but not unheard of) view that some of the *old* versions of the arguments for God's existence are fine the way they are is downright silly: if those versions of the arguments are fine, then why do most philosophers who have thought long and hard about them insist, with their detailed criticisms, that they don't work? Are those philosophers just daft? You can't say with a straight face that they aren't familiar with all the wonderful old theistic arguments and, amazingly enough, keep encountering only the lousy ones! Many philosophers also think the search for new versions of the arguments is foolish: after centuries of investigation, what are the odds that someone will *finally* come up with a successful version of the Cosmological Argument, for instance? How rational is it for a philosopher today to say "Yes, yes, but you haven't seen *my* latest version of the argument! It really works!"? If you have looked for an old sock in your house for 37 years and haven't found it, it's probably time to conclude that it isn't there to be found. Of course, it *could* be found tomorrow but that means next to nothing: just about *anything* is possible. Similarly, if we have yet to find a good version of the Cosmological Argument, after centuries of truly expert investigation, it's probably time to conclude that it isn't there to be found.

I personally am not quite as pessimistic as that, although I certainly feel the pull of that attitude. In any case, now you have an idea of what the majority of philosophers have concluded about arguments for the existence of God. I think this consensus is fairly significant. Philosophers are a highly quarrelsome and independently minded bunch; they agree on very little of importance. Sure, they can agree on relatively minor issues (e.g., they often agree on things of the form "X is a formidable objection to theory Y"), but when it comes to really big questions, there is almost never anything approaching consensus (however you want to plausibly define "consensus"). However, there is an impressive consensus that no version of any philosophical argument for the existence of God—including the 4-Part God—is very good. Obviously the consensus could be wrong: maybe one of those arguments is actually excellent and all those philosophers have misjudged it.

In any case, in the rest of this chapter I'm going to briefly reveal *some* of the faults philosophers claim to have found in the theistic arguments, so you can see for yourself *why* philosophers tend to have these negative opinions about the arguments.

The Design Argument

Let's start with the Design Argument. Here is one "form" of the argument, a pattern that many versions of the argument fit:

a. The universe, or at least large or significant parts of it, has feature F.
b. It's very unlikely that this feature came about in a purely natural way, with no design behind it.
c. Thus, by (a) and (b) it's highly likely that this feature of the universe was designed.
d. If this feature was designed, then it is highly likely that it was designed by God (obviously we didn't design it, and it's really unlikely that aliens did it).
e. Thus, there is excellent evidence that God exists and designed the universe.[20]

You get different versions of the argument by plugging in different things for "F." Whether an argument that fits this pattern is a good one depends on what gets plugged in for F: it has to be chosen so that there is excellent reason to think (a), (b), and (d) are all true. It's not disputed that *if* (a), (b), and (d) are all true, *then* (e) is true as well. (And everyone agrees that if (a) and (b) are true then (c) is true too.) The only question is whether (a), (b), and (d) are all true.

It's easy to come up with Fs so that two out of the three premises (a), (b), and (d) are clearly true but the remaining premise is totally implausible. Here is one way to do so, an intentionally silly one:

a. The universe, or at least large or significant parts of it, has feature F: on September 30, 2010 everyone in the universe heard, in their own mind and language, a voice proclaiming that it is God and it created the universe, etc.; moreover, this amazing moment was accompanied by various apparent flagrant violations of the laws of physics, all described by the voice in our heads.
b. It's very unlikely that this feature came about in a purely natural way, with no design behind it.
c. Thus, by (a) and (b) it's highly likely that this feature of the universe was designed.
d. If this feature was designed, then it is highly likely that it was designed by God (obviously we didn't design it, and it's really unlikely that aliens did it).
e. Thus, there is excellent evidence that God exists and is a designer.

Obviously, no one has ever offered that argument! I'm just using it just for illustration, so we acquire a good understanding of the form of the Design Argument before we look at serious applications of it. Its premises (b) and (d) are plausible but of course (a) is false, so the argument fails. Here is another way to plug something in for "F":

a. The universe, or at least large or significant parts of it, has feature F: it contains lots of laptop computers.
b. It's very unlikely that this feature came about in a purely natural way, with no design behind it.
c. Thus, by (a) and (b) it's highly likely that this feature of the universe was designed.
d. If this feature was designed, then it is highly likely that it was designed by God (obviously we didn't design it, and it's really unlikely that aliens did it).
e. Thus, there is excellent evidence that God exists and is a designer.

Once again, we have a silly argument: although (a) and (b) are reasonable (d) isn't. By choosing yet another candidate for F, we can make (a) and (d) reasonable while (b) lacks obvious support:

a. The universe, or at least large or significant parts of it, has feature F: it contains lots fantastically enormous stars.
b. It's very unlikely that this feature came about in a purely natural way, with no design behind it. *lacks support b/c the beginnings were so long ago. We have no idea. Objection: so many stars that we don't even know about.*
c. Thus, by (a) and (b) it's highly likely that this feature of the universe was *surely some of them were natural?* designed.
d. If this feature was designed, then it is highly likely that it was designed by God (obviously we didn't design it, and it's really unlikely that aliens did it). *makes b false*
e. Thus, there is excellent evidence that God exists and is a designer.

The trick for the person trying to make the Design Argument work is this: *find some feature that can be plugged in for F to make (a) and (b) and (d)* ***ALL*** *look definitely true.* If she can pull this off, then we have a good Design Argument; if not, and no one can, then there is no good Design Argument that fits that pattern.

Q23: The template of the Design Argument has three premises: (a), (b), and (d). We just looked at three ways of filling it out: one had (a) and (b) true with (d) false, one had (a) and (d) true with (b) false, and one had (b) and (d) true with (a) false. Come up with three ways of your own that do the exact same thing.

Over the centuries theistic philosophers have put forth various serious candidates for a worthy F (i.e., one that seems to have a good chance at making (a), (b), and (d) true), some of which can be summarized with approximate accuracy as follows:

F1: Aspects of the universe are structured or ordered in a very intricate and apparently purposeful way, with various parts (the human eye) structured so that larger parts (humans) can do certain things (see things and act accordingly).
F2: The universe contains great beauty/mystery/love/goodness.
F3: The universe's physical laws and fundamental physical constants are finely tuned for the emergence of life and consciousness in the following sense: if even one of those laws or constants had been even the slightest bit different, then there is virtually no chance there would be consciousness, life, people, stars, planets … maybe even atoms.
F4: Biological life frequently has irreducible complexity.

The Design Argument versions one gets by plugging F1 and F4 into the argument pattern have been demolished with biology and physics through the various results about evolutionary theory and thermodynamics. (For F1, premise (a) is true—note the presence of the word "apparently" in premise (a)—but the overall evidence is against (b); for F4 the overall evidence is against (a).) I am not going to treat F1 or F4 in any detail, as I just don't think it's worth it. If you don't know much about science but you do pay at least some attention to politics in the USA, then you might be under the impression that the theory of evolution is controversial in the scientific community, as a significant number of politicians, journalists, and political commentators say so. Well, it's controversial among people who don't know much about it and people who are utterly unable to examine it in anything other than an extremely biased way. Among people who have studied it thoroughly and competently it's about as firmly established as the theory that most ordinary things around us are made of molecules. It's a sad fact about the popular sources of information in the USA, television and newspapers especially, that they completely fail to communicate these facts about the consensus among scientists. It's even sadder that there are whole organizations, such as the Discovery Institute, who spend colossal amounts of energy to intentionally mislead the public about these matters. Hopefully the present intellectual darkness regarding these issues is temporary and the USA will join other countries in not paying attention to the evolution deniers.

Now, this is not to suggest that scientists have the origin of life and biological species all figured out, in exact detail. They certainly do not. Like nearly every other major scientific theory that is overwhelmingly accepted today, there remain lots of gaps in the theories—and not just little ones. No one (especially me!) is saying that the consensus regarding evolution and natural selection can't be wrong—but then again the scientific consensus could be wrong about the existence of molecules, the link between reproduction and sex, the approximate distances between planets (despite the fact that we've successfully sent various spacecraft to those planets based on those calculations), or the tie between smoking and poor health. But anyone betting on it is either uninformed, brainwashed, or a fool. Here's the cold, hard truth: betting that evolution is mistaken is like betting that the New York Yankees will win about 144 games next season: it's certainly *possible*, as it really could happen and we definitely have no proof against it, but only someone seriously ignorant of baseball or caught in some bizarre alternate psychological reality—brainwashed—would take such a possibility to be *likely*.

The evolution objection to the Design Argument doesn't deny that nature is marvelously organized in an intricate way. Sure it is. And that stunning organization must have an explanation. Or at least that seems a very reasonable view to have. But what biology and physics tell us is that the explanation need not invoke any designer at all. Despite what you might have read, we do not face a choice between "There is a designer" and "It is all random."

Be careful with what this shows, as people tend to go overboard on this criticism of the traditional design arguments (i.e., the design arguments you get when you plug in F1 and F4). The facts behind evolution and physics absolutely do *not* show that God doesn't exist. They don't show that the universe wasn't designed. They don't show that God didn't design the universe. All they prove is that two arguments for the God-as-designer conclusion are weak because they rest on premises that our overall scientific evidence is against. That doesn't mean that that conclusion is false, and it doesn't mean that there is no *other* argument, a *better* one, that shows that God did design the universe. The evolution/science objection to the traditional design arguments is *quite modest*: for F1, all it says is that premise (b) fails to be justified (which is not to say that science says (b) is false); for F4, all it says is that premise (a) fails to be justified. Just because one argument for a certain conclusion stinks does not mean that the conclusion is false or that no other argument exists which is quite good and proves the conclusion is true. This has nothing to do with religious matters; it's a general point about arguments.

Q24: Explain how these two statements differ: "Evolutionary theory shows that nothing designed the universe" and "Evolutionary theory doesn't support the idea that something designed the universe."

Q25: "There are exactly two choices: the universe is random or it's not. If it's not random, then it's designed. But anyone who has studied science for more than an hour can tell you that the universe is not at all random. There are all these intricate patterns and principles in nature. That's what equations like '$E = mc^2$' are all about. So, since the universe isn't random, and that means it's designed, the universe is designed." Assess that reasoning.

I've never seen a good argument with F2 plugged in, but then again I don't know too many people who think you could get a good argument that way. I have often heard the idea that goes "But just look at great art! How could that exist without God?" But I know of no reason at all to think that the works of Renoir or John Lee Hooker, for instance, could only have come about with a designer other than Renoir and John Lee Hooker. I included F2 for the purpose of pointing out that there are many things one could try to plug in for F. Whether they generate a decent Design Argument is a matter for thorough investigation, not flip remarks either pro or con.

Q26: Plug something in for F in the Design Argument template that's roughly along the lines of F2. Then assess each premise: (a), (b), and (d), attempting to figure out which are true and which are false.

When you plug F3 into the argument pattern you get something, called the *Fine-Tuning Argument*, which in my judgment is better than the arguments generated by F1 or F4. This argument is better than those others because it's consistent with physics and biology. In fact, you may be surprised to learn that it appeals to twentieth-century physics for support: *this is a new scientific argument for the existence of God*, as I will now explain.

Everyone knows that science is filled with formulas and numbers. The most famous formula is "$E = mc^2$," from Einstein's theory of relativity. But of course there are many others. There is Newton's law "$F = ma$." And Boyle's law "$PV = nRT$." These formulas and numbers characterize how our universe works. You will be happy and relieved to learn that I am *not* going to rely on you understanding what those formulas say, even approximately.

Now imagine those formulas and numbers being a bit different. Instead of a universe that obeys "$E = mc^2$" imagine a universe that is governed by "$E = 7mc^3$." Instead of a universe in which electrons weigh 9.11×10^{-31} kilograms, imagine one in which they weigh 8×10^{-38} kilograms. Instead of a universe in which light travels at about 186,000 miles a second, think of one in which it travels at 1,788 miles per hour. In fact, think of formulas and numbers as coming in packages. There is the package that characterizes our universe, package P1:

P1: *formula God*

- $E = mc^2$
- Electrons weigh 9.11×10^{-31} kilograms
- Light travels at about 186,000 miles a second
- $PV = nRT$
- $F = ma$
- Etc.

All of those formulas and numbers are actually accurate; they characterize the way our universe really is.[21] And here are a couple other packages, P2 and P3, which are "imaginary" in the sense that they don't characterize the actual universe but merely possible universes:

P2:

- $E = mc^4$
- Electrons weigh 9.99×10^{-31} kilograms
- Light travels at about 146,000 miles a second
- $P^5V = nR^2T^3$
- $F = m^3a$
  Etc.

P3:

- $E = mc$
- Electrons weigh 9.11×10^{-3} kilograms
- Light travels at about 186,000 miles a year
- $PV = nT$
- $F = mav$
  Etc.

Of course, there are zillions of *possible* packages (you can adjust the formulas as you please, and add new ones as well), but only one is *real*: the one that characterizes the real, actual universe. P1 is real; P2, P3, and the rest are merely possible. For any one of the possible packages we can raise all sorts of interesting questions. What would those universes be like—the ones characterized by alternative packages of formulas and numbers? For instance, if a universe obeyed the formulas in P2, and another universe was governed by the formulas in P3, what would those two universes be like? Would there be humans in them? Would there be other forms of conscious life? What would planets be like? Would they be closer together, bigger, hotter, shorter-lived, or what? And what would life be like? Would it be more common in the cosmos or would it be more rare? Would there be bunnies and bugs, or would life be very different, with no mammals or fish or reptiles but completely different creatures instead?

The advocates of the Fine-Tuning Argument have a truly stunning answer to these questions, one that certainly appears to be backed up with detailed scientific calculations by genuine expert scientists: if the formulas and numbers were even a tiny, tiny bit different, the overwhelming odds are that there would be no conscious life, no life, no planets, no stars. In fact, there might not even be any atoms! The most that would exist is virtually invisible dust and empty space; alternatively, the universe would be nothing but a soup of insanely high temperature that burns itself out into nothingness in no time at all. Of all the trillions of possible packages of formulas and numbers, *virtually only one* produces a universe with intelligent life: ours.

Think of each package as being a description of a room in a hotel and each room is a mini-universe accurately characterized by the package for that room. Suppose our package, P1, characterizes room 8987978. So if you're in the hotel of possible universes and go to room 8987978 and look inside, you'll see planets, stars, galaxies, life, humans, and baseball games. Package P2 characterizes room 4893, P3 characterizes room 18788788789787, etc. The Fine-Tuning philosophers, scientists, and theologians are saying that of the trillions and trillions of rooms in the hotel only one has anything interesting it in: room 8987978. For every other room, if you open it up you see nothing in it because there is virtually nothing there to see (alternatively: you see a soup of high-energy particles that fail to form anything stable or interesting, such as carbon atoms, and then it burns itself out in a few seconds).

This strikes most people as utterly extraordinary. It doesn't look like an accident. It looks as though it can't be a mere coincidence that of all the possible packages, of all the trillions of possible hotel rooms to make real, the one that got to be real just happens to be virtually the only one that has anything interesting in it. What a miraculous coincidence! The actual universe could have been any of those rooms; why did it turn out to be close to the only interesting room out of gazillions of rooms?

The advocates of the Fine-Tuning Argument say that it's too much of a coincidence. If the package that got to be the one that characterizes the real, actual universe were picked randomly—like choosing a room at random in the hotel—then surely the outcome would be a universe with no stars, no planets, no life, no consciousness, and no baseball. After all, that's what virtually all of the rooms boil down to. And yet, the room that got chosen is practically the only one with anything interesting in it. Imagine that you're standing outside this ridiculously enormous hotel and you throw a rock at it and hit the window of virtually the only room with anything in it; that would seem pretty unlikely, wouldn't it? Something, or someone, must have *purposefully* chosen that room 8987978 over all the others. And of course any being powerful enough to choose the laws of nature—laws expressed by the formulas and numbers in the equations that characterize the universe—has got to be God. So, surprisingly enough *cutting-edge science itself* has generated evidence for the existence of God. That was unexpected.

Here is the Fine-Tuning Argument in a nutshell, fitting the template of the Design Argument given earlier:

a. The universe, or at least large or significant parts of it, has feature F3: the universe's physical laws and fundamental physical constants (what I've been calling "formulas and numbers") are finely tuned for the emergence of life and consciousness in the following sense: if even one of those laws or constants had been even just a tiny bit different, then there is virtually no chance there would be consciousness, life, people, stars, planets … maybe even atoms.
b. It's very unlikely that this feature came about in a purely natural way, with no design behind it.
c. Thus, by (a) & (b) it's highly likely that this feature of the universe was designed.
d. If this feature was designed, then it is highly likely that it was designed by God (obviously we didn't design it, and it's really unlikely that aliens did it).
e. Thus, there is excellent evidence that God exists and is a designer.

This argument is beautiful, at least to my aesthetic sense. Unfortunately, most philosophers who have thoroughly examined these arguments think there is little reason to accept either (a) or (b), despite all the apparently supporting arguments I gave above. I don't have the space to fully explain why, but I can give a quick taste of just *some* (not all) of the reasons why philosophers are highly skeptical about both (a) and (b).[22]

However, I want to make one thing perfectly clear while you examine the objections I list below: there remains the possibility that the advocates of the Fine-Tuning Argument can maneuver around the defects revealed below in order to produce a version of the argument that turns out quite powerful. Just because I can sit here and offer brilliant, trenchant criticisms of staggering genius does not mean that the advocates of the argument have to hang their heads in shame, retire from philosophy, and retreat to spend the rest of their lives restricted to caves. If it were that simple, then no philosopher would endorse the Fine-Tuning Argument; but there are such supporters. All this applies to the Cosmological and Social arguments as well.

The first thing to note about the argument is that it is a scientific one. In fact, it appeals to some of the most advanced, cutting-edge physics there is. Expertise in religion or sociology or psychology or biology or whatnot will do you almost no good at all in investigating this argument. If you're not a philosopher quite familiar with the upper echelons of contemporary physics *and* the philosophy of physics then you should probably just demur when someone asks you about this argument. Unfortunately, that fact virtually never stops anyone from pontificating, as I will prove by example now.

Scientists have argued that if one looks at packages that aren't too different from ours (ours is P1), then you don't get any familiar things like planets, stars, or life-forms. For instance, you get no carbon, which is one of the basic building blocks of life as we know it. Let's take their word for it, as they have the detailed calculations backing them up. (I have a Master's Degree in physics, but I have not even looked at the calculations; so I can't evaluate them with much justification. And let me tell you: a Master's Degree in a subject is very unimpressive compared to the knowledge acquired by true experts in that subject who look upon their PhDs as their first baby steps in the field.) But I don't see much reason to think that they are able to tell what entirely *new* kinds of matter would result, or what new kinds of material organization might result. If you alter the laws of nature (or the "physical constants"), there is very little to go on in determining what new things you might end up with—even if you can be somewhat confident in figuring out what familiar things you will *not* come up with. You don't get to assume that you will be dealing with the same stuff—electrons, protons, neutrons, photons—but they will just be obeying different laws. Instead, you have to think about the likelihood that the new laws will bring entirely new kinds of matter. And I don't think anyone has the foggiest idea how to calculate those odds.

So we have our first criticism: *even if the physicists are perfectly right that slight changes in packages would result in the lack of familiar entities such as carbon, that doesn't give one much reason to think there would be no life or consciousness.* Truly, we know very little about what novel things would have come about if there were no familiar elements due to differences in packages—and, again, by "novel" things I mean things not made of electrons, protons, and the rest. That's one reason to be wary of (a). You can't justifiably assume that no new kinds of matter—and perhaps life—would come about if the laws of nature were slightly different.

Here is a second criticism of (a). As I mentioned above, physicists like to say things like "If you change this equation by a one part in a gazillion, then you get no life; isn't that amazing?!" But physicists have not considered *radically different packages*, ones with very little in common with ours. Such packages might govern universes rich in material, biological, and conscious existence but utterly different from ours; hardly dust and empty space. Physicists say things like "Well, if you keep every fundamental law of nature and fundamental physical constant the same, but change this one here by one billionth of a percent and that one there by a millionth of a percent, but change nothing else, then you get no stars, no planets, and no carbon; isn't that incredible?" That's fine, even incredible, but what about universes in which *many* laws and constants—even the fundamental ones—are very different, with different numbers *and even different variables* (e.g., ones other than energy, force, mass, electric charge, etc.)? As with the first criticism, nobody has even the *slightest* idea what such packages would produce even if some of us do know what they would *not* produce (e.g., they wouldn't produce carbon). Clearly, it is going to be near impossible to reasonably speculate what would happen if there were entirely new kinds of physical factors. We might be able to confidently say there would be no carbon-based life, but we have no idea what new things—including forms of life—might come into existence. We just have no idea at all.

> Q27: We just looked at two criticisms of premise (a). How are they different?

Those are just a couple of reasons why (a) is so doubtful that we have no good reason to accept it. But let's assume for the moment that the above pair of criticisms are mistaken and (a) is true; we want to give the advocate of the Fine-Tuning Argument every chance at success. Hence, we are now assuming that if the laws and constants were even slightly different—or completely different— there is almost no chance of life or consciousness of any kind at all, carbon-based or otherwise. Unfortunately for the Fine-Tuning advocates, even if (a) is true there is little overall reason to think (b) is true. I'll describe three reasons why (b) is so doubtful even on assumption that (a) is true.

First, it might well be the case that our package is *necessary* in the sense that it's the only possible package. That is, it might be the case that all the other packages are literally impossible. (That means that the "if" part of (a), "if the laws and constants were even slightly different," is vacuous, as the laws and constants could not have been different.) Saying "But we can imagine a universe with $E = 7mc^3$ instead of $E = mc^2$" might be like saying "But we can imagine a universe in which water has no hydrogen in it" or "But we can imagine a world in which the ratio of a circle's circumference to its diameter is 3.14159 exactly instead of pi." Yes, you can *imagine* those things (at least under some conceptions of imagination), but what you're imagining is, according to firmly established science and math, literally impossible. It's impossible to have water without hydrogen, so why think that it's possible that $E = 7mc^3$? The formulas in mathematics are said to be necessary (it's not an *accident* that twice two is four instead of five), and we know that many of the statements in science are too; the fundamental formulas and constants in science may be as well, regardless of what imagination suggests. Some physicists have speculated thus.

Now, if we knew a *great deal* regarding how those formulas and constants were fixed, then perhaps we would be in a position to confidently say that they genuinely could have turned out different. But whether we like it or not, we don't have such knowledge at the present time. Sometimes it is easy to know that something could have been different: I could have lived my life without being a professor. But when it comes to the fundamental notions of physics, only the ridiculously overconfident make such claims. We simply have *no idea* whether the fundamentals of physics could have been at all different. I'm not saying that contemporary physics says that those fundamentals could not have been different; I'm saying that it says nothing worthwhile on the topic as of yet. Scientists do two things: figure things out and *speculate*; we shouldn't confuse them. So that's one reason why we should be wary of (b).

> Q28: "In order to cast doubt on premise (b) one has to show that it's false. But all the above line of reasoning shows is that we don't know much about (b). That means the criticism is no good." What's wrong with that thought?

One might think: but what if the absolutely necessary laws of nature had all the appearance of design? Well, *if* they did *then* that might constitute a good version of the Design Argument! For instance, what if we found out that if you take all the fundamental and absolutely necessary constants of physics and order them from smallest to largest, and then convert the list to English using some prime number translation scheme (just go with me here for a moment), the resulting sentences would come right from the English translations of the Torah, or the Bible, or something similar? Yes, what if?!

a.　The universe, or at least large or significant parts of it, has this feature: if you take all the fundamental and absolutely necessary constants of physics and order them from smallest to largest, and then convert the list to English using some prime number translation scheme, the resulting sentences come right from the English translations of the Torah, or the Bible, or something similar.
b.　It's very unlikely that this feature came about in a purely natural way, with no design behind it.
c.　Thus, by (a) and (b) it's highly likely that this feature of the universe was designed.
d.　If this feature was designed, then it is highly likely that it was designed by God (obviously we didn't design it, and it's really unlikely that aliens did it).
e.　Thus, there is excellent evidence that God exists and is a designer.

Now (b) looks reasonable, at least if we fill out the story appropriately, but (a) is silly, as no one has discovered anything remotely like that. But *if* we did discover that (a) is really true, *then* we would have a serious (if not successful) Design Argument on our hands. Of course, what appears above is just a silly argument that I invented for the sake of illustration, but all I'm trying to do with it is show that there *could* be an excellent design argument. When we criticize the Design Argument (or the Fine-Tuning version of that argument) *we need not be criticizing all possible arguments that fit that pattern.* At least I'm certainly not arguing that way. *I'm not against Design Arguments in general.* We're just looking at the ones that have premises that have a significant chance of being actually true.

Here is the second important objection to (b). If the laws of nature were finely tuned with the purpose of producing life and consciousness, then you would probably expect laws that produce *a significant amount of life and consciousness.* And yet, there is barely any life and consciousness in the universe—even if there is plenty of life on other planets. There's some life here on the sliver known as the earth's crust, but for literally billions of miles in any direction there isn't any (or, there is a minute amount but it's incredibly primitive, like bacteria, and unbelievably rare), life has been present on earth for only a very short time, and consciousness has been around for a vanishingly short time, compared to the age of the universe. If you were God designing a universe so that there would be life and consciousness, why would you design the laws so that life and consciousness are so incredibly rare and fragile? Instead, it looks like the *last* thing the universe was designed for—assuming it was designed at all—was either life or consciousness. Really, *all* the hotel rooms—including ours—look virtually completely devoid of life or complex matter: for each one either 99.999 percent of the space in the room is occupied by nothing bigger than a proton (that is, for all we can see with our senses there is nothing bigger than a proton there; here I'm setting aside the possibility discussed above that there might be all sorts of new kinds of existences in those rooms), or it has lots of matter but 99.999 percent of that matter is lifeless.

To illustrate a couple of these points: if our sun were the size of the period at the end of a sentence, how far away do you think the *nearest* star would be? A few feet? How about fifty feet? Five hundred feet, which seems crazy? No: about *five miles*, and we are in the midst of a galaxy, the crowded "urban" part of the universe; the "rural" space between galaxies is even sparser. And virtually the whole universe is around a balmy -455 Fahrenheit. To say the universe is *virtually all* frozen empty space is an extremely mild thing to say.

The advocate of the Fine-Tuning Argument wants you to think that our universe is extraordinary compared to all those other possible universes, as ours has things like galaxies and life and the others don't. She wants you to think that if you look in our hotel room you can see lots of galaxies, stars, and planets whereas when you look in the other rooms all you see is a tiny bit of dust floating in the air. But even if we accept that the other universes wouldn't contain any impressive physical things—which we saw in the previous pages we have no reason to believe—almost all the universes look exactly the same when you open the hotel room doors, and the ones that don't are occupied by nothing but dead matter. Our universe is almost entirely cold empty space—and the parts that aren't empty are almost entirely without any life.[23] Our universe-room is surprising only if you are surprised that in a few *infinitesimally small* places in the room there is some biological activity going on—life about the size of a proton compared to that of the room. If God designed the universe, it looks like he is really fascinated by frozen dust and empty space, not life or consciousness. And when it comes to life, all he seems to be interested in is bugs and bacteria, since throughout history virtually all life (I'm guessing well over 99 percent) has been just bugs and bacteria.

This line of reasoning is supposed to get us to be highly suspicious of (b) *even if we are convinced that (a) is true*: that is, even if we agree that it's incredible that the laws and constants turned out to give rise to life and consciousness, this is not the result of design but just a highly interesting side-effect. The extreme rarity of life and consciousness is what makes them look like a side-effect, not the result of design. Here is an illustration of that general side-effect idea.

Think of vacuuming a dusty room. This is done with a plan or design: you're trying to get the dust and other stuff off the floor. In the midst of vacuuming you will of course move the furniture around slightly, at least if you're trying to do a good job. When you're finished, each piece of furniture will be slightly tilted when compared to the nearest wall (e.g., the couch won't be perfectly parallel with the wall near it; it will be off a bit). Now suppose that it turns out that when measured with respect to the nearest wall each piece of furniture is tilted by 7 degrees. Not 8 or 6: always 7. The odds of that happening are very tiny, given that you didn't plan it. Your eccentric friend Fred is completely obsessed about angles and room measurements; he is also convinced that the number 7 has mystical properties that no other number has. He of course finds this outcome of the vacuuming incredible, even stunning, and obviously in need of explanation. Given the extreme odds against 7 just showing up randomly for *all* the furniture, and the extremely special status of that number as opposed to any other number, Fred will insist that this is no accident. This is a case in which the analogy to (a) is true but the analogy to (b) is false: the odds that a vacuuming task would align each piece of furniture with the sole mystical number (according to Fred) is miniscule (so the analogy to (a) is true), but much to Fred's disappointment this is just a coincidence and not the result of your designing it that way (so the analogy to (b) is false).

The odd thing is that no matter how you vacuum the room, if a large and dedicated team of geniuses studied your vacuuming long enough, they would find something along the lines of what Fred found. It's inevitable: the number and variety of obscure facts guarantee it. Maybe when you vacuum your home you don't get bizarre patterns of furniture angles. But if people looked hard enough, they would find *something* remarkable about it. In fact, every seemingly boring and unremarkable thing has features that when put together in the right way look amazing to someone (many conspiracy theories thrive on this fact). But even so, that gives no reason to think that the thing in question was designed to have those amazing features.

You might say, with reason, that the vacuum example is silly. Clearly, there is nothing objectively amazing about having furniture exactly seven degrees off from surrounding walls! It's highly interesting for Fred, due to his peculiar interests, but that's all you can say for it. When it comes to a universe with life and consciousness matters are quite different. Biological life and consciousness are truly remarkable no matter what one's interests. So the fact that our universe is virtually unique in being just about the only one compatible with life and consciousness (remember that we're assuming (a) is true) is the type of thing that can't be coincidental. So, the "empty cold space" objection to (b) sucks.

This response to the "empty cold space" objection seems to me to have something going for it: it really does seem to lots of people that consciousness is an amazing thing, whereas the "seven degree furniture angle" thing just isn't. But this response to the objection to (b) is based on a misunderstanding of that objection to (b). The "empty cold space" objection to (b) focuses on the fact that life and consciousness are fantastically *rare*. (We should call it the "life and consciousness are unbelievably rare" objection, not the "empty cold space" objection.) Maybe consciousness is objectively interesting while furniture angles aren't. That seems right. But the main point of the objection is that even if consciousness is objectively amazing and our universe is virtually unique in having it (so (a) is true), the fact that consciousness is so rare makes it unlikely that it's the result of design: given its extreme rarity it looks exactly like an unintended and curious side-effect.

Here is an example that illustrates this point. Suppose I flip a coin not a hundred or thousand times but 97 gazillion times (this would take forever, but pretend I have eternal life and not much to do). Suppose further that people take turns watching me do this (presumably they would be paid, as it's so boring). When it's your turn to watch me, the coin comes up heads fifty times in a row. Naturally, you find this extraordinary. You say to yourself that this can't possibly be a coincidence. You conclude that someone has messed with the coin so that it turns up heads. You would say that the odds that it just happened to turn up heads fifty times in a row even though the coin is a "fair" one is so absurdly improbable that we can dismiss that possibility out of hand.

But you're wrong! If I really do flip a coin that much, crazy things are *bound* to happen: they are inevitable. Eventually, exceedingly rare things like getting fifty heads in a row are going to happen even if it's not the result of design. You probably already know this, at least implicitly: if you examine any extremely large group of things long enough weird results will come up. For instance, if you look at snakes all your life (so that's a large group of things) you will discover some that have two heads (I'm not making that up). Similarly, for any extremely large collection of coin tosses there will be long stretches in which the coin comes up heads every time. It's inevitable given the large number of tosses. Similarly, just because right here on earth things seem pretty remarkable with so much life and consciousness, when you take a big picture view of the universe, earth looks like one of those *inevitable* flukes (like the string of fifty heads in a row), not something designed. Given the extreme rarity of life and consciousness, the universe looks exactly as though it was *not* designed for them. Now, if we found life and consciousness throughout the universe, and (a) were true (so our universe is the only one with any life or consciousness at all), then perhaps the extreme rarity objection to (b) would be no good. But that's not what we find in the universe.

Now maybe God has excellent reason for creating a universe virtually without consciousness or life even though it was designed for life and consciousness (e.g., perhaps there is some hidden benefit to our discovering the vast emptiness of the frozen universe). You can *make up* all sorts of divine reasons here, pulling them out of your imagination. But the line of reasoning of the previous paragraphs does suggest that it's not at all obvious that the universe was designed with consciousness in mind *even if the laws and constants have the amazing feature mentioned in (a)*. It also suggests that *if it was* designed for life and consciousness, then there must be some reason why the things it was designed for are so incredibly rare in both space and time that they don't look anything like the product of design.

Q29: Explain why the extreme rarity of life and consciousness in the universe casts doubt on the idea that it was designed.

Now for the third reason to be wary of (b). Some physicists have hypothesized that there are an enormous number of universes. Think of blowing some bubbles for children: their idea is that each universe exists sort of like a bubble. If there are a great many of these bubble universes (say, 10 raised to the 10th power raised to the 10th power raised to the 10th power …), and they have all sorts of different laws of nature, then even if there is no divine hand designing them, even if the universes are generated without any design, since there are so many of them it stands to reason that eventually some "interesting" universes—with life and consciousness—will be generated. We can use the hotel of universes idea I described earlier to see what's going on. In that discussion we assumed that there is just one real universe: just one room in the hotel is real. And then it seemed mysterious that the one room that got to be the real universe just happened to be one of the incredibly rare rooms that have life and consciousness in them. But the physicists I am alluding to now are suggesting that a fantastically large number of the hotel rooms are real, one for each bubble universe, and so it's no surprise that the rare rooms get realized.

The upshot of this idea: even if our universe is extraordinary in the fact that it is one of the tiny few possible universes that permit life and consciousness, there is no mystery as to how it came into existence, given the incredible number of bubble universes that actually exist. The vast majority of these bubble universes have no life or consciousness, but given the fantastically large number of them it's almost inevitable that *some* will end up with life and consciousness. It's a bit like flipping a coin a gazillion times: if you do it enough times, eventually weird and unlikely things will happen (e.g., fifty heads in a row, or the coin lands on its side a few times in a row). Thus, even if (a) is true, if the speculations of these physicists are on track, there is no reason to posit a designer.

I articulated that third criticism of (b) because it is common in the philosophical literature. However, I am skeptical regarding its worth, as it is based on what everyone agrees are highly speculative hypotheses (regarding the number and nature of the bubble universes). The other two criticisms of (b) strike me as more solidly grounded, for what it's worth.

Finally, you probably noticed that the Fine-Tuning Argument does not try to establish "God exists and is a designer"—in fact, all it concludes is that there is excellent evidence for that idea, which hardly proves it because there could be strong evidence *against* the idea that cancels out the strong evidence *for* the idea. Not only that: it doesn't even *try* to get "God is supremely good," "God is supremely knowledgeable," or "God is supremely powerful." Clearly, additional mighty arguments would have to supplement the Fine-Tuning Argument in order to get anything like a decent argument for the existence of the 4-Part God. Thus, even if the Fine-Tuning Argument is *completely successful* we are still a helluva long distance from a good argument for the existence of the 4-Part God. Smart Fine-Tuning advocates are aware of this; they certainly don't hang their entire case for God on this one argument.

Q30: For the sake of argument pretend that the Fine-Tuning Design Argument is successful in establishing the truth of its halfway conclusion in (c) that it's highly likely that the universe's laws were designed. In fact, pretend that we somehow know that not only is it highly likely but it's really true: there *really was a designer*. How might a theist go on to argue that the designer is a person? Or is good? Or is supremely knowledgeable? Or is supremely powerful? Answer all four questions.

Often when I present these criticisms of the Fine-Tuning Argument I get the response "Well, maybe God set up the laws anyway; you haven't shown that he didn't." And that's exactly right: I have done nothing to show that God didn't set up the laws of nature. I have no such ambition here, especially since I'm agnostic on this issue. But keep in mind what is going on. The theist is trying to construct a scientific argument for the existence of God (or the 4-Part God). Hence, it's *up to her to deliver the goods*: she is the one who has to come up with the evidence backing up her claims. That's what she has set out to do. When we evaluate her argument, trying to figure out how good it is, we need not attempt to show its conclusion is false. Indeed, we may well agree with its conclusion (I have colleagues who are competent in the philosophy of religion, who are theists, and who reject the Fine-Tuning Argument entirely). To respond to our criticisms with "But you haven't shown that God didn't design the laws of nature" is to misunderstand the dialectical situation. The critic of the Fine-Tuning Argument has the burden of showing why we fail to have good reason to accept the premises; she has no obligation to argue against the conclusion. Indeed, she may well agree with it.

Let me emphasize that what I wrote above is an *incomplete* evaluation of the Fine-Tuning Argument, as I'm leaving out all sorts of additional important considerations, including further criticisms as well as intelligent responses by the advocates of the Fine-Tuning Argument. I myself have no firm opinion on its quality, but you should not concern yourself with my personal opinion or any other particular philosopher's opinion. In any case, I hope the above discussion will suffice, for our limited purposes here, as a quick but intelligent explanation of why philosophers are so skeptical of the Fine-Tuning Argument. Now we leave it behind and move on to the other two arguments for God's existence.

The Cosmological Argument

Like the Design Argument, the Cosmological Argument comes in lots of versions; I will examine just two. Here is a simple presentation of what we'll call the *Finite* version, since it says that the universe has a finite past (which means, roughly, that it doesn't go back in time infinitely):

a.   The universe had a beginning: there was a *first* event.
b.   If the universe had a beginning, then the first event must have been caused to happen by something; at least, this is highly probable.
c.   Whatever caused the beginning of the physical universe must be God; at least this is highly probable.
d.   Thus, there is excellent evidence that God exists.

Let's just assume that (a) is true, to give the advocate of the argument the benefit of the doubt. (The advocate of the Infinite version of the Cosmological Argument, which I'll get to below, has the opposite claim (viz. that the universe goes back in time infinitely); so the theist can appeal to the *pair* of arguments in order to cover all the possibilities.) But should we think that (b) is true? Many, perhaps most, philosophers think there is little reason to believe it's true. There are good reasons to doubt it—and I mean doubt it for *serious* reasons, and not merely doubt it because like virtually every idea it's conceivable it is false.

Our first reason to doubt (b) is that we are now talking about the first physical event of the universe, what is usually called the "Big Bang."[24] If your toilet suddenly flushes even though no one touched the handle or any other part of it, it's still a good bet that something caused the toilet to flush even if you haven't figured out what it was. (I once had a toilet that did this for a while; it was very puzzling.) That's the way toilets work: when they do something, something must have caused them to do what they did. The same holds for a flower: if a flower opens its petals, you can bet that something made that happen. But the Big Bang is hardly your ordinary, everyday event. Just because ordinary, everyday events have causes doesn't mean that bizarre, utterly extraordinary events do. The Big Bang is nothing ordinary: *it's unwise to extrapolate from the ordinary to the utterly extraordinary.*

Our second reason to doubt (b) is that a good number of obviously competent and accomplished physicists have, after much thought, come to the conclusion that many events occurring at the quantum level—involving electrons, photons, and things like them—are uncaused. Now, maybe they're right and maybe they're wrong; there are lots of technical matters here. But in any case the idea

"Well, anything physical that comes into existence must have a cause" is nowhere near obviously correct. It's obviously correct for ordinary events, but as we just said above, the Big Bang is by far *the strangest and least well-known thing in the universe*; it's unwise to extrapolate from the ordinary to the utterly extraordinary.

Now, you might not be too impressed with those first two criticisms, as you might wonder just *how* extraordinary the Big Bang is compared to other physical events. That's a very good thing to wonder about. In order to get an idea of the extraordinary nature of the Big Bang, and as a consequence see the wisdom of the first two criticisms, first consider that to *informatively* hold that the Big Bang was caused by something one would have to have at least one of the following:

(i)   Some good argument that shows that absolutely all physical things, no matter how bizarre, simply must have causes. If we had this argument, then the fact that the Big Bang was so odd would be no good reason to question whether it had a cause.
(ii)   Detailed knowledge of what the Big Bang was—knowledge which shows that it, like ordinary events, probably had a cause.

Philosophers think (i) is not viable (even though philosophers tried for several centuries to find such an argument). Naturally, it is hard for many people to imagine something just popping into existence with no cause (I have no trouble at all with this, but maybe that's just me). Such an idea may seem philosophically unseemly, especially if we confine our imagination to things like toilets flushing. But we are looking for evidence here, not prejudices that make us comfortable in our philosophical beds. So (i) is out, as there simply is no such argument. And no one who is wise about contemporary physics thinks (ii) is now available. The more one knows about the Big Bang the more one sees how we have no good reason to think it had a cause.

Let me explain a bit why (ii) is lacking (which means we lack a good reason for premise (b) of the Cosmological Argument). Physicists have a lot of good (but hardly conclusive) evidence for their theories regarding the time around 14 billion years ago when the entire universe was concentrated in a superhot and very tiny energy "ball." And they have offered speculations on what happened immediately before that time: many (but not all) think the universe, including space and even time, was *created* in the Big Bang, which very quickly produced that very tiny energy ball. The idea of the Big Bang comes from Einstein's General Theory of Relativity (GTR), which has some impressive evidence in its favor.[25] However, GTR is incompatible with another theory in physics, Quantum Mechanics (QM)—which has truly stunning evidence backing it up. In fact, QM is probably the most impressively verified scientific theory ever. I would put my money on QM over GTR! Because QM is so well verified and GTR is incompatible with QM (by "incompatible" I mean that they can't both be true, as they conflict with one another), we have good reason to doubt the predictions of

GTR, including that of the Big Bang. Don't get me wrong: we have *good evidence* that around 14 billion years ago the whole universe consisted of a superhot tiny ball of extremely high energy, and our universe today came from that ball (at least, the *known* physical universe came from that ball). So I am definitely not putting any doubt on that part of the Big Bang theory. But the idea that the universe was *created* shortly before that time is a more contentious hypothesis, one that we don't have a lot of evidence for. Furthermore, GTR gets you evidence for the Big Bang only on the assumption that there are no undiscovered laws of nature that have significant effect on what happened before the time of the superhot energy ball. But since our understanding of *that* period of the universe is so weak, and that period is so utterly unlike the rest of the history of the universe, it is pretty risky to suppose that GTR's assumption is correct. For several decades physicists have been trying to construct a consistent theory that includes only what is right with both GTR and QM, but thus far there is little experimental support for the speculations. It's pure speculation, as the physicists themselves will tell you. Thus, information about GTR and QM should make us realize that contemporary physics by no means justifies the idea that there was a beginning and it had a cause.

Q31: We have looked at three criticisms of premise (b) of the Cosmological Argument. First, the Big Bang is bizarre compared to anything else in the universe; so what may be true for everything else—they have causes—might not be true of the Big Bang. Second, many intelligent physicists claim that many things in nature don't have causes; so, maybe that's true of the Big Bang as well. Third ... what is the third criticism? State it in one paragraph using your own words.

Now for our fourth reason to doubt (b), the reason that shows how extraordinary the Big Bang was. Some physicists claim that the Big Bang is the beginning of time itself, as I mentioned above. That is, there is no "before" the Big Bang. That's very hard to imagine, but there it is. If they are right, then it is hardly obvious that there was a cause of the Big Bang, in any sense of "cause," since it is usually (to put it mildly!) true that the cause of an event precedes it in time, and yet there was no time before the Big Bang. Challenge: think of a case of x causing y when neither x nor any other physical thing existed before y. You can't do it. In fact, it's much worse than that: strictly speaking the Big Bang is probably not an "event" at all, contrary to what I've been saying over and over, since events happen in time and the Big Bang is the origin of time. Odd as it may seem, the Big Bang did not happen *at* a time; it is the origin of time. Challenge: think of a case of x causing y when neither x nor y occur at any time at all (not even over a temporal interval). You can't do it, and yet (b) is insisting that there is such a case when y = the Big Bang and x = the cause of the Big Bang. This is yet another reason to not apply ordinary rules about events to the Big Bang. In response, some philosophers have tried to spell out a notion of "the cause or ground or explanatory source of an event" that doesn't include the cause or source or whatever coming *before* the event, but it's all just highly doubtful and contested philosophical speculation without even the slightest bit of experimental confirmation. Some of it is interesting and inspiring speculation, at least according to some philosophical tastes, but that's all that can be said for it.

We move to the fifth reason to doubt (b). Suppose that contrary to what I've been arguing our *very best science today* said that the Big Bang really happened and something, X, caused it to happen. (Science isn't saying this, at least not today, but for the sake of argument pretend it is saying it or will say it in the future.) All by itself, this means nothing. Whether or not we should take stock in the speculations of physicists depends on how much evidence they have for their theories. A significant number of physicists openly speculate without much in the way of evidence. Naturally, they are aware that they are offering mere speculations—ideas that are definitely worthwhile because they suggest new avenues of research but do not claim to be supported by real data. What counts as our "very best theories regarding X" need not have much in way of evidence backing it up.

Now for the sixth reason to doubt (b): the weirdness of contemporary science. Ever since Darwin, science has gone contrary to many commonsensical beliefs from ordinary life (actually, the heliocentric view of the Solar System was also deeply against common sense, and the transition from a geocentric to a heliocentric model occurred well before Darwin). The results of evolutionary theory (in which, to put it crudely, stupid things just naturally organize to make smart things without any help from intelligent agents), GTR, QM, and transfinite mathematics (in which, for instance, there are infinitely many infinite numbers) show that ideas derived from common experience just aren't at all reliable when applied to odd cases. And the origin of the universe, or the Big Bang, has got to be the oddest case ever. When people stamp their feet and insist "But something can't come from nothing! So there simply had to be a cause of the Big Bang!" the right response is to point out that in ordinary life that's perfectly true but when it comes to the origin of the physical universe we have good reason to hesitate in thinking that that rule still applies.

Further, and this strikes me as crucial, the alternative idea—God caused the Big Bang—*is just as fantastic as the idea that the Big Bang had no cause.* When I hear someone insist that he or she just can't imagine how the Big Bang could just pop into existence with no cause, I *completely sympathize with their inclination*, as it strikes me as deeply weird as well. But then I have to go on to insist that I for one have no grasp whatsoever on how a non-physical, non-temporal being could cause a physical event—especially when the physical event in question is so bizarre that some experts say it's not something that happened at a particular time. To a real extent, we are faced with at least two potential incomprehensible marvels here: a non-temporal, non-physical cause (God or some non-physical "force" of some sort) of a possibly non-temporal event (the Big Bang), or an uncaused possibly non-temporal event (the Big Bang). Only the overconfident has any view on which really happened.

Q32: The last criticism of premise (b) of the Cosmological Argument was peculiar. It said that maybe the idea of the Big Bang having no cause is a bizarre idea. But it also insisted that the idea of a non-physical intelligent agent causing the Big Bang is comparably bizarre. We are faced with two possibilities: it was caused by God, it wasn't caused by anything. Is there a more likely, less bizarre, possibility?

Q33: Again, the last criticism of premise (b) of the Cosmological Argument said that the possibility that the Big Bang was caused by God is bizarre. Question 1: what reasons were offered for the idea that the God-cause is bizarre? Question 2: are those good reasons?

I'm *not* saying with these six criticisms "Well, we can't be 100 percent absolutely certain that the universe had a beginning and that beginning had something, X, cause it to happen." I'm saying something much stronger: our evidence just leaves us *utterly in the dark* regarding whether X really existed. The upshot of these scientific reflections is *not* that we should think that GTR is false or that there was no Big Bang or even that the Big Bang had no cause (either divine or not). Instead, we should *withhold judgment* on the matter of what the Big Bang was like, if indeed there was any such thing. And that means that we should not think that physics gives much support for (b), the premise that the beginning of the universe had a cause. That is, (ii) is lacking, just as I said earlier.

But let's not get carried away here with the force of these six criticisms of (b) (six may seem a lot, but mere large numbers doesn't guarantee collective strength). There is certainly nothing crazy about thinking that the universe began billions of years ago and that, like other physical events, was caused by something! On the contrary, (b) is a *reasonable* claim, at least in my judgment, even if there is significantly less evidence for it than many people say. So let's assume for a moment that the above criticisms are no good and (b) is true. Hence, we're now setting aside *all* previous criticisms and assuming for the sake of argument that (a) and (b) are perfectly true: the universe began in the finite past and something, call it X, caused it to start up. That's a reasonable position to have, even if science doesn't back it up sufficiently. Is there any good reason to think X is God, as premise (c) says?

It is hard to think of any such reason coming from philosophy or science. There is reason to think that X would have to be non-physical (as God is virtually always thought to be). Here's the reason: since the Big Bang is supposed to be the *first* physical event (even though, as we mentioned above, it might not really be an event at all), X caused the Big Bang, and causes of events precede those events (not always, but let's set that criticism aside), X can't be physical. (Actually, there is nothing in the physics that says that all matter originated in the Big Bang—all it says is that all *known* matter (especially that governed by gravity and other familiar forces) so originated—but let's set that problem aside too.) But is there any reason to think X has to have a mind, or know anything (let alone virtually everything), or be loving, or be forgiving, or be morally good (or even be just *one* thing X, instead of a bunch of things X, Y, Z and so on)?

I have encountered just two arguments for even a small part of such a conclusion. The first: all causation of physical events consists of either a *physical cause* plus a physical effect, or a *personal/mental cause* plus a physical effect; so all causes are physical or mental; since cause X isn't physical (as we saw in the previous paragraph), it must be personal in the sense of having a mind. But this is a lousy argument. For one thing, there is hardly any decent reason to think that all non-physical causation, if there is any, involves persons or minds. Indeed, I can't think of *any* good reason, and neither can you since you're in the same boat as me in not being at all familiar with even a tiny bit of the full range of possible non-physical causation, assuming there is such a thing at all. A similar point holds for the second argument that X has to have a mind, which runs "There are just two kinds of non-physical things, minds and abstract things like numbers; obviously, X can't be a number; so, X must be a mind." There is no good reason to accept the first premise in that argument—especially since almost everyone who devotes their life to studying the mind thinks that the mind is physical!

But hey, let's be generous and set aside *all* the previous criticisms. Suppose we somehow know that X exists and has a mind. Even so, there is no reason I know of for thinking that this non-physical person/mind knows anything much less everything, is loving, is good, is forgiving, etc. A modest upshot of these reflections is that even if the Finite Cosmological Argument were *wildly successful* (which seems pretty unlikely, given the criticisms above) it would need important and non-trivial supplementation by further arguments in order to secure the 4-Part God.

Just like when we finished evaluating the Fine-Tuning Argument, it's important to know the argumentative situation. The 4-Part theist is saying that she has good evidence for the existence of God: the premises (a), (b), and (c). But we have encountered no good reason to accept either (b) or (c). So we have not found any good evidence *here* for the existence of God. As before, this is not to say that God doesn't exist or that there is no evidence for God's existence.

For the sake of speeding up this section on evidence of God's existence, let us take a much briefer look at the *Infinite* version of the Cosmological Argument:

a.   The universe has no beginning: it goes back in time infinitely.[26]
b.   Even though the universe goes back in time infinitely, there is some *explanation* of the whole temporally extended thing. At least, it's highly likely that there is such an explanation.
c.   Whatever explains the infinite chain must be God; at least this is highly probable.
d.   Thus, there is excellent evidence that God exists.

Now the key premises are (b) and (c) (recall that at this point we are simply assuming the truth of (a)). I'll just assume that (b) is true in order to focus on (c). To see very briefly why (c) is doubtful, consider a very simple model of cause and effect. Event E1 is caused to happen by preceding event E2, which is caused by preceding event E3, which is caused by preceding event E4, et cetera, going back in time:

$$E6 \rightarrow E5 \rightarrow E4 \rightarrow E3 \rightarrow E2 \rightarrow E1$$

Time going forwards

$$\longrightarrow$$

So E1 is explained by its cause E2, and E2 is explained by its cause E3, and E3 is explained by its cause E4, et cetera, going back in time infinitely. So *every* event in the chain has a non-supernatural explanation—assuming every event has a cause. (If not every event in the chain of causes and effects has a cause then premise (b) is in trouble.) So why think that there has to be an *additional* explanation, a supernatural (God) one, of the whole chain? We just explained *each and every one* of its parts without invoking God; we have explained literally *everything in the physical universe*. So what have we left out? Nothing. So, even if (b) is right, so there has to be an explanation of the whole universe, the obvious explanation is "Each part of the whole is explained by another part of the whole."

You can't just respond with "Well, the whole is greater than the sum of its parts; you can explain each part without explaining the whole": that's a nice slogan, but is there any reason at all to think that it's actually true for the physical universe, which by supposition here is infinite in time (as premise (a) demands)? The same holds for the response that goes "But now you're wedded to the absurd idea that the universe as a single composite thing *explains itself,* as each part of it is explained by another part!" The comment is accurate, as that is indeed what we're saying, but that's no objection because that's just the way infinite objects work. If the universe is an infinitely long object (infinite in temporal length, going into the past if not the future), then it can be a purely contingent thing (that is, it could have not existed and been replaced with a different physical universe) that "explains itself" in the sense that each part is explained by another part without circularity or limit. Sure, that sounds deeply weird. In medieval times, and even according to some folks today, the idea of a purely contingently existing thing that can explain its own existence would have been pronounced absurd, contradictory, and contrary to reason, but our intuitions about physical objects are formed regarding finite ones alone, not infinite ones, and infinite objects are utterly different from finite ones.

There are all sorts of violently counterintuitive results about infinite collections. For instance, you can prove, about as rigorously as you can prove anything, that there are just as many positive numbers as there are positive and negative numbers—and yet, there are fewer positive and negative integers than there are decimal numbers between 0 and 1! Take the collection of all positive integers; now add something to that collection, such as the number 0; the resulting set is *no bigger* even though you have indeed *added* something to it that it didn't have before. Sounds crazy, doesn't it? (It certainly did for me, and for many years, but after learning and reflecting philosophically on some transfinite math I was able to "see," in a sense not tied to the rigorous proof, how it isn't crazy at all and is actually quite intuitive.) After learning about the mathematical work on infinite quantities (started by the mathematician Georg Cantor in the 1870s), much of which is indisputable yet utterly against common sense, we should no longer be *at all* confident in our pre-scientific prejudices about infinity when applied to the infinite physical world. And if that's the case, then we should not rely on our commonsensical ideas that seem to call out for a separate explanation of an infinite chain of causes and effects.

There is a common criticism of the Cosmological and Fine-Tuning arguments that doesn't focus on any one premise. It's this: how on earth are we supposed to know anything substantive about the origin or ultimate explanation of the universe or the universe's laws of nature (or the nature of infinity for that matter)? If we had some reason to think that contemporary physicists had finally settled the major issues regarding the universe's origin or laws, then perhaps we could just study physics and reflect appropriately. But most physicists will tell you that only fools put so much faith in the most advanced and least confirmed speculations of physicists. In my view, the right answer to most of the questions involved in the Cosmological and Fine-Tuning arguments is "How the hell should I know?" Doesn't God punish hubris anymore?

Q34: What's wrong, if anything, with this theistic reply to the Problem of Gratuitous Suffering?

Look, I don't have anything fancy to say about suffering and God. Do I *look* like an expert?? No. I admit that it's really puzzling how God can fit the 4-Part conception and yet allow such a colossal amount of suffering, much of it truly horrific. It's a mystery. But there are *lots* of mysteries in the world! It's a mystery why the laws of nature, like gravity, don't change all the time. It's a mystery how

> consciousness arises from electrochemical activity in the brain. It's a mystery how the universe started or how biological life started. We're practically *surrounded* by mysteries. And yet: I still believe in gravity, in consciousness, in life, and the universe. Why should I let a mystery about God be so potent that I give up belief in him? I am more than willing to admit that there are loads of things I don't understand about the world, but they don't make me go around denying the existence of things. Why should the mystery of God and suffering be any different?

It should be plain at this point that I am *not* trying to argue that the universe had no beginning, or that although it did begin it had no cause, or that although it began and was caused the cause had no mind, or that although it began and was caused by a mind the mind fails to have the characteristics typically accorded to God. In the above pages I presented no convincing evidence *against* the idea that the universe was caused to exist by a mind that is loving, good, knowing, and powerful (which is not to say that there is no such evidence against that theistic idea). All I'm saying is that we don't have any impressive evidence *for* the key claims of the Fine-Tuning Argument or the Cosmological Argument. It can be difficult, especially for really smart people like sophisticated Design Argument or Cosmological Argument advocates, to admit that our current evidence just completely runs out, leaving us not *merely* short of certainty (regarding the key premises of the two arguments) but short of anything that can justify substantive belief, but in my judgment that's what happens when we contemplate matters such as the origin or explanation of the physical universe.

The Social Argument

Let's move on to the Social Argument, which starts from the simple idea that since so many people have believed in God—literally billions—and *many highly intelligent* people have been among them, it is pretty likely that God exists, as very large groups of highly intelligent people are generally not that prone to huge mistakes upon serious reflection over many, many years. The argument is significantly bolstered by the observation that many intelligent, sober, sincere people have claimed to have actually *perceived* God, usually (but certainly not always) through years of meditation training. The argument allows for the truth that there are lots of cranks in the world who delude themselves into thinking that they have perceived God. But the argument also says that it's very unlikely that *all* the alleged perceivers and geniuses are deluded. Given the large numbers of geniuses and self-proclaimed perceivers, there are certainly going to be some frauds among them, but what are the odds that *all* of them are grossly mistaken?

In sum, the Social Argument is an attempt to show us that there is excellent evidence for God's existence—even though this evidence is not conclusive.

a. Throughout history literally billions of people have believed in God.
b. Throughout history many thousands of our most intelligent and careful thinkers have believed in God.
c. Throughout history thousands of intelligent people who show no signs of derangement have claimed that they have actually perceived God, usually through meditation.
d. If (a)–(c) are all true, then a significant portion of those people (not: all of them) are believing in God on the basis of significantly powerful genuine evidence. After all, it strains credulity to think that so many people, especially so many highly intelligent and apparently quite sane people, could believe something with lousy or zero evidence.
e. Hence, by (a)–(d) there is significantly powerful genuine evidence for God's existence.

Some theists almost recoil from the challenge "What *evidence* is there for the idea that God exists?"; they probably hate this book. In reply to the challenge for evidence they often insist that religion is a matter of "faith." But "faith" is a slippery term. When pressed with a follow-up question such as "Why choose faith in theism, as opposed to some other religion or some superstition or something utterly silly like astrology?" they will, after a fashion, often say that theistic faith is more reasonable *because it is so common and accepted by sober smart folks*, while faith in obvious silliness is not. This is, I think, a (fallible) sign of an implicit reliance on something strongly akin to the Social Argument. Thus, something along the lines of the Social Argument is implicitly relied on by many people.

I happen to have a slightly higher opinion of the merits of this argument than most other philosophers. Usually, when zillions of people believe X there is some decent *evidence* for X that many (not: all) of them are basing their opinion on. This is especially likely when many of the people in question are extremely smart and have put a lot of thought into whether X is true—which is definitely the case when X = theism. I could bore you with a list of contemporary theistic philosophers who are unquestionably among the very best philosophers in the world. I don't see any reason at all to reject any of (a)–(c); each is just an obvious, brute sociological fact about people. But one might reasonably think that (d) is false. I will give several reasons for being skeptical of that premise.

Q35: The Social Argument says, roughly, that when zillions of people all believe X is true, there is an excellent chance that there is good evidence that X is true. (This is just a rough statement of it because the Social

Argument also mentions perception and high intelligence.) Think of four cases, two of which conform to that rule and two of which seem to go against it.

In the nineteenth century lots of people, especially the clear majority of our best and brightest geniuses, thought that eugenics was a simply *wonderful* idea. After the Nazis and World War II this endorsement of eugenics was quietly abandoned in intellectual circles, but for several decades before then—right through the 1930s—a great many of the "really smart folk" in Europe and the USA thought it was super. Similarly, throughout most history most smart people have been racists, but this hardly suggests that the members of some races are morally or intellectually inferior to those of other races. Today we still have the bigotry towards gays, lesbians, and transgendered people. Those are just a few examples, but the sad fact is that humans make colossal mistakes, even in very large groups of unquestionably smart and intellectually virtuous people.

This observation of mine doesn't prove much. All it shows is that one has to use a premise along the lines of "Well, it's really unlikely that so many people, even really smart ones, could be wrong" with real care, which you probably knew already. But there are additional reasons why it is a highly doubtful premise *when it comes to religion*.

Here is one of the reasons. Near the beginning of this book I mentioned that my mother recently died. Like almost all professional philosophers I believe that there is no afterlife (it may surprise you to learn that many theistic philosophers don't think there is an afterlife). And yet, I felt very strongly the pull of the idea that perhaps, just maybe, my mother could somehow see me or hear me after her death. It was a powerful emotional reaction of mine that provides no evidence whatsoever that there really is an afterlife or God; for instance, there is no reason to think that I was on the brink of becoming perceptively in tune with the after-life. This isn't the movies folks; it's real life. The desire to communicate with loved ones who have died (especially recently) is *very* strong, and belief often helplessly follows such extreme desires. Those intense desires push us in the direction of theism regardless of whether we have any supporting evidence.

In addition, many people have an extremely strong reaction to injustice. If we see a gross injustice and the perpetrators get away scot-free, this can be very distressing, especially when *we* are the victims of the injustice. Again, there is an incredibly fierce desire for justice to be made. And since justice very often doesn't come before death, we are strongly if unconsciously tempted by the idea that it *must* come eventually, in the afterlife.

In sum, there is a profound human yearning for an afterlife of love and justice. Even so, I suppose that most theists did not become theists *solely* on the basis of either of those desires, strong as those desires are. But there are several similar forces pushing us towards various religious doctrines, and for many of them there is no corresponding impressive evidence supporting the push. Indeed, *reflective theists almost always will accept that claim*, as they need to account for the hundreds of millions of religious people who disagree with their specific religious beliefs (e.g., the specific beliefs about Jesus of Nazareth). The upshot: given the strong emotional pressures to believe in theism as well as specific theistic doctrines— pressures we recognize to not be based on evidence—humanity has a strong disposition to believe in theism even in the absence of evidence for theism. Let me be perfectly clear: this does nothing at all to suggest that there is no good evidence for theism! All it does is suggest that contrary to the Social Argument (specifically, premise (d)) it would not be all that surprising to learn that most people who become theists do not do so on the basis of any significant evidence.

Now for the third reason to be skeptical about the argument: it is growing "less applicable" all the time. Again, the key premise says "Well, it's really unlikely that so many people, even really smart ones, could be so wrong." That is a reasonable idea, but it is pretty suspicious that the percentage of educated people who accept theism is decreasing all the time. When we look at the percentage of scientists and academics who are theists we see that it is much less than it was a century or so ago. And the percentage of highly educated theists from a couple of centuries ago was more than it was one century ago. The amount of societal pressure to publically advocate theism has dropped over the years, and in response the number of admitted theists among the most educated has plummeted. This data raises the possibility that a great many highly educated people endorsed theism over the centuries not because they had some decent evidence but because it was socially unacceptable to refrain from doing so.

> Q36: The last criticism went like this: although lots of people used to think X was true, the fact that fewer and fewer people today think X is true suggests that in the past it was social pressures that made so many people think X is true. Think of a non-religious case in which precisely this happened.

Yet another reason to be unhappy with the Social Argument is that it merely postpones the real issue. What we really want from a theist is something like *direct* evidence for the existence of God, and yet all the Social Argument delivers, at best, is some *evidence of evidence* for God. In order to grasp the distinction between direct evidence and evidence of evidence, consider an analogous case. Sherlock Holmes announces that he is completely confident that the butler killed the maid. You read this announcement and come to believe that the butler killed the maid. Although you and Holmes share a belief—you both think the butler did it—you have entirely different bodies of evidence backing up your beliefs. Holmes has things like a bloody knife, some diary entries of the butler outlining plans for murder, testimony of a love triangle, etc. You don't have any of that evidence. All you have is this: Holmes has an excellent track record on things like this, he has said that he's completely confident the butler did it, and there's no special reason this time around to doubt him. That's enough evidence to make your belief reasonable, but it's second-rate evidence: it's good testimonial evidence that there is good detective evidence for the butler's guilt. If the butler's wife heard that you thought her husband was guilty, which she thinks is false, and she confronted you about it, she would demand you back up your belief with detective evidence, not mere testimonial evidence. The latter evidence is fine, but what we really care about is the former evidence. Similarly, what we really care about is direct evidence for God's existence; testimonial evidence is a highly unsatisfying substitute.

Q37: The Social Argument is an argument that attempts to show us that there is excellent evidence for God's existence—even though this evidence is not conclusive. As expressed in the book it has four premises: (a)–(d). Which of these four premises do you agree with? For the one or ones you don't agree with, why do you disagree with it?

But what about people who have had *spiritual experiences*, as the Social Argument mentions in premise (c)? There are a great many detailed written first-hand accounts of alleged perceptions of God. Many philosophers are highly skeptical about the veracity of such accounts. To a certain extent, this is entirely justified. There are loads of people who make utterly ridiculous claims about communicating with God. Did former US president George W. Bush really have God tell him to invade Iraq in 2003, as he claimed? Please.

Although it can be somewhat entertaining, depending on one's tastes, to focus on the deranged people who claim to have perceived God, it has the negative effect of drawing our attention away from the interesting sources of alleged divine communication. The ugly fact is that most philosophers know little about the experiences *these* non-deranged people have had. I'm not one of those philosophers: I've studied many accounts of spiritual experiences, both the ones alleged to provide evidence for theism and those had by people (e.g., Zen Buddhists) who do not take them to provide any such evidence. For what it's worth, my own view is that these people, or a good number of them anyway, are having experiences that are not at all unhinged or irrational or primitive or anything insulting like that. But the question remains: do the spiritual experiences of those who claim that their experiences were genuine perceptions of God provide us—or even them—with good evidence that God really exists? Or is there some other, non-insulting and *significantly more likely*, explanation of their experiences? I'm now going to argue that it's the latter. I personally find this result very disappointing, even crushing, as I think it would be so cool if I could actually perceive God, but I'm trying hard to adjust my beliefs to the *evidence*, and not adjust my beliefs to my *wishes*.

As I just said, we are faced with the question of what to make of the spiritual experiences people have—where we are restricting ourselves to people who have meditated for a number of years in a community devoted to exploring the intricacies of spiritual development. But how on earth are we supposed to figure out whether those experiences call out for the existence of God? It would be nice if we could just ask the experts, as in lots of other cases in which we are faced with a really tough question. If you want to know whether Uranus is heavier than Neptune, you ask someone who is an expert. You could ask a college student who majors in physics or astronomy. Better yet, you could ask an astronomer. Even better: ask a professional astronomer, and not an amateur astronomer. Probably best: ask a professional astronomer who specializes in our solar system, as opposed to specializing in remote galaxies or black holes or the like.

I assume that the advocate of the Social Argument, who thinks much spiritual experience is genuine and indicates the existence of God, will insist that some people have more spiritual experiences than other people. In addition, she will think that some people have a spiritual experience akin to a lightning bolt out of the sky while others have spiritual experiences as a result of a highly disciplined and long-term participation in one of the meditation traditions. Furthermore, when it comes to spiritual experiences she will hold that some people are like the college student, others are like the amateur astronomer, yet others are like the professional astronomer, and then there are those who are like the professional astronomer with the relevant specialization. In order to figure out whether spiritual experiences are good evidence for the existence of God, it would be best to consult the people who are like the professional astronomer with the relevant specialization. Let's call those people "spiritual experts."

I take it the people with the most plausible claim to be spiritual experts are the ones with lots of spiritual experience, especially advanced spiritual experiences, *and* lots of competent reflection on spiritual experience, *usually* acquired by helping others develop their own spiritual capacities. And I take it that most of these people will be advanced members of meditative disciplines, since these are the disciplines primarily devoted to developing spiritual experience. For instance, the meditation masters/teachers of various forms of Zen, Christianity, Vajrayana Buddhism, and many other traditions or disciplines will count as spiritual experts if anyone does. These experts are, to all appearances, as intellectually and morally and psychologically upstanding as you like (that's my experience with them anyway). They say all sorts of very intelligent and substantive things about religious experiences or states of consciousness.

Of course, you might deny that there are any experts regarding spiritual experience! That's fine; lots of intelligent, informed, and fair-minded people have that view. And I'm not going to suggest that that view is incorrect. But my criticism of the Social Argument will not rely on that controversial denial. For the sake of argument I am going to assume, *with* the advocate of the Social Argument, that there are experts regarding spiritual experience. By admitting the existence of spiritual experts, I'm meeting the advocate of the Social Argument half way.[27]

Q38: Suppose Jones says that there are genuine experts in spiritual experience but we normal people just don't have the ability to figure out who is an expert or whether what the so-called experts say is true. Jones says that the spiritual experts are akin to people who have a sixth sense, something other than seeing, hearing, touching, smelling, and tasting. She says that *all* of us have the capacity to awaken this sixth sense, have spiritual experiences, and thereby gain spiritual knowledge. The problem, she says, is that virtually all of us have yet to awaken that capacity, and until we do we won't be in any position to judge the assertions made by the people who have awakened that sixth sense. Is there any good way to decide whether what Jones says is true?

The key point of my criticism is this: *many* of these spiritual experts insist, based on their genuine expertise on these matters, that the spiritual experiences had by many people who aren't part of some meditative discipline *are not experiences of God*. Instead, these spiritual experts say, the correct explanation of those religious experiences is non-theistic, and people who form theistic beliefs upon having such experiences are victims of a particularly interesting and pervasive illusion *typical for beginners* at spiritual experience. Many religious experiences are very advanced, in the evolutionary psychology sense. That is, the spiritual states of consciousness are in some sense more advanced than any of those states of consciousness most of us live through in our ordinary lives. When developmental psychologists make the concerted effort, they will discover that there are stages of psychological development *far* beyond those typically studied in psychology; and it turns out that these stages are the home of spiritual experiences. People who have them are not deranged or irrational in virtue of having those experiences; on the contrary, these people may be evolutionarily advanced because they have those experiences. Many of these folks are beginners, yes, but what they are doing is beginning to explore the intricacies of the "higher realms" of psychological development, not regressing to the womb or other such nonsense that applies to the deranged preachers on television such as Pat Robertson or Jerry Falwell in the US. The spiritual experts I'm considering here aren't saying anything insulting or condescending about people who have spiritual experiences! They aren't saying, for instance, that such people are really just deluded and deeply yearn for a supreme father figure (although such an explanation does of course depressingly apply to some theists). But they are saying that *those experiences don't signal the existence of any being other than the one having the experience*. Given any of a fairly large range of appropriate cognitive backgrounds and expectations, one will have experiences *as if* there is a non-physical and roughly person-like being in their presence; the spiritual experiences are "malleable" as we might put it. And one can eventually realize that fact, but only after one has had more mature spiritual experiences—in fact, this realization almost never happens unless one takes up some meditative practice in a serious way for several years. Eventually, with more advanced spiritual experiences one has years later, one can see one's earlier mistakes. Indeed, there are many testimonials from spiritual experts describing how their initial spiritual experiences were deceptive in many ways despite their being illuminating and "on the right track." These experts say that the spiritual experiences many people have are somewhat akin to the visual experiences had by someone who was congenitally blind but who has just had an operation to gain the power of sight. She is having genuinely new visual experiences. But her experiences are those of a novice, and novices make lots of perceptual mistakes.

The spiritual experts who offer what I'm calling "alternative" explanations of some spiritual experiences need not be atheists; in fact, they can be *and actually sometimes are* theists—even theists who believe that we can know God through spiritual experiences. Just like I sometimes say to my students,

> I agree with your essay's conclusion. And I think your argument is sophisticated, illuminating, and worth an "A" grade. Unfortunately I also think your argument doesn't really support your conclusion, as there is a subtle mistake present ...

some actual spiritual experts will say to many of us,

> I agree that God exists. And I think one can experience God, come to know God through spiritual experience, and your experience was extraordinary and meaningful. So we agree on some quite fundamental matters. Unfortunately I also think that you have not really experienced Him this time around.

Many others will be agnostics who say that many spiritual experiences are extraordinary and genuinely spiritual but don't come from God, regardless of whether he exists, because these experiences are indicative of the higher realms of human inner experience, and not experiences of divine entities. They take no stand on God's existence but just hold that the spiritual experiences have non-divine sources and explanations. And of course many of the spiritual experts will be atheists (of a great variety of kinds). But they aren't any old atheists, like the ones who sometimes write editorials in newspapers or misleading but popular books: the ones I have in mind acknowledge the "legitimacy" and extreme importance of spiritual experience but don't think it is experience of any supernatural entity.

I am certainly not saying that these spiritual experts are right about any of this. Part of what I am saying is this: they are genuine spiritual experts *if anyone is* and their considered opinion is that a huge portion of spiritual experience is not of God.

Now ... what are *we* supposed to do with this information—where the "we" in question do not consist of spiritual experts? Well, for what it's worth it makes me think that although a lot of people say they have perceived God, and these people are perfectly sincere and intelligent and aren't trying to fool anyone, there are serious grounds for doubting that they have characterized their experiences correctly. As much as I would like to take their word for it, I can't because of the serious controversy surrounding their claims of perception. And this makes me doubt the truth of the part of premise (d) that mentions meditation.[28]

Naturally, someone may object that the "spiritual experts" I have mentioned above aren't the *real* experts. The real experts are the ones who say that we often truly experience God—even us ordinary folk who don't meditate for years under the direction of some spiritual master/teacher. But on what grounds should we say which "experts" are the genuine ones? Are we to say "Well, the genuine ones are the ones who agree with me!"? It must be comforting to live with thoughts like that.

Lessons

I'm finished evaluating those three arguments for God's existence. Now, things are relatively simple in one respect: either one or more of those arguments is great or they all stink. Both possibilities have interesting consequences, ones that should influence how we think of the Confident Approach.

Suppose first that the philosophers are right: those three arguments (as well as many other arguments) provide little evidence in favor of God's existence. But what does that *mean*? For instance, does it mean that anyone who bases some of her religious beliefs on those arguments is stupid or irrational or something else insulting?

I don't think so. In order to explain why, consider a story—one whose ending you will probably find shocking. Fred thinks he might have disease X. He goes to Dr. Quack, who administers a test meant to determine whether or not Fred has X. Dr. Quack tells Fred, correctly, that the test has two excellent features: if someone has X and takes the test, the test will correctly say "You have X" a whopping 99 percent of the time and it will incorrectly say "You don't have X" a measly 1 percent of the time; and if someone doesn't have X and takes the test, the test will correctly say "You don't have X" 99 percent of the time and it will incorrectly say "You have X" 1 percent of the time. Dr. Quack also informs Fred that only 1 out of 100,000 people have X. X is a rare disease. Fred is impressed with these facts and comes to have belief B: *if the test says you have X, then there's an excellent chance you have X.*

Now the reason I chose the insulting name for the doctor is that the test he or she is using is actually lousy for testing for X. If the test says "You don't have X," there is indeed an excellent chance you don't have X; so in that respect the test is okay. But what about Fred's belief B that if the test says "You have X," then there is an excellent chance you have X? If you know a little probability theory you can figure out that Fred's belief B is utterly and completely false! In reality, if the test says "You have X," then there is actually only a *miniscule* chance that you have X—even given the 99 percent facts given earlier. The truth is that almost every time the test says "This person has X" the test is *wrong*. That's surprising, but that's the way the math works. There is all the difference in the world between "If you have the disease, then the test will say yes" (which is very nearly true in this case, as it's 99 percent accurate) and "If the test says yes, then you have the disease" (which is completely false in this case).

Let's pause to see why (I promise the explanation will be relatively painless). Suppose a million people take the test. Since about 1 in 100,000 actually have the disease X, about ten of the one million people will have the disease. When those ten people take the test, the odds are that the test will say "You have X" all ten times (as it is 99 percent accurate in that sense); in that respect the test is great. But now consider the remaining people, the 999,990 folks who don't have X. When they take the test 1 percent of the time the test will mistakenly say "You have X." One percent of 999,990 is about 1,000. So all told, the test will say "You have X" about 1,010 times: that's the first 10 (who really do have X) plus the next 1000 (who don't have X). But only 10 of those times is the test right in saying "You have X." Thus, when the test says "You have X," which is about 1010 times, the test is wrong 1000 out of 1010 times: it's wrong about 99 percent of the time! So Fred's belief that if the test says you have X, then there's an excellent chance you have X, is about as false as it can get.

This story illustrates how facts about probability are pretty counterintuitive, at least for me. More to the point, it shows how *misleading evidence* can, oddly enough, make someone's belief completely "reasonable," at least under one standard way of understanding that term. Since Fred doesn't know probability theory, the percentages that Dr. Quack boasted about strongly suggest to him that the test is excellent. The fact that the disease is so rare is the reason why the test is actually no good (if 1 out of 10 people had the disease then belief B would be true), but Fred doesn't have the mathematics background or ability to see that. The argument (1)–(4) below, which implicitly went through Fred's mind in the doctor's office, makes his belief B *reasonable* (it's reasonable because he has knowledge that he takes to be good reason for his belief, even if the reasons don't establish his belief), *blameless* (because given his background it would be over the top to criticize him for concluding with B), and *rational* (in some sense of that word) even though the premises don't really, objectively, support the conclusion in the slightest way:

1. If someone has X and takes the test, the test will correctly say "You have X" 99 percent of the time and it will incorrectly say "You don't have X" 1 percent of the time.
2. If someone doesn't have X and takes the test, the test will correctly say "You don't have X" 99 percent of the time and it will incorrectly say "You have X" 1 percent of the time.
3. Only 1 out of 100,000 people have X.
4. Thus, if the test says you have X, then there's an excellent chance you have X.

The three premises are perfectly true but offer no objective support for the conclusion, which as we saw was utterly false.

(Just to be clear: the facts that Fred knows, (1)–(3), collectively amount to *good* evidence for this *alternative* conclusion: if the test says you have X, then the chance you have X is significantly greater than if the test says you didn't have X. They also are good evidence for yet another conclusion: if the test says you have X, then the chance you have X is much greater than 1 in 100,000. Before finding out anything about Fred we know that the odds he has the disease are 1 in 100,000, as that is the odds for humans in general. After the diagnostic test says "You have the disease X," the odds are now about 1 in 101 (as explained above, they're about 10 out of 1010). So if the test says you have X, your odds of having X have increased by about a factor of 1,000—which of course is a lot. But there is still very little chance you have X (i.e., just 1 in 101). Fred thought that the facts he knew about the test, (1)–(3), provided good evidence for his belief that if the test says you have X, then there is an *excellent* chance you have X (that's belief B), but he was wrong about that, as 1 in 101 is hardly an "excellent chance.")

When I say that Fred's belief B is "blameless" I don't mean that there are *no* legitimate criticisms of his belief or reasoning. The fact that his premises collectively offer no objective support whatsoever for his conclusion even though they are perfectly true is surely a flaw that can be pointed out. Even so, given his background it is not a *serious* flaw. We can hardly say of him "He really should have known better than to come to that conclusion." If he were a mathematician such a criticism would be legitimate and serious. So the hurdle one has to clear in order to have a belief that has *objectively good evidence* backing it up is different from the hurdle one has to clear in order to have a belief that is *reasonable*—under a "subjective" conception of being reasonable. With the latter notion I have in mind the idea that given his background knowledge and ignorance, his reasons for coming to accept B make his belief in B "reasonable" even though as a matter of objective fact his reasons don't support B.

With respect to the three arguments for God's existence (Design, Cosmological, Social), I suspect that many of us may be in a position similar to Fred's in this respect: even if the particular versions of those arguments that people actually rely on (or would rely on if challenged on their basic theistic beliefs) don't really, objectively, support the conclusion that God exists (or that the 4-Part God exists), they nevertheless are *good enough* that they can make a lot of people's belief in God reasonable in a sense similar to that of Fred's belief in (4), which was made reasonable by his knowledge of (1)–(3). All that is required is that they have the appropriate background—including ignorance of certain important but subtle flaws in those arguments. This kind of ignorance is hardly a serious blow against one's rationality; it's common to *all* of us.

So *if* a person mistakenly thinks she knows for sure that the 4-Part God exists but her belief is reasonable only in the sense that Fred's belief was reasonable (because, perhaps, it is based on some flawed but hardly silly considerations such as those in the Social Argument), then when she says to herself "I know the 4-Part God exists; so, either the Gratuitous Premise or the Consequence Premise must be false," her inference will be reasonable as well. It won't be reasonable in the *evidential* sense, as she fails to have genuine evidence that backs up her belief— just like how Fred fails to have genuine evidence that backs up his belief. So in that evidential sense—a very important one—the Confident Approach for her is a failure: it is not an evidentially rational way for her to respond to the Problem of Gratuitous Suffering. But that doesn't mean that she is utterly doomed either, as she could be in the same situation as Fred.

Q39: Think of another case that meets all of the following conditions: (i) someone bases their belief B on argument A, (ii) argument A actually provides no real evidence for B, but (iii) A is good enough to make her belief in B reasonable.

Now let's take the other possibility: let's say that one of those arguments for the existence of God is actually excellent in providing strong evidence for theism; so the philosophers are wrong about this argument. Does this mean that the theist who bases her belief on that good argument is in the clear?

Well, there can be excellent evidence for a false idea. One sees this in courtroom cases all the time: there is truly formidable evidence that someone is guilty, for instance, even though it's just an objective fact that he is utterly innocent of the alleged crime and the evidence against him is highly misleading. Thus, even if one of the arguments for God's existence was impressive, this would not automatically mean that God exists.

That's an obvious point. A more interesting one lies closer to home. Let's suppose that the Design Argument (perhaps with some supplementary arguments) proves, successfully, that the 4-Part God exists. Suppose further that you base your belief in God on that argument. Or perhaps you have some other way of knowing that the 4-Part God exists. So you *know* that God exists! Even so, acquiring misleading evidence can ruin this knowledge. Consider a story meant to illustrate that phenomenon.

You and your good friend Fred go to a party. At the party you meet Mary. You talk with her on and off for a couple hours. You learn that she works in a hospital, although she doesn't go into details regarding her job. On the way home after the party you mention to Fred that you met this woman Mary at the party. Fred tells you that he talked with her as well (you and Fred mingled separately at the party). You say that she works in a hospital. He agrees, saying that she is an administrator at the Children's Hospital of Philadelphia, CHOP. What he says is true. At this point you *know* that Mary works at CHOP as an administrator, as your friend Fred is intelligent and trustworthy (as is Mary).

The next day you are in downtown Philadelphia sitting in a coffee shop and through the shop's window you see a woman in obvious hospital garb immediately outside CHOP. She looks exactly like Mary, is helping a patient into a wheelchair, and then brings him into the hospital. You got an excellent look at her. Further, you see her do this task several times over the next hour. Now you're confused, right? The night before you heard that she was an administrator but you just saw her doing clearly non-administrative work. Unknown to you, Mary's identical twin Margaret works part-time at CHOP and you were watching her that day. The previous night you did indeed learn, and come to know, that Mary works at CHOP as an administrator but the next day you were presented with powerful yet misleading evidence against your belief. If the misleading evidence is powerful enough (just play around with the story a bit) then it can happen that the protagonist's previous belief becomes positively irrational to hold on to in the face of the new evidence. You start off with excellent evidence for your belief, evidence good enough for knowledge, but then encounter contrary evidence that is powerful enough to ruin your previous belief, making that belief not merely fail to count as knowledge but become downright irrational for you to hold on to.

Q40: Think of another case in which you start off with excellent evidence for your belief, evidence good enough for knowledge, but then encounter contrary evidence that is powerful enough to ruin your previous belief, making that belief not merely fail to count as knowledge but become downright irrational for you to hold on to.

Hence, even if you somehow come to know the 4-Part God exists, the evidence supplied by the Gratuitous Premise and the Consequence Premise may well be powerful enough to make your true belief in God irrational. As I mentioned previously, the vast majority of theists accept the Consequence Premise (for reasons we'll encounter in the next chapter). So if the evidence for gratuitous suffering is strong enough (even though misleading!), then one's previously rational theistic belief can become irrational to retain when faced with the Problem of Gratuitous Suffering. For many philosophers, this "if" idea is not regarded as an idle possibility but as a real, live possibility. In fact, some think it's really the crux of the whole debate over suffering and God. We'll encounter the explicit argument for the Gratuitous Premise in chapter 7.

Q41: The Fred-Disease story illustrates a crucial epistemological lesson. (a) What is it? (b) What relevance does it have for the Problem of Gratuitous Suffering?

The Mary-Hospital story illustrates a crucial epistemological lesson. (a) What is it? (b) What relevance does it have for the Problem of Gratuitous Suffering?

Q42: Suppose that contrary to what is suggested in the book, one of the standard arguments for God's existence—cosmological, design, social—is actually so good that it *proves* that the 4-Part God exists. Just assume that's true for the sake of answering this question. Doesn't that mean that the Problem of Gratuitous Suffering is powerless to ruin our 4-Part theistic beliefs? After all, the two premises of the Problem of Gratuitous Suffering argument entail that the 4-Part God doesn't exist; since that's false (or so we're assuming for the sake of argument), at least one of those premises is false; hence, they are no good for overthrowing theistic belief in the 4-Part God. Answer the question and then explain your reasoning.

Let me sum up the main results of this chapter:

(i) We have seen that there is a central problem with the Confident Approach: even if we are theists who agree that the 4-Part conception of God is accurate, precious few (if any) people actually *know for certain* that the 4-Part God exists, and there are plenty of traditional theists who believe in God (that's why they count as theists) but who insist that the 4-Part conception is inaccurate. Perhaps some lucky people have had extraordinary experiences that show beyond any doubt that there is a being that (a) created the universe, (b) is perfectly good, (c) is perfectly powerful, and (d) is perfectly knowledgeable. But these people are rare, assuming there are any at all.

(ii) Whether the Confident Approach is a reasonable response to the Problem of Gratuitous Suffering rests with the question of whether the theist who makes this response *already has truly excellent overall support* for her belief that God exists *and* fits the 4-Part conception.

(iii) Many of the standard arguments for the existence of God are well known to have serious if not fatal flaws. The people who have examined them most thoroughly—philosophers—have concluded that even when put together they give little good objective reason to think God exists. This consensus is by no means unanimous: whether the arguments are successful is still a matter of debate. Even so, there definitely is a consensus that the arguments are so flawed that they supply little genuine reason for believing in God.

(iv) But this does not prevent those arguments from making theistic belief "reasonable" in one sense of that term (the kind illustrated by the story involving Fred and Dr. Quack). And that means that a person who mistakenly thinks she knows that the 4–Part God exists could adopt the Confident Approach and thereby "reasonably" conclude that either the Gratuitous Premise or the Consequence Premise is false—but her response will fail to be backed by genuine evidence.

(v) Most advocates of the Confident Approach have to insist that there are no gratuitous sufferings, since they accept the Consequence Premise. They have to deal with the central problem mentioned in (i) as well.

(vi) *If* it's possible to have very high-grade knowledge that God exists and fits the 4–Part conception, *then* it is quite likely that one can reasonably conclude that one of the premises is false even though one has nothing informative to say about them—just like the person who is certain that $1 \neq 2$ but can't find the mistake in the "proof" that $1 = 2$.

(vii) If one has a rational belief in the 4–Part God, even a belief that amounts to knowledge, provided the evidence for the Gratuitous Premise and Consequence Premise is strong enough, that belief in God will become irrational to continue to have despite the fact that it initially amounted to knowledge.

Q43: Construct a list of bullet points, each stating a part of or crucial fact about the Confident Approach. Go through the entire chapter to do this; you should end up with a long list (include a lot more than what appears immediately above).

5

GOD PERMITS GRATUITOUS SUFFERING

What the Approach Says

In this approach the theist tries to give good reasons that strongly suggest that even though there is genuinely gratuitous suffering, God exists and fits each of the four parts of the 4-Part conception. That is, she attempts to give good reasons to think that even though God the creator knows everything, can do anything, and is morally perfect, God permits suffering that he knows full well is not outweighed by any good whatsoever. This amounts to saying that the Consequence Premise is false. Since this theist is saying that the 4-Part God is *compatible* with gratuitous suffering, we call her idea the **Compatibilist Approach** to the Problem of Gratuitous Suffering.

My sense of the debate is that most people who have thought hard about these issues think it's quite difficult to defend this option of rejecting the Consequence Premise. That is, many people just don't see any good reason to think the Consequence Premise is false. In order to cast doubt on the Consequence Premise one has to give some good reason to think that the 4-Part God would allow gratuitous sufferings—that is, that God could be morally perfect and yet *knowingly* allow there to be *gratuitous* suffering. There are various possible reasons to give here in support of the Compatibilist Approach, but for what it's worth (maybe not much) most of them strike me as not very promising (I'll examine eight of the reasons below). Many philosophers admit that while it's not hard to see why the 4-Part God would allow lots of suffering, what's hard is to see how the 4-Part God would allow for *gratuitous* sufferings—sufferings whose badness isn't outweighed by the goodness of something they led to or are otherwise coupled with. As I have suggested several times, philosophical consensus is a tricky thing, but for what it's worth virtually no theistic philosopher has thought that the Consequence Premise is false. That's an impressive consensus given how disagreeable philosophers are.

Of course, if we dilute the notions of being "all powerful" and "all knowing" enough, then it will be easy to see how God could permit gratuitous suffering: if he's got merely all the knowledge available to idiots or merely all the power of weaklings, then of course we can see how he would permit gratuitous suffering: he either has no clue what is going on or he is powerless to do anything about it. I'll look at serious versions of those ideas in chapter 8. But the advocate of the Compatibilist Approach is holding on to the vague idea that God is *supremely* knowledgeable and powerful, that at the very least, the collective knowledge and power of humanity are mere specks compared to those had by God.

Q44: "All the Compatibilist Approach is really saying is that the 4-Part God can make a universe that has some suffering in it. But that's pretty obviously true: he could just arrange things so that the benefits outweigh the costs, so every instance of suffering has an outweighing good. Thus, it's pretty clear that the Compatibilist Approach has an excellent chance at being true." Does this line of reasoning give any support to the Compatibilist Approach? Explain why your answer is right.

Criticisms of the Approach

Here's the first way to try to cast doubt on the Consequence Premise (which you'll keep in mind means showing that the 4-Part God might allow gratuitous sufferings) and thereby defend the Compatibilist Approach. Some philosophers and theologians have argued that evil is a purely *negative* thing akin to how a hole in a piece of cheese or a lack of skills or a grain shortage are negative things—that is, someone might say: "Well, evil is merely the *lack* of goodness, which makes evil a purely negative thing"—and the omnipotent and omniscient creator isn't morally deficient just because he permits something purely negative to happen or exist. But this isn't very convincing as a response to gratuitous suffering, as it hardly seems to matter whether suffering is purely negative or not: it still sucks big time. This is *not* to say that evil isn't negative! (Although, to my mind the idea that a throbbing pain is a mere lack of something is absurd on its face: it's hard for me to imagine anything more fully present and utterly unlike a gap or hole or lack of something, each of which are "negative" things.) It is to say that even if evil is purely negative (whatever that really means!) this fact doesn't cast any doubt on the Consequence Premise. We normal moral agents would be blameworthy if we knowingly allowed incredibly terrible "negative" things to come about when we knew full well that the "negative" things weren't coupled with any outweighing good and we knew full well that we could have easily prevented them. I don't think any of this would be news to many of those philosophers who have argued that evil is negative: most of them would not have thought that it means the Consequence Premise is false.

Here's a second way to attempt to be a Compatibilist: by claiming that the 4-Part God allows there to be gratuitous sufferings because there might be real value in our *thinking* that there are gratuitous sufferings, or perhaps actually *witnessing* things we take to be gratuitous sufferings. The idea behind this claim is that perhaps we need to think that there are truly gratuitous sufferings in order to really understand sin and salvation, or be appropriately free and not robots, or something similar. Or so this line of reasoning says. I've had several people put forward this idea.

I think this idea has significant merit but I don't see how it can work to show that the 4-Part God would allow gratuitous sufferings. If the sufferings are allowed for some excellent purpose that the 4-Part God has in mind (e.g., we need to think there are gratuitous sufferings in order to be truly free to make important decisions in our lives, or to truly love God, or so that morality isn't undermined, or for some other purpose), as the advocate of the idea of the previous paragraph claims, then by her own lights the sufferings *are not* gratuitous. After all, she is saying that God allows the sufferings to happen *because some outweighing good is coming from them*; the sufferings allow him to make some good thing happen that makes the sufferings worth it. This is ruinous for the advocate of this idea because she started out trying to cast doubt on the Consequence Premise. Casting doubt on the Consequence Premise requires gathering evidence that the 4-Part God would allow sufferings that *are* gratuitous. But then she went on to argue that the sufferings *are not* gratuitous!

The proposal I just rejected is still an intriguing idea, which is why I said it had significant merit even though it does nothing to undermine the Consequence Premise. Suppose some terrible thing happens: thousands of animals slowly burn to death in a big forest fire. These deaths might be coupled with no goods whatsoever—with the one exception that some of us humans become aware of these types of horrible events. Maybe we don't become aware of this one fire in particular (if it happens in a forest far from humans, or maybe even long before there were any humans), but we do become aware of many other fires just like it. And as a consequence of that awareness we acquire some good (e.g., the good of knowing the difference between good and evil, the good of being motivated to prevent evil, etc.) Still, doesn't this seem ridiculously unfair? After all, many trillions of animals have died horrible deaths. Does the benefit for humans somehow make it fair that all those animals had to suffer horribly? I'll return to these questions when I evaluate the PHOG Approach in chapter 6.

> Q45: "Sometimes cognitive illusions can be highly beneficial. For instance, people who have inflated opinions about themselves are often more psychologically healthy than people who have more accurate assessments of themselves. So maybe there is a real benefit for there being lots of gratuitous suffering. By making lots of suffering gratuitous God gets us to do things, or see things, that make us somehow better." Does this line of reasoning give any support to the Compatibilist Approach? Explain why your answer is right.

Here's a third way to attempt to develop the Compatibilist Approach, popular with a great number of theists: God works in mysterious ways, and we shouldn't be so arrogant to think we can know what he has in mind in allowing evil things to happen. Presumably, there is real truth behind this proposal! So it's a good idea to discuss it. If the 4-Part God exists then since he is all knowing and all powerful we comparatively stupid and weak humans are going to have a heck of a time trying to understand him; in fact, it would be a miracle if we could understand him. That sounds right. But the person who thinks the Consequence Premise is true will admit all that. She is definitely *not* saying that she's got God all figured out! Instead, she's saying that there are certain very specific and relatively modest consequences of the 4-Part conception that we *can* figure out. She's saying this: if God really is the supremely moral, knowledgeable, and powerful creator, then we can conclude that he allows evil things to happen *only* when he's got a good reason (even if that reason is invisible to us). That hardly seems like an overly ambitious claim to make—especially since she'll admit that the reason in question (the one that justifies the suffering) might be completely mysterious to us mere mortals, and thus she will have *admitted the truth of* at least one reading of "God works in mysterious ways." All she is saying is that the reason has to exist if the 4-Part conception is really accurate.

Here's a fourth and better attempt to explain how the Consequence Premise might be false: perhaps all a supremely morally good God has to do is create a universe that is good *overall*. That is, maybe all that morality requires is for God to make a universe in which life is on balance good, even if there are some bad parts that aren't linked with any outweighing goods. Suppose you live a truly wonderful life filled with great happiness but there was one episode in which you suffered some nasty physical pain that didn't lead to any good at all (let alone an outweighing good). Would you have cause to complain? Probably not. So the 4-Part God can exist and allow gratuitous sufferings as long as he makes the universe morally good overall.

There are several problems with this proposal; I'll mention just two. Problem one: what about people whose lives are just wretched? Under the above proposal they experience loads of gratuitous sufferings that are truly horrible and yet the 4-Part God is supposed to be morally perfect. It's hard to swallow the idea that God is morally justified in permitting that person's life to be so hideous just because that person's suffering was counteracted by the happiness experienced by a bunch of *other* people, the lucky ones. Over here we have the suckers who experience colossal pain and agony their whole lives; and over there we have the billionaires who party and experience delightful orgasms every few hours. On the contrary, that would make God really unjust. Keep in mind that many millions of people have lived lives of almost unending fear and suffering. It's easy to fail to appreciate this if one lives a life without hunger or fear of injury. Problem two: if God really knows everything, can do anything, and is morally perfect and loves us, then why would he allow *any* suffering at all unless he had the good reason that that suffering is coupled with an outweighing good? Given that he knows everything and can do anything, why would he allow any suffering that wasn't coupled with any good? It's still hard to see how he would permit *any* quantity of gratuitous suffering.

Q46: "As long as the universe is good *on balance* God is off the hook when it comes to the charge of suffering. That is, a wholly good God has to make a universe that is good when we add everything up, but he is under no obligation to make every nook and cranny of the universe good overall." That's the idea we just looked at in the text above. (a) Does this line of reasoning give any support to the Compatibilist Approach? Explain why your answer is right. (b) Independent of whether it supports the Compatibilist Approach, does the view seem like a promising one for responding to the Problem of Gratuitous Suffering?

Here is the fifth way to be a compatiblist: maybe this universe, with lots of gratuitous sufferings, is the *very best* universe possible. Of course, he could have made a universe containing nothing but dust, and hence no bad things at all, but if he wanted to make a universe with a large number of conscious beings who have some complexity to them (thoughts, emotions, plans, some control over their lives, etc.) then it was impossible for him to create a universe with even a tiny bit less gratuitous suffering. To say that God is "all powerful" doesn't mean that he can do literally anything imaginable. It means that he has all *truly possible* power, but not all *imaginable* power. As I mentioned earlier, people can imagine all sorts of things that are actually impossible: for instance, some folks can imagine finding water that scientists then discover has no hydrogen or oxygen in it. This is impossible, as water must contain both hydrogen and oxygen, but we can imagine it anyway. Since our universe is the absolute best one that even limitless power can make, this Compatibilist continues, as every other possible universe is worse overall compared to ours, all the gratuitous suffering in it is compatible with God being the all powerful, all knowing, morally perfect creator. There is a price to be paid if one wants to create a universe with complex, conscious life-forms, like us, and that price is gratuitous suffering: it's literally impossible to make creatures like us without also allowing in lots of gratuitous sufferings.

I think this proposal is useful because it draws a distinction that is important for thinking hard about the relation of God to suffering. The proposal is saying that although God knowingly permits *gratuitous* suffering—suffering not paired with outweighing goods—he does not permit *unjustified* suffering—suffering that he wasn't justified in allowing to happen. He is justified in allowing the gratuitous suffering to occur because it was beyond his power to prevent it. If you absolutely can't prevent some suffering from happening, then you are of course off the hook as far as blame is concerned; this holds for us as well as God. The lesson: just because some suffering is gratuitous doesn't automatically mean it's unjustified, even for a creator who has all possible power.

The problem with this idea is simple: there doesn't seem to be much good reason to think that this is the *best universe possible* with conscious beings. In fact, there doesn't seem to be much reason to think that the presence of conscious beings requires any gratuitous suffering at all: even if the presence of conscious beings requires suffering (we can grant that assumption if we like), why think that some of that suffering simply must have no outweighing goods coupled with it? I have never seen any evidence for that idea, and I haven't been able to think of any myself. In the case of water, we have excellent evidence that you can't have water unless you have both hydrogen and oxygen, but there is no evidence I know of for the idea that it was literally impossible to have a universe with less or even no gratuitous suffering even though it has creatures like us.

Q47: In the text above there is an argument that an instance of suffering might be *gratuitous but justified*. Present the argument in your own words and then evaluate it.

What we have been slowly doing thus far in this chapter is constructing the reasoning behind the Consequence Premise, the reasons why we think it's true:

a. If the 4-Part God exists, then each of the following are true:
    (1) God is supremely powerful.
    (2) God is supremely morally good.
    (3) God is supremely knowledgeable.
    (4) God made the universe with conscious beings living richly textured lives (that's us).

b.   If (1) God is supremely powerful, then (5) God has the power to make a universe with conscious beings living richly textured lives but with no gratuitous suffering. That is, if (1) is true then (5) is true.

c.   Notice that (a) says "If the 4–Part God exists, then (1), (2), (3), and (4)" and (b) says "If (1), then (5)." So when you put them together you get "If the 4–Part God exists, then (2), (3), (4), and (5)."

d.   Now we have a general principle: *if* all this were true of some individual:
  • He is supremely morally good.
  • He is supremely knowledgeable.
  • He made a universe with conscious beings living richly textured lives.
  • He had the power to make such a universe without gratuitous suffering.

Then he would have made a universe with no gratuitous suffering. His knowledge, goodness, and power demand it.

e.   But those four bullet points are just (2)–(5). So here is where we're at: (c) says that if the 4–Part God exists, then he fits the bullet points; and (d) says that if he fits the bullet points, then he created a universe with no gratuitous suffering. So when we put (c) and (d) together we get our conclusion: if the 4–Part God exists, then there is no gratuitous suffering. This is the Consequence Premise.[29]

So we have seen that the Consequence Premise looks pretty reasonable even if we can't prove it: a morally perfect, omnipotent, omniscient creator would very likely not allow gratuitous sufferings anywhere in the universe.

Q48: Is there some way to cast serious doubt on premise (d) in the argument for the Consequence Premise? (Keep in mind what it takes to cast doubt on (d): you need to come up with an argument that the four bullet points in (d) could be true of someone and yet he made a universe with gratuitous suffering.) State and then defend your own view.

The fact that we can't *prove* beyond a shadow of a doubt that the Consequence Premise is true opens the door to a sixth way of being an Compatibilist. One could be quite certain that God exists and fits the 4–Part conception but also be quite certain that there are many instances of gratuitous suffering. Indeed, as I stated in chapter 2 some philosophers and theists have gone down this road, especially in the twentieth century after Auschwitz and the rest of the Holocaust. As a result of these two convictions—there is gratuitous suffering, the 4–Part God exists—one might just reluctantly conclude that the Consequence Premise has got to be false, despite the fact that one can't find anything wrong with either it or its supporting argument (a)–(e) given above. Unlike the previous five ways of being a Compatiblist, under this sixth way one does not pretend to have any good idea how it is that the 4-Part God would permit gratuitous suffering, but one concludes that there must be *some* reason that explains how this can be, even if we don't know what it is.

Is this position defensible? Well, for starters it is not much different from the Confident Approach. With the latter a person starts out supremely confident in the 4-Part God's existence and then concludes that either the Consequence Premise or the Gratuitous Premise must be false. Earlier I noted that as a matter of sociological fact most people who go this route end up saying that it must be the Gratuitous Premise that's the false one. But here we're seeing the opposite, the other choice: some folks conclude it must be the Consequence Premise that's the false one. In each case, though, the main question lies at the start: are these people justified in being so confident that God exists and fits the 4-Part conception? That's exactly the question we raised when evaluating the Confident Approach, so I won't go over it again here.

Now for the seventh way of being a Compatibilist. She might challenge premise (b) in the argument for the Consequence Premise:

b.   If the creator is supremely powerful, then he has the power to make a universe with conscious beings living richly textured lives but with no gratuitous suffering.

She might say: how on earth do we know that it's really possible for there to be a universe with lots of great things like love and happiness and baseball with no gratuitous suffering? She acknowledges that there doesn't seem to be anything *obviously* impossible with a universe containing lots of wonderful things such as happiness and love but no gratuitous suffering, but she thinks that for all we know such a universe is impossible anyway. Earlier I gave the example of how a universe with water but no hydrogen is impossible but not obviously impossible. She is saying that for all we know the same applies to a universe with many excellent goods but no gratuitous suffering.

Q49: A key claim regarding the Consequence Premise: if the creator is supremely powerful, then he has the power to make a universe with conscious beings living lives more or less like ours (with good things like happiness and love) but with no gratuitous suffering. That is premise (b), used to derive the Consequence Premise. Is the claim true? Justify your answer.

I agree with the challenge to a certain extent. I readily admit that the idea that it's possible for the universe to have great goods and *no suffering at all* is quite doubtful. I also think that we have no rock-solid reason to think it's really possible to have a universe with great goods, suffering, but no gratuitous suffering. Even so, if a scenario initially *looks* perfectly possible—as "lots of water but no hydrogen" did for some time in the past—and there is no evidence against its possibility, then our overall opinion should be that it's really possible. I hasten to add: the opinion should be provisional or tentative. We should be wholly ready to switch our opinion if new evidence goes against it. For instance, our opinion that Mount Everest is the highest point on Earth is likewise provisional, despite the enormous amount of evidence in its favor. The advocate of the (a)–(e) argument for the Consequence Premise need not be, and usually is not, someone who is dogmatic about (b). Instead, she says that we have no reason whatsoever to doubt the possibility of a universe with great goods, suffering, but no gratuitous suffering: no scientific evidence, no mathematical evidence, no philosophical evidence, *nothing*. So, since it is coherent and there is no evidence against it, we should judge it to be possible.

Finally, it's worth noticing that the seventh proposal supplies no reason to doubt the Consequence Premise. Merely pointing out that one doesn't have a definitive proof of a claim (in this case, premise (b)) hardly amounts to a real proposal at all. There are loads of things we fail to have "definitive proof" of but we still would be irrational to seriously doubt them. I know that the actress Julia Roberts has made a great many very successful movies and was paid millions of dollars for each one. And I have never heard that she has lost all that money through bad investments or the like. So, I believe that she is rich. Then my friend Fred, who is a bit odd, points out to me that I don't have any "definitive proof" that she hasn't recently lost all her money through catastrophic investment decisions. In response I will admit that he's right about that, but I would be irrational if I proceeded to seriously doubt my belief in her richness. I don't have definitive proof of just about anything, but that doesn't make me go around doubting almost all my beliefs.

Q50: How do we know that this isn't the best universe the 4-Part God could make, assuming he exists?

Our eighth and last compatibilist idea is this: the whole notion of a good *outweighing* an instance of suffering is fraught with dubious assumptions. The notion pretends that we can compare goods and sufferings on some kind of scale, with goodness points and badness points, and do the math to see if the goodness outweighs the badness. This is pure fiction: there is no such scale, and goods and sufferings very often don't have anything remotely like degrees of goodness and badness that can be weighed against each other.

There is wisdom here, but I don't see how it helps. Presumably, the idea is that some instances of suffering are gratuitous because there is no way to compare their badness with the goodness of goods they are linked with. (Clearly, it won't do to say that there *never* is a way to make the comparison; we have no trouble making such comparisons in millions of everyday cases such as going to the dentist.) So according to the proposal there are gratuitous sufferings. How is that supposed to *help* the 4-Part theist? In order for the Compatibilist Approach to succeed, the theist has to offer a theory regarding how there can be gratuitous sufferings *and yet God is morally perfect anyway*. We have seen some unsuccessful attempts at such a theory: God is excused to permit gratuitous sufferings because (i) it isn't possible to get rid of them, (ii) there is extreme value in permitting them, (iii) all morality requires is a universe that is good overall, etc. In each case, the theist tries to explain why gratuitous suffering doesn't take away from God's goodness. But on this eighth proposal we get no explanation at all. We get an admission that there is gratuitous suffering, but when faced with the question "But why does he permit it?" all we get in reply is "Well, sometimes the badness of an instance of suffering can't be measured against the goodness of any goods it happens to be linked with." How on earth is that supposed to explain why gratuitous suffering is morally just fine?

Perhaps the idea behind the eighth version of compatibilism is this: since the badness of an instance of suffering often *cannot* be outweighed by the goodness of linked goods, God can hardly be blamed for not linking the suffering with an outweighing good. God can't do the impossible. But there is no reason I know of for thinking that for every instance of apparently gratuitous suffering, it was impossible for there to be a linking good. On the contrary, for virtually any instance of suffering, can't you imagine that you would be happy to accept it provided it would cause or otherwise be linked with a much greater good? And in many instances can't you pinpoint actual instances of suffering that were very similar to yours and really were linked with outweighing goods? That's what a critic of the eighth version of compatibilism would say.

Q51: What's wrong with rejecting the Consequence Premise with the following line of reasoning: we know the 4-Part God exists; but there is excellent reason to think that at least *some* instances of suffering are gratuitous (there are so many cases of suffering! And for most of them we haven't the faintest idea what an outweighing good might be!); thus, the 4-Part God exists and permits some gratuitous suffering; hence gratuitous suffering is compatible with the 4-Part God; the Consequence Premise is false.

We have arrived at two main conclusions regarding the Compatibilist Approach:

i)   The reasons the Compatibilist Approach advocate gives for thinking that a morally perfect, omnipotent, omniscient creator would allow gratuitous sufferings are not very good.

ii)   If she doesn't claim to understand why the 4-Part God would allow gratuitous suffering but believes it anyway based on her confidence that the 4-Part
God exists and there is gratuitous suffering (this was the sixth way of trying
to be a compatibilist), then she has to deal with the main points we made
regarding the Confident Approach at the end of chapter 4 (and she also has
the burden of finding a flaw in the (a)–(e) reasoning that says the 4-Part God
would not allow gratuitous suffering).

Q52: Construct a list of bullet points, each stating a part or crucial fact
about the Compatibilist Approach. Go through the entire chapter.

On to the next option for the theist who aims at providing a rational and
informative response to the Problem of Gratuitous Suffering.

6

GOD'S REASONS FOR SUFFERING REVEALED

What the Approach Says

This theist is highly ambitious since she is attempting to actually tell us what the PHOGs (profoundly hidden outweighing goods) are—the PHOGs that morally justify almost all cases of suffering, thereby strongly suggesting that there are no gratuitous sufferings at all. Given the number of instances of suffering (remember: many, many trillions of cases of horrific suffering—in addition to many cases of ordinary suffering), obviously she can't do this on a case-by-case basis. Instead, she will probably try to indicate a small number of very general good things that morally justify virtually all instances of suffering—especially the ones that appear gratuitous. Note that this theist doesn't merely *say* that there has to be, or probably are, such outweighing goods; she tries to come up with good reasons for thinking the outweighing goods really, actually exist—and then she *tells us what they are*. It's this last bit that makes her so ambitious. We call this the **PHOG Approach** to the Problem of Gratuitous Suffering. She probably wouldn't call the outweighing goods "profoundly hidden," as she thinks she knows what they are—she says they aren't hidden *to her*—but I'll stick with the phrase "profoundly hidden outweighing good" because she will readily admit that the alleged goods in question are hidden to many intelligent folks who think long and hard about these matters.[30]

Philosophers who think they know the PHOGs that justify suffering fall into two groups. First, there are those who take the existence of the 4-Part God *as a fact already known* and then *on the basis of that alleged theistic knowledge* try to figure out what the outweighing goods are—often by studying preferred religious texts for clues. They say "Since such-and-such theistic doctrines are true, we can see that the outweighing goods (or a good portion of them anyway) must be as follows …" These folks are definitely advocates of the PHOG Approach, since they claim to actually know what the outweighing goods are. But notice that they are not that different from the advocates of the Confident Approach: both assert that they *already know for sure* that the 4-Part God exists and proceed from there (with the PHOG advocates speculating on the outweighing goods and the Confident Approach advocates resting content to conclude that either the Gratuitous Premise is false or the Consequence Premise is false). Because of that commonality, the primary objection to the Confident Approach applies to members of the first group of PHOG Approach advocates.

Second, there are those who think they can figure out the outweighing goods without relying on any theistic premises at all. The latter folks think that the out-weighing goods can be discovered even if we set aside any and all theistic ideas. They say "Even if you are an atheist you can discover the outweighing goods without giving up your atheism!" At least, they say that the goods that outweigh *almost* all sufferings can be discovered this way.

It's important to not confuse the two groups. It's also important to distinguish PHOG Approach advocates from another group of people, who look a little like PHOG Approach advocates but actually aren't taking up that approach at all. The people I have in mind here proceed this way: they *assume for the sake of argument* that God exists and then armed with that assumption try to see if there is any way that there are actual goods that outweigh all suffering. They do not claim to *know* that God exists, like the first group of PHOG Approach advocates did. They take the 4-Part God's existence as a mere assumption. And they don't think that they have actually discovered the outweighing goods. Instead, all they claim to have done is figure out one possible story according to which the 4-Part God exists, there is lots of suffering, but there is no gratuitous suffering because all instances of suffering are linked with such-and-such specific goods.

I don't see much worth in that latter project, as it is so easy to pull off and has no great significance that I can see. All one needs to do in order to carry out that project is note some possibilities: perhaps all creatures who can suffer have free will; all suffering, of all creatures, is the product of the misuse of free will, either that of some creature or of Satan; and although the suffering generated by the misuse of free will is colossal, free will itself is so incredibly valuable that it is the supreme outweighing good. Maybe that story is not realistic enough for you, but it gets the job done. Here's another try: all suffering that isn't outweighed by goods we enjoy in our Earthly existence is outweighed by goods that we enjoy in an afterlife; and the connection between the Earthly suffering and the afterlife goods is beyond our comprehension. As long as I don't have to even try to come up with evidence regarding the *actual* outweighing goods, as long as my task is merely "Here is one way the 4-Part God *might*, just might, have supplied outweighing goods for all suffering," why bother leaving fantasy or pure speculation behind? What I have not done, with these two stories, is give any reason to believe that there is no gratuitous suffering, or to think that such-and-such goods collectively outweigh all suffering. We are in the realm of fantasy, not reality.

The main point is that the project discussed in the previous two paragraphs is *not* one of discovering the actual goods that justify suffering. Simply assuming 4-Part theism and then dreaming up possible outweighing goods can hardly be called *discovering* what the outweighing goods really are. An agnostic or even a diehard atheist could engage in this project! (I'm an agnostic and I just did it in the previous paragraph.) And of course an atheist or agnostic would hardly think that she has, at the end of her investigation, thereby discovered what the outweighing goods really are—or even discovered that there are any such outweighing goods. Further, even a theist engaged in this project would probably not be inclined to think that her speculations regarding possible outweighing goods reveal what the actual outweighing goods are.

Q53: There are two groups of 4-Part theists associated with the PHOG Approach. Explain how each differs from the other.

So, in sum, here is where things stand with regard to people who pursue something along the lines of the PHOG Approach. One group of PHOG Approach advocates use theism plus various detailed theistic doctrines as premises in speculating about the outweighing goods. They understand themselves as already knowing that theism and those doctrines are true; so they are claiming to be discovering the PHOGs that actually justify suffering. They are subject to the main criticism of the Confident Approach, which was the idea that few if any of us are in a position to be so confident that the 4-Part God exists. Indeed, the criticism is stronger here than when applied to the Confident Approach, because now we need to know not just that the 4-Part God exists but that many controversial theistic doctrines are true as well (e.g., regarding the afterlife, union with God, free will, etc.; see discussion of particular alleged PHOGs below). Then there is the second group of PHOG Approach advocates, who think they have found the outweighing goods *without making any assumptions about theism*. If we are interested in theistic responses to the Problem of Gratuitous Suffering that are both *rational* and *informative*, then we will have a preference for the insights of the second group of PHOG Approach advocates, since the first group—which confidently says that they already know for sure that God exists and that certain controversial theistic doctrines are true—will not strike us as terribly informative, given that they will simply take for granted many controversial theistic premises. If the folks in the first group *in fact* know for sure that God exists and certain theistic doctrines are true, then they might be *rational* in concluding that such-and-such goods exist and justify virtually all suffering throughout history. In fact, such a procedure might even generate *knowledge* of what the goods are! So the procedure might be quite excellent and worthwhile to that extent. In that particular sense the PHOG Approach can be fully successful, at least as a possibility. But unless they can share with us the basis for their secure knowledge of theism and the theistic doctrines with which they start their deliberations, their reasoning regarding the goods won't be terribly informative for those of us who are interested in the actual goods, if any, that justify all suffering and yet don't already know for sure that the 4-Part God exists. It will be informative for us only in this limited sense: we might learn what the outweighing goods would be *if* 4-Part theism were correct and *if* certain other theistic doctrines were also true; but this would hardly tell us that any such goods actually exist and are actually doing their outweighing work.

In the rest of this chapter I will do two things: discuss what constitutes a PHOG (e.g., the conditions that something must meet—the characteristics it must have—in order to be a good that justifies some suffering), and then evaluate some particular alleged PHOGs that people often put forward when confronted with the Problem of Gratuitous Suffering. My comments will primarily apply to the PHOG Approach advocates who are trying to find the *actual* outweighing goods, although those engaged in speculative fantasy (from a few paragraphs back) will also find high hurdles they have to clear.

The PHOG Approach is a tough road to take. Can you name anything that could justify the many trillions of cases of horrific suffering that animals (including humans) have endured over hundreds of millions of years? When exploring answers to that question we need to keep foremost in our minds what the requirements are on a PHOG that justifies suffering; otherwise we won't be able to evaluate the PHOG Approach in a competent way. So we need to ask: how exactly does a good thing morally justify a bit of suffering anyway? The five examples from the beginning of this book—blood donation, medicine, champagne, autonomy, and roughhousing—generate decent models of what's required. But there are other kinds of examples. For instance, perhaps I'm morally justified in knowingly letting something awful happen if I know that the only way to prevent it is to break some *moral law or rule*—so the good that justifies the subsequent suffering in this case is the avoidance of a bad thing, where the bad thing would be a violation of a moral law. We need to keep an open mind regarding what the goods are that allegedly justify all suffering; the examples I gave earlier are just the most straightforward ones.

When a person is operated on in a hospital in order to save her life, we say that the badness of the pain induced by the operation is outweighed by the goodness of the recovery. This is what that means:

- The recovery actually *exists* (i.e., it really happened).
- The recovery is *linked with* the pain of the operation in the sense that the one goes with the other (she endured the pain on the way to the recovery).
- The goodness of the recovery is *strong enough* to outweigh the badness of the pain (the pain was "worth it").

So, when we're looking for a group of PHOGs[31] that show that the apparently gratuitous suffering isn't really gratuitous, we need PHOGs that meet three absolutely necessary requirements (which you'll definitely need to remember when we start to evaluate particular PHOGs below):

The Existence Requirement: the PHOGs have to *really exist*. This means that the PHOG Approach advocate has to *give us good reasons* to think that the PHOGs she is focused on (e.g., a glorious afterlife in heaven) really exist. Obviously, if there is little or no reason to think they actually exist, then there is little or no reason to think that they actually justify any suffering.

The Linking Requirement: the PHOGs have to be *linked with* the many trillions of cases of horrific suffering that appear gratuitous, so the goodness of the PHOGs *counteracts* the badness of the suffering. This means that the PHOG Approach advocate has to *give us good reasons* to think that the PHOGs she is focused on are really linked with the trillions of cases of suffering that seem gratuitous.

The Strength Requirement: the goodness of the PHOGs has to be *strong enough* to outweigh the badness of all those many trillions of cases of horrific suffering—so the PHOGs have to be really, really spectacularly good. It isn't enough to point out some PHOGs that are genuinely linked with trillions of cases of suffering; the goods have to be amazingly good as well. This means that the PHOG Approach advocate has to *give us good reasons* to think that the PHOGs she is focused on are really strong enough to outweigh the badness of the trillions of cases of suffering that seem gratuitous.

Now I'm going to offer a few comments on each of the three requirements so that we know what they mean.

Regarding the first requirement, on occasion a theistic philosopher will respond to the Problem of Gratuitous Suffering by listing some *imaginable* good things and then arguing that they *could* be the PHOGs that justify all apparently gratuitous suffering. As I mentioned a few pages back, I don't see much point in that argument. We know of trillions of actual cases of horrific suffering. We then ask: what justifies all this intense suffering? We aren't interested in what is merely possible, what might, just *might*, justify it. Instead, we are interested in knowing what goods *actually justify* all that suffering. To be told "Well, it's *possible* for such and such things to exist and do the justification job—but I realize that I have little or even no evidence that they actually exist or do the job" is profoundly unsatisfactory and suggests a pathetic attempt to avoid the seriousness of the Problem of Gratuitous Suffering. We want *good reasons* to think that suffering is outweighed by some *actual* goods, and nice stories about how there is a *possible* universe in which our suffering doesn't exist or is outweighed by good things are hardly relevant to our genuine and very serious concern about suffering in the real world. This is why we have to have good overall reason for thinking the alleged PHOGs satisfy the Existence Requirement.

The second requirement, "linking," is important too. After all, I have a lot of fun at amusement parks with my kids, but the goodness of those outings certainly doesn't justify the badness of you suffering a toothache, as the two things (my fun outings, your nasty toothache) are completely unrelated. In order for a bad thing to be justified by some good thing the good thing has to be *connected* to the bad thing in an appropriate way (e.g., the badness of the late-night headache is connected to, and justified by, the goodness of the champagne that led to the headache; the goodness of autonomy for my children led to, and justified, the badness of their subsequent poor but not awful decisions; the badness of the pain of blood donation led to, and was justified by, the goodness of the use of the blood in the hospital). This connection between the good thing and the bad thing is the basis for the second requirement.

I already made an important comment on linking in chapter 2, but I need to repeat it here. One idea we will get to below says that there are tremendously important goods that are only *indirectly* linked with individual episodes of suffering. For instance, some philosophers have claimed that in order to develop our souls properly—and as we will see below there are several ways to spell out what that means—we must endure certain kinds of suffering. Let's assume for the moment that this is true. Now note that the link between the good of a developed soul and individual bouts of suffering will be much less straightforward than in the familiar examples of linking we looked at previously (e.g., blood donation). For any given instance of suffering it isn't as though we can say "Well, if he didn't experience that particular pain (or grief, or frustration, or loss), then he would never develop his soul properly." There is some leeway here. Instead, we say that these individual experiences of suffering *combine appropriately over many years* until the good is realized. So the theist can say that those bouts of suffering have outweighing goods—they are *not* gratuitous—but this linking is something that can only be seen in the long run and is much less direct than in many other cases.

Here is another case of indirect linking, one that has to be kept in mind when it comes to horrors such as the Holocaust: perhaps in order for there to be consciousness at all, there has to consciousness with free will; and if we're going to have free will, then things like the Holocaust are all but guaranteed to happen eventually. If God is going to create a species with genuine free will, the odds are that eventually that gift will result in atrocities. On many occasions very smart people have insisted to me that it's just perfectly obvious that there is gratuitous suffering, and as evidence they point out that there is no reputable evidence that the Holocaust is linked with any collection of goods that outweighs the incredible suffering of that event. The proper answer to them, I think, is to admit that they are probably *right* that there is no strong evidence for any *direct* connection between the Holocaust and some supreme goods that justify it, but they might be mistaken in thinking that there is no *indirect* connection. This is just another way in which the coupling of goods and sufferings makes demands on our intelligence. The question this book is concerned with, "Is there gratuitous suffering that rules out God?", is not easy to answer.

The third requirement on outweighing goods—making sure the goods are *good enough* to offset the badness of suffering— is easy to acknowledge and remember. When I mention it to people they nod their heads appropriately. And yet, I doubt whether very many people who read this book really appreciate the hurdle here. I think this is also true of many of the philosophers who investigate the Problem of Evil, which doesn't make them look good. My reason is the one I gave in chapter 2: very few people who read this little book have suffered incredible pain, either physical or psychological; neither are they vividly aware of it through other means. According to this line of thought, the PHOG Approach is doomed from the beginning. Even if all the goodness in the universe hung on one particular evil, if the evil is horrendous enough—keep in mind the cases mentioned earlier in the book—this hardly means that the evil is outweighed by all the goodness. The evil of the suffering has gone off the scale and no goodness can justify it. This issue of our lack of understanding of the intensity and depths of suffering will come up from time to time when we examine particular possible PHOGs below.

I can't go over *all* the candidate PHOGs in this book that you might think of, but in the rest of this chapter I've listed eight that people typically think of when confronted with the Problem of Gratuitous Suffering. For each one I've tried to explain why in my opinion each of them needs a lot of work before it can be seen as much of a help in providing decent evidence that there is no gratuitous suffering. This is a very modest conclusion, but it is enough to suggest to you that if you want to defend the PHOG Approach, then you're going to have to do some serious philosophical work in order to get your view off the ground.

Q54: There are three conditions on an outweighing good; explain them in your own words.

The PHOG advocate's task is this: give us good reasons to think that the goods she has in mind (a) really exist, (b) are linked with the bulk of the trillions of cases of apparently gratuitous suffering, and (c) are so fantastically good that their goodness outweighs the badness of those trillions of cases of suffering.

Notice that the PHOG Approach advocate doesn't have to come up with just *one* good thing that does all this work; all she has to do is come up with a number of goods that *when combined* do that work. So it is no good to criticize her by noting that free will, for instance, fails to justify *all* apparently gratuitous suffering. She will agree with that statement because she only thinks that free will justifies *a significant portion* of suffering—and the *other* goods she indicates will take care of most of the other suffering not justified by free will.

Notice further that the PHOG advocate doesn't have to show that the combination of goods justifies *100 percent* of all the apparently gratuitous suffering. If she could give us good reasons to think that the goods she indicates justify 90 percent (say) of all the apparently gratuitous suffering then I think she could reasonably say to us "And if my short list of goods can justify 90 percent of suffering, then there is some reason to think that I've missed a few that justify the remaining 10 percent—at the least, we should no longer be even remotely confident that there are any gratuitous sufferings, which means we should not be at all confident that the Gratuitous Premise is true."

You will no doubt notice, while reading the eight entries below, that several of the PHOG proposals have the same or very similar problems. You'll also notice that I use the phrase "many trillions of cases of horrific suffering" on several occasions. I hope the repetition won't become annoying (or too annoying)![32] I keep using that phrase in order to remind you of three vital things:

- *First,* there really have been many trillions of cases of horrific suffering (and the PHOG Approach advocate has to reveal to us the outweighing goods for the bulk of these trillions of cases).
- *Second,* although it's not hard to see how *some* of those cases of suffering have outweighing goods (e.g., painful surgery that prevents an even worse case of suffering), there are still many trillions of cases of horrific suffering left over that don't seem to have any outweighing goods.
- *Third* and most important, almost all of the cases of horrific suffering have nothing at all to do with humans.

This last point is important because it's tempting, when thinking about suffering, to think of just us humans and the suffering we endure. Clearly, humans endure some kinds of suffering that non-human animals don't or even can't endure (e.g., the psychological pain of grappling with a really hard intellectual problem!). But it's uncontroversial that many animals suffer physical and even emotional pain much like how humans do—we now know that much about the nervous systems of non-human animals—and the PHOG Approach advocate has to show us what goods justify their suffering as well as ours. Some theistic philosophers, even today, think that animals don't suffer any real physical pain. Quite frankly, I think these people are so incredibly desperate for a theistic-friendly solution to the Problem of Gratuitous Suffering that they will lunge at any idea to help them out, no matter how utterly ridiculous and even morally depraved it is. If we know anything at all about dogs, cats, monkeys, zebras, and many other kinds of animals both living and extinct, we know that they suffer horribly while starving, while being ripped apart by predators, when shot, when burned, when beaten, while drowning, etc. The vast majority of theistic philosophers are not so demented; they acknowledge the importance of animal suffering. However, that acknowledgment doesn't get one very far. If a philosopher spends a great deal of time thinking about the Problem of Gratuitous Suffering, and yet *almost all that time is devoted to how the problem applies to humans alone,* this is a sure indication that he or she is not taking the problem with the seriousness it deserves. The Problem of Gratuitous Suffering is not a mere intriguing intellectual challenge: it's a grave threat to what hundreds of millions of people say is their *identity*, their *whole way of life.*

One more point before I start looking at the eight potential PHOGs. There is a criticism of the PHOG Approach that surprisingly enough has nothing to do with the particular goods that the PHOG advocate addresses! Here it is:

> If you are personally convinced that there are going to be outweighing goods for absolutely all cases of suffering, no matter how bad or prevalent the suffering is, then how are you going to live your life? Suppose you'd really like to ignore someone who needs you; or suppose that you'd like to hurt someone. Maybe you'd really like to go over to the next village and burn it to the ground after killing everyone and stealing their stuff. It will of course cause a great deal of horrible suffering, but so what? You know that God has created the universe in such a way that if you go over there and do those horrible things, *it will all be worth it,* as you know there will be outweighing goods linked with all that suffering! So ... do as you please! No moral constraints! Rape and pillage freely!

This is a fascinating challenge! For once, I'm going to shut up and not evaluate an argument that I have presented in this book. (Well, I say some related stuff when I examine the Skeptical Approach in the next chapter.) But note that what the argument is really saying is this: if you are convinced that there is no gratuitous suffering, then you will have no reason to avoid inflicting suffering on the world. It doesn't say that contrary to the PHOG Approach there are gratuitous sufferings. All it does is point out an oddity in *firmly believing* that there are no gratuitous sufferings, in rejecting the Gratuitous Premise. Note further that this problem is a challenge for *anyone* who thinks there are no gratuitous sufferings. So it applies to the advocates of the Skeptical Approach (to be discussed in chapter 7) as well as to most of the advocates of the Confident Approach (since they typically reject the Gratuitous Premise).

When reading the following, keep in mind that I'm offering *initial* criticisms of the eight PHOGs. A great deal more has been written about some of them in the philosophical literature. My criticisms will sometimes seem harsh and unyielding, but I do that just to be brief and set up the hurdles that the PHOG Approach advocate has to meet. I do *not* mean to imply that the PHOG Approach advocate will have nothing intelligent to say in response to my criticisms and so will have to submit to my superior intelligence and slit her wrists in shame.

Knowledge

A huge portion of those many trillions of cases of horrific suffering (i.e., the ones not *obviously* coupled with outweighing goods) are coupled with, and justified by, our **knowledge of the difference between good and evil**. That is, there had to be a huge portion of that suffering so we could gain that important knowledge. You can't really know the difference between good and evil—in fact, maybe you can't really know what good and evil even are—unless you have a vivid awareness of both of them in all their glory. And without that knowledge, you're spiritually unenlightened or not in intimate contact with God or suffer some other very bad defect. So the knowledge in question turns out to be extremely valuable.

This proposal is doubtful for several reasons (and you can usefully substitute different pieces of knowledge in for "knowledge of good and evil," depending on what pieces of knowledge you think are most valuable).

- First criticism: there is no reason I know of to think that the good of that knowledge is *good enough* to justify a sizable portion of those many cases of horrific suffering endured by human beings. So the *Strength Requirement* doesn't look like it's met. Many of us humans have just a confused view of the difference between good and evil, and although knowing the difference between good and evil is a good thing, I wonder how great a thing it is. I admit that knowledge is a wonderful thing, but is it so great that it justifies so much colossal pain and suffering? I don't know any reason to accept that view—especially when I consider that I don't even know what extreme suffering really is.
- Second criticism: it's hard for me to see how the knowledge and the human suffering are linked: how is it that all, or even a good portion of, those cases of horrific human suffering led to our knowledge of good and evil? It seems to me that humans have hardly reflected on all suffering in order gain that knowledge. The pain I endure while being operated on in a hospital is justified by the good it does—saving my life—because the pain *led to* the good; but in the knowledge case why should we think the knowledge and horrific suffering are linked to any significant extent? Maybe our knowledge of good and evil, for what it's worth, came from our witnessing *some* suffering. Maybe that's part of the way children learn. But that would justify just a tiny bit of suffering it seems. I have never seen any reason to think that the goods are linked with an appreciable amount of human suffering; the crucial *Linking Requirement* isn't met.[33]
- Third criticism: in response to my last point you might think that God *set up* the linkage between human suffering and human knowledge of good and evil. Maybe that's just how he made the universe, even if it doesn't look that way

to us mortals. It's almost like a law of nature: in order to be saved (or be in communion with God, or achieve some other great thing) there must be knowledge of good and evil, and such knowledge can only be obtained via awareness of extreme amounts and degrees of human suffering. I admit that God *might* have set things up that way; so the Linking Requirement might be met (although I know of no evidence to believe this is the way things actually are). But now it looks like God has intentionally set up *a profoundly unjust system*. It looks just incredibly cruel to make a rule that says there has to be extreme amounts of extreme human suffering so that humans can be saved/ get into heaven/commune with God/obtain some other important good. Why on earth should the pathway to God be one of horrendous suffering? What a malicious system! Maybe you think that although the system has its defects, it was the best God could do. I suppose that that's *logically possible*, but is there *any* evidence at all to think that that's the way things really are? I know of none. So even if the Linking Requirement is met through God's setting it up that way, it seems like this would mean that God is unjust. And the idea that God had no choice—that it's somehow completely necessary that there is this hideous linkage with horrendous suffering—is an idea I know of no evidence for.

- Fourth criticism: thus far I have questioned whether knowledge of good and evil is linked with, and strong enough to outweigh and thereby justify, a good portion of *human* suffering. But what about non-human suffering? Even if the knowledge of good and evil is really fantastically valuable and justifies a good portion of human suffering (so now I'm setting aside my first three criticisms), how could that knowledge justify hundreds of millions of years of extreme suffering on the part of animals that, unlike humans, don't acquire knowledge of good and evil? How can all *their* suffering be justified by *our* gain of knowledge—especially since so many humans have little knowledge of animal suffering (think of how things were in the relatively recent past, when people thought the earth wasn't very old or that no species had gone extinct)? There doesn't seem to be any link there at all between their suffering and our knowledge. So the good of knowledge can do precious little as a PHOG given that it's not linked with the vast majority of suffering (which is endured by non-humans).

- Fifth criticism: even if by some miracle there is a mysterious hidden linkage between human knowledge of good and evil and non-human suffering so that as a matter of objective fact all that non-human suffering somehow led to our gain of that knowledge (e.g., some link that God set up), how can a large portion of *non-human* suffering be justified by *our* gain of knowledge? Why should trillions of animals have to suffer horribly in order for us to have the benefit of knowing about good and evil? That looks horribly unjust; so even if the Linking Requirement is mysteriously met it seems like it's met only by means of an unjust system knowingly set up by God, which would mean that he is not perfectly morally good. Many people think that non-human animals are here just for our benefit, and their suffering isn't worth *anything*: they can suffer horribly and there is nothing wrong with that. Like most philosophers, I find such a view morally hideous: people who have that view are vile or stupid or brainwashed. I'm happy to admit that there are loads of interesting differences between humans and non-human animals, and perhaps those differences mean that we are superior to non-human animals in significant ways. So I'm not saying that animals are "just as good as" humans, whatever that's supposed to mean, or that you should be a vegetarian or anything like that. That may or may not be right; I take no stand on it here. All I'm saying in this book is that it's beyond question that non-human animals definitely suffer (physically and often emotionally) and their suffering is a genuinely bad thing.

Q55: Answer the following questions about knowledge.
(a) Knowledge can be extremely valuable. Give some examples of how knowledge of good and evil turned out valuable.
(b) Knowledge is often linked with suffering: the latter leads to the former, and it would have been difficult to achieve the former without the latter. Give some examples of this.

Note that there were two separate sets of criticisms: doubts about whether the good in question (knowledge of good and evil) can justify *human* suffering, and doubts about whether it can justify *non-human* suffering—especially the non-human suffering that happened before there were any humans. Note also that the first class of criticisms indicates that the alleged PHOG does not justify much of the suffering it is commonly thought to justify, while the second class indicates that the alleged PHOG is very limited, since the amount of suffering that it says virtually nothing about is enormous. These two kinds of doubts will be repeated below for other alleged PHOGs. One thing we will see several times is that the PHOG Approach advocate seems to have no PHOG that can do much to handle non-human suffering. Another thing we'll see over and over is that the PHOG Approach advocate has no obvious justification for the crucial claim that the good she says is coupled with lots of suffering is *good enough* to justify that suffering (so the Strength Requirement is met).

Q56: In the 1998 movie "What Dreams May Come" there is something akin to Hell. When someone commits suicide their soul goes to a ghastly place where they are tormented forever. In the movie a man dies in an accident and has various adventures in the afterlife. Later on his wife commits suicide, as she has lost both her husband and children to terrible accidents. When the man finds out that his wife is in this horrible place, he gets very angry, saying that it's horribly unjust. He is with a "guide" to the afterlife, and the guide says that God is not *punishing* his wife. Instead, it's just the way things are that she ended up in that Hellish existence.

Thoughts like this suggest to people that God is not to blame for many horrible things because that's just the way the universe is, "the way things work," as the guide puts it. This suggests a further thought: suffering is just the way that certain good things come to be; it's the price we have to pay in order to get the good things in life. So, when faced with the reality of suffering, these people will say that that's just the way things are, the way the universe operates.

Explain why this response to the Problem of Gratuitous Suffering is inadequate.

Free Will

A huge portion of those many trillions of cases of horrific suffering are coupled with, and are justified by, **our having free will**. That is, a huge portion of that suffering is the price of having free will. God gave us free will, which is an incredibly valuable good, but we misuse it all the time, thereby creating a great deal of suffering. So, the free will exists, is extremely valuable, and is intimately linked with a huge portion of suffering.

This proposal is problematic for several reasons.

- First criticism: it's not certain that we have free will. That may sound weird to you if you've never studied the relation of free will to determinism, but lots of people, especially philosophers, have reached that conclusion over the centuries (although to be sure, it's a minority opinion among philosophers who have written about it; I think it's more common amongst the philosophers who don't write about it). Many philosophers have thought that everything that happens in the physical universe is predetermined by the laws of nature (like "$E = mc^2$") and facts about the physical origin of the universe (e.g., what happened at the Big Bang); and they have also thought that such predetermination rules out any interesting sense of free will ("interesting sense" because the term "free will" is ambiguous). So it's not clear that the *Existence Requirement* is met because it's not clear that there is any free will. But, as I said, this is a minority view so maybe it shouldn't be so troubling.
- Second criticism: it appears that horrific suffering and human free will are not linked extensively: why think that free will has led to all those many

trillions of cases of horrific suffering? (Think of all the suffering caused by natural disasters, which aren't the result of anyone's employment of their free will.) After all, we humans didn't freely produce even a tiny fraction of those cases of horrific suffering, as virtually all of them happened before there were any humans! Perhaps free will is appropriately linked with much of the suffering caused by humans (but again, natural disasters and diseases seem to cause most suffering by far), but it's *very* hard to see how it's linked with a large portion of sufferings in general. Most people think that most of the animals who suffer don't have free will and the pain they experience is not the result of anyone exercising their free will. So it's not at all obvious that the *Linking Requirement* is met in a significant portion of cases. It is worth noting that most theists concede these points, but what is often neglected is the fact, mentioned above, that non–human suffering makes up virtually all suffering on earth and occurred before there were any humans.

- Third criticism: even if by some miracle there is a mysterious hidden linkage between human free will and non–human suffering (e.g., some link that God set up so that human free will is inextricably connected to non–human suffering), how can a large portion of *non-human* suffering be justified by *our* gain of free will? In order for us to have the benefit of free will many trillions of animals had to suffer horribly? That hardly looks remotely fair; so even if (contrary to the second criticism) the Linking Requirement is met to a significant extent it seems like it's met only by means of an unjust system knowingly set up by God, which would mean that he is not perfectly morally good to put it mildly.

Q57: Cats and dogs feel pain; spiders and worms do not. Arguably, cats and dogs have some measure of free will, as they are not mere biological machines like spiders and worms are. At least, some people think this way. What if it's right? Maybe it's the case that every creature who suffers really does have free will. Would that make the free will PHOG succeed in showing that an enormous amount of suffering is worth it?

- Fourth criticism: although some have said that there are supernatural demons and devils with free will moving about through time causing all that horrible suffering not caused by human free will, I know of no reason at all to believe in such creatures. I suppose that there *could* be such creatures, but that's irrelevant: we are dealing with the real world here, not the merely possible. (Indeed, I know that many readers will think I'm wasting time here even discussing the idea, because they think it's just silly.) So it's hardly plausible to think that the *Existence Requirement* is met for this particular idea.
- Fifth criticism: even if the Existence Requirement were met with regard to the supernatural demons with free will, it strains imagination to think the

goodness of a demon's free will is so fantastically valuable that it justifies many trillions of cases of horrific suffering on the part of humans and other animals! So there is no reason to think the *Strength Requirement* is met either when it comes to demons.

- Sixth criticism: it's not at all clear that human free will is valuable enough to justify even the horrific suffering that *humans* endure as the result of our exercising our free will; that is, it's not clear that free will is worth all the horrific suffering caused by the exercise of that free will. Given the choice of free will with lots of suffering versus no free will but a life of bliss, I think I'd give up the free will and opt for bliss. (Remember: how much do you truly understand about the intensity of "real pain," given that you're one of the lucky ones who hasn't been tortured either physically or mentally?) Sure, I'd be akin to a robot, but I'd be a robot living a life of unending bliss! (I need not be *aware* that I'm akin to a robot; I could be a blissfully happy robot who is convinced that he has free will.) So it's not clear that the *Strength Requirement* is met even for suffering caused by the use of human free will. Someone might point out that it's possible that free will is sufficiently valuable. But what is the evidence that it is actually valuable enough to outweigh the colossal amount of horrific suffering that comes in its wake? Let us not rest content with comforting stories; let us look to the evidence instead. (Notice that this criticism also applies to non-human animals with free will, so even if it's the case that all animals that can suffer have free will, such a fact wouldn't automatically satisfy the Linking Requirement or Strength Requirement. And don't forget the fact that almost all non-human animal suffering is the result of things like disease, not free will.)

Soul-Making

A huge portion of those many trillions of cases of horrific suffering are coupled with, and are justified by, the fact that in order for us to **develop our souls properly** we need to experience and know of that suffering. That is, a huge portion of that suffering is the price of having appropriately developed souls. God gave us the ability to develop our souls so that we may experience or be in intimate contact with him, which is an *incredibly* valuable good—maybe the greatest good there is—but in order to develop our souls properly we need to know and experience suffering. So, the ability to cultivate our souls exists, is extremely valuable, and is intimately linked with suffering.

I haven't said what a "properly developed soul" would be. Some people think it's a *virtuous* soul; others say it's a *saved* soul. Still others say it's a soul that is in *communion with God*. My criticisms below apply to all these as well as other readings.[34]

There are significant problems with this proposal, all of which are akin to the ones that plague the proposal about free will.

- First criticism: it's hardly clear that horrific suffering and human soul-making are linked enough: why think that our appropriately developed souls somehow came from or are otherwise coupled with all those many trillions of cases of horrific suffering? After all, we humans don't have anything to do with even a tiny fraction of those cases of horrific suffering, as virtually all of them happened before there were any humans. Perhaps developed souls are appropriately linked with much of the suffering caused by humans (we need to know of and experience suffering in order to develop our souls properly), but it's hard to see how they are linked with a large portion of sufferings in general. Most people think that most of the animals who suffer don't have souls and the pain they experience is not linked with the development of any souls. So it's not at all obvious that the *Linking Requirement* is met to a significant extent, since there doesn't seem to be any link between soul-making and most non-human suffering (even if there is a significant link between soul-making and a good portion of human suffering).

- Second criticism: even if by some miracle there is a mysterious hidden linkage between human soul-making and non-human suffering (e.g., some link that God set up), how can a large portion of *non-human* suffering be justified by *our* gain of developed souls? In order for us to have the benefit of saved souls many trillions of animals had to suffer horribly? That hardly looks fair; so even if the Linking Requirement is met it seems like it's met only by means of an incredibly unjust system knowingly set up by God, which would mean that he is nowhere near perfectly morally good.

- Third criticism: it's not at all clear that developed souls are valuable enough to justify even the horrific suffering that *humans* endure. Given the choice of a developed soul who experiences lots of extreme suffering versus having an undeveloped soul but a life of bliss, I think I'd give up the developed soul. This might be foolish, but how am I to judge the value of a "developed soul" when I don't even know what that is? It depends on what the wonderful aspects of having a properly developed soul are. Maybe you think there is an everlasting heaven for such souls, which of course is a highly relevant point; I'll get to that idea below. In any case, this consideration casts doubt on the idea that the *Strength Requirement* is met. If you think that an appropriately developed soul is one that is in some intimate communion with God, then of course we have the problem with the *Existence Requirement*: we need some excellent evidence that such divinely connected souls exist—which would mean that we need excellent evidence for the existence of God as well!

> Q58: Lots of theists think the Soul-Making PHOG is one of the most impor-
> tant ones. Suppose it's true that there is an afterlife, virtually all of us get
> there—or maybe all of us get there eventually—and it is so wonderful that
> everyone there is utterly convinced that all the suffering they experienced
> on Earth was worth it. If all that were true, would that mean that there
> really are outweighing goods for all suffering?

At this point it's well worth reminding ourselves of the state of play, as there are
two very different kinds of PHOG Approach advocate and we shouldn't mix
them up when evaluating their views.

To begin again: we have the Gratuitous Premise and the Consequence Premise.
The reasonable 4–Part theist admits that there is at least *some* reason to believe
each of them, although she has to hold that such reason is misleading since at least
one of the premises is false. Most 4–Part theists will think the Gratuitous Premise
is false and the Consequence Premise is true; the PHOG Approach advocate
agrees. The PHOG Approach advocate says she can show us the goods that
outweigh most instances of suffering. Hence, she needs to give us good evidence
that her alleged goods satisfy the three requirements for the bulk of sufferings. So
much is clear.

Now the PHOG Approach advocates split into two groups. One proceeds by
relying on many plainly theistic doctrines (such as a spectacularly good communion
with God, as we just saw above) without bothering to defend those doctrines.
That may be fine, *provided she really does know that those doctrines are true*. Naturally,
she need not be moved by the third criticism given a few paragraphs back. But
even then it won't amount to a very *informative* response to the Problem of
Gratuitous Suffering, since it takes for granted not only the existence of the 4–Part
God but a plethora of theistic doctrines as well. (It's certainly *partially* informative
since it indicates how a certain religious tradition deals with the Gratuitous
Premise, which is interesting and well worth knowing about; but since it takes the
theistic doctrines for granted it is not very informative for the person who doesn't
already know that those doctrines are true.) The main criticism of the Confident
Approach applies also to that theist. But it's crucial to see that we are in the midst
of pointing out *additional* difficulties with the approach of the PHOG Approach
advocate. For instance, it's not enough to say that the good of soul-making exists
(or that there is a spectacularly good afterlife, or just punishment for original sin;
see discussion of those alleged PHOGs below). She has to present evidence that
the divine goods she appeals to not only exist but *have more goodness than the badness
of the suffering they are coupled with*, so they are up to the task of being *outweighing*
goods. It just isn't enough to prove that communion with God really happens; that
isn't sufficient for such communion to help the PHOG Approach. And of course
she has to present evidence that the coupling is there too; the Linking Requirement

hardly comes for free. So just proving the existence of heaven or sin or communion with God will not, by any stretch, be good enough to establish the PHOG Approach. Most people find this initially highly surprising: establishing that there is a wonderful afterlife, for instance, is *not* sufficient, as it may fail to establish the Linking or Strength requirements!

The much more ambitious PHOG Approach advocate, a member of the second group, tries to show us the actual outweighing goods that justify most suffering *without relying on any controversial theistic doctrines* such as original sin, soul-making, and the afterlife. Hence, she is going to appeal to ideas that atheists and agnostics are in a position to accept (e.g., free will and knowledge). This ambitious PHOG Approach advocate has to supply real reasons for her approach instead of merely showing how it's possible that there are PHOGs that do the trick. I think few theists will take this option, because they almost always think that our suffering is often justified by purely divine goods such as soul-making, an afterlife, and communion with God. (In this chapter I look at eight alleged PHOGs, half of which are theist and half of which are not.) Now I continue with the alleged PHOGs.

Afterlife

> A huge portion of those many trillions of cases of horrific suffering are coupled with, and are justified by, the fact that in the **afterlife there is tremendous goodness** that is the direct result of all that suffering. All the injustice and suffering in the world is rectified in the afterlife—so much so that when you're there you will gladly say "It was all worth it!" even if you suffered horribly during your earthly existence.

On the one hand, this looks like a great proposal. After all, if we have an eternal afterlife, and perhaps a very long "beforelife," then many interesting possibilities regarding why there is earthly suffering can be imagined. Nevertheless, there are lots of problems with this proposal:

- First criticism: the evidence that there is an afterlife is not terribly good; in fact the evidence is pretty bad. I'm not saying that it's impossible for there to be an afterlife; I'm merely saying that the theism-neutral evidence for it stinks. Please don't take the afterlife for granted just because some religious people tell you so; it's much, much more controversial than that! For one thing, some *theists* (who are philosophers) say that we are purely physical beings who have no afterlife. Thus, it's hardly clear that the *Existence Requirement* is met.
- Second criticism: the evidence that there is a *tremendously good* afterlife is even less impressive. Why should we think that God made the afterlife so great when he didn't see fit to do it for our time before our afterlife? So even if there is an afterlife there is little reason to accept the *Existence Requirement* for

a fantastically great afterlife. And even if the afterlife is tremendously good, why should we think that that goodness lasts very long, let alone forever? And if we're going to accept that there is an incredibly great afterlife, why should we be confident that there isn't a very bad afterafterlife? Surely we should consult the evidence on these matters.

- Third criticism: it's not at all clear that all that the trillions of animals who went through those many trillions of episodes of horrific pain get to have a tremendously good afterlife. So there is little reason to think that the goodness of the afterlife is linked with any more than a tiny fraction of the many trillions of cases of horrific suffering.

- Fourth criticism: even if there is such a linkage—our making it to the blissful afterlife depends on many trillions of cases of horrific pain endured by non-human animals—(again, a link set up by God), how does *our* having a tremendously good afterlife justify *their* horrific suffering? Sounds like a blatantly unjust system knowingly set up by God, which rules out him being anything close to perfectly morally good.

- Fifth criticism: why should we think that the horrific suffering experienced by humans (setting aside non-human animals) is linked to the afterlife bliss for humans? That is, why did there have to be all that unbelievably intense and widespread suffering in order for us to experience tremendous bliss in the afterlife? If there is this fantastic afterlife, then why does its existence depend on hundreds of millions of humans to suffer hundreds of millions of cases of unbelievably horrifying pain? (In fact, why did he bother with earthly existence at all if the afterlife is so sweet?) Seems like a really unjust system.

Summing up: *even if there really is an afterlife*, we need reason to think it's great; and even if it's everlasting and full of bliss, this would not solve the problem, as the last two criticisms would remain in force. This just shows, once again, what an uphill battle the PHOG Approach advocate faces.

Q59: When thinking about the afterlife, don't forget Hell. Many theists think that Hell really exists: some people will be there for an infinite amount of time, it is truly awful to be there, there is no escape, and they are there because they failed to do something.

Some people think this amounts to another "problem of evil," as it is difficult to imagine a 4-Part God setting up a system in which people end up in Hell. Try to formulate an argument that has premises about the 4-Part God and people being in Hell and concludes that the 4-Part God doesn't exist.

Original Sin

> A huge portion of those many trillions of cases of horrific suffering are coupled with, and are justified by, the fact *we are all guilty of original sin* and must be punished for it.

In this case the alleged PHOG is the good of punishment that is just (obviously, original sin itself isn't the PHOG). Lots of problems here too:

- First criticism: it's hardly clear that there is anything like original sin; so it isn't clear that there is any good of appropriately punishing original sin. Unless you have some good reason, of some kind, to think there is such a thing this PHOG won't be very convincing (so the *Existence Requirement* might not be met). I realize that some people will say that of course there is original sin, but that "of course" is coming from the same part of the mind that says of course there is a God. In *this* part of our discussion you don't get to assume that there is original sin any more than you get to assume the 4-Part God exists. At least, if you're a member of the second group of PHOG Approach advocates (the ambitious ones).
- Second criticism: even if there is original sin, and even if it's a good thing that we are justly punished for it, the punishment seems far too severe when compared with the good of justice. That is, although just punishment of the guilty may be a good thing, it's not *good enough* to justify many trillions of cases of horrific suffering. So it's doubtful that the *Strength Requirement* is met even if the Existence Requirement is met.
- Third criticism: it's hard to believe that all those animals are guilty of original sin (for one thing, most of them existed millions of years before humans). So there is no linkage from their suffering to our punishment (and *if* there is such a linkage, as we've seen before, it seems terribly unjust).[35]

Lawfulness

> A huge portion of those many trillions of cases of horrific suffering are coupled with, and are justified by, the fact that *if God had made a universe without those horrific sufferings, he would have had to intervene in nature so much that there would be no stable, unbroken laws of nature*. The idea here is that if God were to make a universe without a huge portion of those cases of apparently gratuitous horrific suffering then he would be intervening against the laws of nature almost constantly in order to prevent those sufferings, with one miracle after another virtually every minute; and that would mean that the laws of nature are a joke since he is breaking them all the time with his interventions. And why are unbroken laws of nature so important? Well, many of the most important goods in life wouldn't exist if the universe didn't operate according to such laws.[36]

Usually, the linkage between an instance of suffering and an outweighing good is not hard to understand. For instance, the painful medical procedure is the direct cause of the good of the recovery of some illness or injury. Another simple case: the good of the champagne causes the annoyance of having to go to the bathroom in the middle of the night. But in the laws of nature case, the idea is that there is a two-stage linkage. First, there is a link between the laws and goods like happiness, love, and knowledge: *if* the universe is going to have those important goods, *then* it's going to have to operate according to unbroken laws of nature. So, we need the laws. Second, there is a link between the laws and suffering: *if* the universe is going to have laws that permit those great goods, *then* it's inevitable that it is going to have trillions of cases of suffering. When you put those two "if-then" claims together you get the result "if the universe is going to have those goods, then it's inevitable that it's going to have trillions of cases of suffering."

In the other proposals, we have met with a particular good—spectacular afterlife, free will, communion with God, etc.—that is supposed to justify a huge chunk of suffering. That's not what is going on with this proposal; we are not revealing (or reminding ourselves of) a new and profound good. Instead, the idea here is that there is a *profoundly hidden linkage* between suffering and goods we are already familiar with. It is saying that oddly enough, one of the necessary requirements for things like happiness and love—the requirement of unbroken laws of nature—will inevitably cause great amounts of suffering. The proposal in a nutshell:

(a) If the universe is to have such-and-such wonderful goods (distributed among many people and creatures), then it will have to have unbroken laws of nature; moreover, the only laws of nature that will lead to those goods will also inevitably lead to great amounts of suffering.

(b) But the collective goodness of the goods secured by the laws outweighs the collective badness of the suffering caused by the laws.

If the person advocating this proposal is serious, she will have to offer evidence in favor of both of (a) and (b). I think this is going to be pretty difficult to do. Obviously, the proposal isn't very specific with its "such-and-such" clause in (a). But setting that aside, why should we think that the *only* unbroken laws of nature that will allow the generation of love, happiness, or other goods will also generate trillions of cases of suffering? For instance, it doesn't seem hard to imagine that creatures could have been created, via evolution, in such a way that they didn't require any intense pain and suffering in order to adjust to their environment in intelligent and/or fruitful ways. In addition, perhaps we could have been created so that we naturally care about not just the welfare of the people in our immediate family but almost all sentient creatures; why couldn't we be like that? We're already made in such a way that we feel that way towards our own children and parents, so why not just extend it? Simple thoughts like that make one wary of (a).

But there's more: why do we need *unbroken* laws of nature in order to get all sorts of goods? What is wrong with God's breaking laws a lot in order to alleviate great suffering? Can you think of any reason to believe that if the laws of nature were a bit different or frequently broken—so that there was considerably less suffering—then the amount of good in the world would have to be drastically reduced? Me neither. Sure, I suppose it's *possible* that that's the way things simply must be, but in the absence of any evidence it is silly to think that that's the way things *actually* are. You can't just go around saying "Hey, maybe it's just a completely necessary truth that the only way to get a series of fundamental unbroken natural laws is a universe in which there are many trillions of cases of horrific pain"; you have to give us some reason to accept the claim. On the face of it, there isn't reason to believe it—unless, of course, you are convinced that the 4-Part God exists and that in order to get around the Problem of Gratuitous Suffering claim (a) would just have to be true. So, I don't see much reason to accept (a) that doesn't involve just assuming that the 4-Part God exists and then reasoning from that assumption in a certain manner.

I can imagine further arguments in support of (a). For instance, one might think that (i) in order to prevent a sizable chunk of those trillions of cases of suffering God would have to intervene in the universe a lot, stopping the suffering from happening; and (ii) if he intervened a lot then there would be no real (unbroken) laws of nature; and (iii) if there were no unbroken laws of nature then we wouldn't know much of anything about cause and effect (since the relation between cause and effect would be so unpredictable, as God is breaking it a lot); and (iv) if we didn't have knowledge of cause and effect then we wouldn't be able to *learn* much of anything or *build* hardly anything; and, finally, (v) knowledge and the ability to do things are such extreme goods that they justify all the suffering. So by these lights the Linking Requirement is met because the unbroken laws are linked with knowledge; and also by these lights the Strength Requirement is supposed to be met because that knowledge of cause and effect is an extremely good thing to have. (Of course, now we're back with a variant of the first proposed PHOG above, regarding knowledge of good and evil, with all its problems.) But why on earth would God have to intervene a lot in order to not have trillions of cases of suffering—that is, why should we think that (i) is true? I don't know of any evidence that God couldn't set up the laws of nature and the nature of creatures in such a way that they didn't suffer so much. This is awfully hard to know *anything* interesting about, so it seems overconfident, to put it mildly, for the PHOG advocate to just make unsubstantiated assumptions about it. (Again, the response "Well, it could be true!" is silly, as it isn't taking the problem seriously.) And even if God did have to intervene a lot, I don't see how that would prevent us from knowing *enough* about cause and effect in order to do things like build stuff. That is, I know of no evidence at all for (iii).

Q60: Maybe God had no choice in the laws of nature. Perhaps "E = mc²" is just as absolute and necessary as "2 + 2 = 4." God could not have made a universe in which twice two is eleven; neither could he have made a universe with different laws of nature.

Pretend that that's all true. (It might be; I don't think anyone knows for sure.) Then it looks as though statement (a) is true. Does that change what we should think about (b)? Is (b) true?

Finally, *even if (i)–(v) are perfectly true*, it seems bizarre that the Strength Requirement is met: how can *our* benefit—learning about cause and effect, being able to partially control our environment, etc.—be good *enough* to justify all the trillions of cases of horrific suffering endured by non-human animals for hundreds of millions of years? They had to suffer so we could gain knowledge of causation and have civilization? Seems grossly unjust.

Q61: The laws-of-nature PHOG idea is crucially different from *all* the PHOGs before it. How?

Motivation

A huge portion of those many trillions of cases of horrific suffering are coupled with, and are justified by, the fact **pain, fear, and suffering are the primary motivators for improvement**, which of course is a very good thing. A huge part of what makes us try to improve our lives, either our own lives or those of others, is the desire to avoid suffering and increase things like happiness. Oddly enough, what gets us off our asses and doing constructive things is very often fear, pain, or the threat of pain. Without them we would do almost nothing productive and sit on the couch watching television and eating snacks. And this holds for non-human animals as well—maybe to an even greater degree than for humans. So, the motivational power of fear, pain, and suffering exists, is extremely valuable, and is intimately linked with suffering.

As with the previous proposal, regarding laws of nature, this proposal is really about hidden linkage instead of a new hidden outweighing good:

(a) If the universe is to have such-and-such wonderful goods (distributed among many people and creatures), then we will have to be motivated to make ourselves better.

(b) If we are going to be motivated to make ourselves better, then we will have to have great amounts of suffering, as suffering is the prime source of that motivation.

(c) Fortunately, the collective goodness of the things mentioned in (a) outweigh the collective badness of the things mentioned in (b).

And just as before, if the person advocating this proposal is serious, she will have to offer evidence in favor of each of (a)–(c).

Parts of the proposal are clearly right. For instance, no one is going to argue that pain and fear fail to motivate us to improve our lot in life or that being motivated to improve isn't a very good thing. Furthermore, I like the fact that this proposal applies to both humans and non-humans: non-human animals are motivated by pain just like we are. The main problem here I think is one we have already seen several times with the other proposed PHOGs.

For one thing, it doesn't appear that the *Strength Requirement* is met: although pain and suffering very often motivate us to better ourselves as well as others (so perhaps the *Linking Requirement* is met), the badness of that suffering is so extreme that it is hard to see how the goodness of what it leads to can outweigh it. Furthermore, and this also is relevant to the strength point, pain and fear also motivate us to do an enormous number and variety of truly awful things. Fear, in particular, causes people to do nasty things to one another. For instance, over the last ten years the fear of terrorists has made the US federal government spend literally trillions of dollars on security issues while giving up many civil liberties (e.g., President Obama feels free to order the murder of US citizens such as Anwar al-`Awlaqi who have not been convicted of any crime and who are not on any battlefield). All the suffering caused by fear subtracts from the good that fear is linked with; and that's a *big* subtraction.

If we temporarily adopt the alternative conception of "gratuitous suffering"—that is, if we said, roughly, that suffering is justified only if God had no way to get rid of it without allowing some other suffering just as bad as the one he got rid of—then the criticisms are even stronger. After all, why in order to get people and animals motivated to make good things happen did we have to have trillions of cases of fear and pain? It doesn't seem to be *necessary* to use fear and pain to motivate. Why not motivate with something else? Couldn't the all powerful God come up with something better?! For instance, why not create creatures that have a natural, innate desire to seek out and produce things that are effective in bringing about well-being—without all the agony? Or as mentioned earlier, why couldn't animals have a natural affection not just for immediate members of their group but many others as well? In response, the PHOG advocate could say that it's just an unyielding law of nature that fear and pain are the primary motivators for improvement. But now we have two problems from before. First, we have the justice problem again! Isn't the choice of fear and pain as motivators just about *the cruelest one imaginable*, making God the equivalent of Satan? I could motivate my children with fear and pain, but that would make me a prime candidate for *worst* parent of the year—and hardly anything like supreme moral goodness. God could hardly be good if he set up the laws of our universe this way. Second, there isn't the slightest reason to believe that of all the possibilities only pain and fear are adequate motivators.

Divine Suffering

A huge portion of those many trillions of cases of horrific suffering are coupled with, and are justified by, the fact **God himself has suffered more than anyone**. Often the idea here is that Jesus is appropriately related to God (his "son") and suffered not just incredible physical pain via crucifixion but went through the pain of being separated from God the father (he was "forsaken," allegedly in his own words), which is the ultimate sacrifice for someone who was in communion with God (even somehow "identical" with God).

I have difficulty in figuring out how this potential PHOG bears on the Problem of Gratuitous Suffering, despite the fact that the crucifixion and resurrection of Jesus are the key to Christianity (but of course they aren't crucial to other forms of theism).[37] To get a taste of the difficulty, suppose I torture you for no good reason; alternatively, I knowingly allow others to torture you even though I could have stopped it and I knew that your suffering was gratuitous, setting aside what comes next. Naturally, you're a bit upset: you're being tortured. But then someone—maybe me, maybe someone else—attempts to justify my torturing you (or allowing you to be tortured) by pointing out that I have tortured *other* people as well, including myself. How on earth is that supposed to justify my torturing you? What is the good thing that is paired with your suffering that outweighs it? Perhaps God's willingness to be tortured himself, in the person of Jesus, would show that God cares very deeply for our suffering—so much that he tortured himself via his son. Assume that's completely true. That's great that he cares so much, but is his caring supposed to be the good that outweighs the badness of the suffering? (If not, what is the PHOG?) How is it consistent with justice that God allows trillions of cases of suffering and then makes up for it by engaging in some *more* torture, of Jesus? Why allow the torture in the first place? If it was the result of our having free will, or giving us the opportunity for salvation, or something similar, then we are back with the PHOGs we looked at earlier. And how does any of this help at all with the 99 percent of sufferers who know nothing of Jesus (e.g., non-human animals, people before the time of Jesus, etc.)?

I'm absolutely not saying that these incredibly simple, elementary—even childlike—questions *have* no answers. I am saying that they *need* answers—and they need answers backed up with good reasons, not just answers that someone just finds in a book or speech. It won't do to just spout some theory we learned as children, say: we need answers backed up with real evidence. In order to see if the answers are evidentially justified it is best to keep an eye on the three PHOG requirements. I won't explore the answers here.

Q62: As noted earlier in this chapter, there are two groups of 4-Part theists associated with the PHOG Approach. One of those groups cannot embrace several of the potential PHOGs discussed above. (a) Tell us which group; (b) tell us which PHOGs they cannot accept.

Q63: Think up a new potential PHOG (that isn't silly; try to think of one that has a real chance to justify a lot of apparently gratuitous suffering) and assess it according to the three PHOG requirements.

Lessons

I'm finished with the eight potential PHOGs. A PHOG Approach advocate might object to my analysis of those potential PHOGs as follows: although she has yet to *prove* what the outweighing goods are, she has done enough to shake our rational confidence that there are many instances of suffering with no outweighing goods. This theist admits that she hasn't come close to showing that 90 percent, say, of instances of suffering have outweighing goods, but she has done enough to show that we should not be at all confident that there are any sufferings that are gratuitous. She admits that her reasons aren't conclusive proof, but she insists that they are pretty damn good anyway.

Unfortunately, I just don't see any basis for that optimism. For each PHOG there weren't just little, annoying criticisms around the edges. The objections weren't quibbles. Instead, the criticisms went right to the heart of each proposal. The criticisms showed that we had little if any reason to think the alleged PHOG satisfied the three requirements.

"Yes, but in that long discussion of those eight PHOGs you didn't consider the PHOGs that *I* think do the trick!" Often enough, when I give talks on this topic someone brings up a potential PHOG that I had not thought of before (or a linkage I hadn't thought of before). And every time that happens I have us investigate the same three questions:

1. Do we have good reason to think the potential PHOG really exists?
2. Do we have good reason to think the potential PHOG is strong enough to outweigh a good portion of suffering?
3. Do we have good reason to think the potential PHOG is really coupled with that suffering?

Using the reflections on the eight PHOGs considered above and those three questions, you can assess more potential PHOGs on your own.

I'm sure you noticed that just about everything I said in response to those eight alleged PHOGs was negative. But please keep in mind that all I've done in the above long discussion is offer some *initial* criticisms of only *some* candidate PHOGs. I certainly don't think I have come even close to *proving* that those eight PHOGs won't collectively (i.e., when combined) do the trick of showing how there is no gratuitous suffering (or more modestly, showing that we should not be confident that there are gratuitous sufferings). You shouldn't think so either. All I've done is list some (but not all!) of the fairly obvious and weighty obstacles that each faces. You would do well to think of candidate PHOGs and then do the hard part: see if there is good reason to think that they satisfy each of the absolutely key requirements listed above: the *Existence Requirement*, the *Linking Requirement* and the *Strength Requirement*.[38] In order to do so, you could not do much better than to think of detailed ways of responding to each of the criticisms I articulated above, modified so as to apply to the new PHOG.

So what can we conclude about the viability of the PHOG Approach? Suppose I'm right that there are all these serious flaws with it. Suppose further that there is no way to repair the PHOG Approach in such a way to get rid of those flaws—a big assumption to make. (In this chapter I argued for the first supposition, not the second.) Does that mean the approach is a failure?

For starters, despite my exceedingly brilliant criticisms it's conceivable that someone might have such detailed knowledge of God and his plan that she knows full well what the goods are that are linked with most suffering and outweigh that suffering. I certainly didn't argue that such a person is impossible. I think it's unlikely, as I have never seen what struck me as decent evidence for the crucial claims of the PHOG ideas given above, but *unlikely* certainly doesn't mean *impossible*. But suppose someone doesn't have that key theistic knowledge of PHOGs and linkages but adopts the PHOG Approach: is she irrational?

It depends on what you mean by "irrational." I think the Fred and Dr. Quack story applies here just like it applied to the person who takes up the Confident Approach. If the person who adopts the approach fails to have the requisite theistic knowledge but is in a position similar to Fred's, then although her response to the Problem of Gratuitous Suffering won't be evidentially reasonable it will be reasonable in the weaker and admittedly less significant sense. In that disappointing but not trivial sense the PHOG Approach could be successful.

Q64: Construct a list of bullet points, each stating a part or crucial fact about the PHOG Approach. Go through the entire chapter.

7

OUR INABILITY TO SEE GOD'S PLAN

What the Approach Says

Sometimes combining theories can strengthen their virtues while weakening their vices (other times it can do the opposite). The approach of this chapter, the Skeptical Approach, has elements of both the Confident and PHOG approaches. The main question is whether this new approach is stronger than either of the alternative approaches whose elements it shares. In order to understand the dynamics of the Skeptical Approach we need to go over some basic epistemology (which is the study of a group of closely related concepts such as knowledge, evidence, certainty, wisdom, and understanding). I will do so by means of a story.

Suppose that just before 6:00pm you come home to your apartment and barely miss a phone call on your landline phone (pretend this is the olden days, before cell phones and other fancy communication devices). You heard the phone ringing while you were fussing with your keys outside the door, you were holding three bags of groceries, and you didn't get in the apartment in time to answer the phone. After you put away the groceries you pick up the phone to get the recorded message, if any, that was left by the person who just called. There is indeed a message, but it is very garbled and all you can figure out is that it was a woman who called. So you believe "It was a woman" (i.e., you believe that the 6pm caller was a woman) and your evidence is that you just listened to the message and the voice obviously had the characteristics of a woman.

While this is happening your roommate is taking a shower, which explains why he didn't answer the phone. After he gets dressed he comes into the kitchen and informs you that the message you just heard was from earlier that morning (your roommate listened to it earlier in the day but didn't delete it; furthermore, the phone message didn't say what time the call was made). So your roommate has given you a new piece of evidence. Importantly, it *shows the inadequacy of* the first piece of evidence. The timeline is this: you started out with the question "Who called?"; you then got some evidence E_A from the voicemail message which suggested that the 6pm caller was female; you immediately formed the belief that the 6pm caller was female; this belief of yours had some decent evidence, E_A, backing it up (I'm not saying that E_A was *excellent* evidence, but I am saying that it was evidence that wasn't horribly weak); next you acquired another piece of evidence, E_B, that the garbled message you heard was from much earlier in the day (you got this evidence by listening to your roommate); E_B shows the inadequacy of E_A in the sense that your belief that the 6pm caller was female has now lost *all* its justification. We can use a fictional numerical model to help understand things. You started out with the belief "The 6pm caller was a woman" and your belief had 100 units of justification coming from the evidence E_A of the message on voicemail. But then after learning E_B that the message came from much earlier in the day, those 100 units go away, leaving your belief with no justification at all. Naturally, at this point you give up your belief that the caller was a woman; you no longer believe it. E_A was genuine evidence, albeit not on the strong side, but the addition of E_B ruined the force of E_A.

Notice that although you should (and did) give up your belief "The 6pm caller was a woman," you did not, and should not, come to believe "The 6pm caller was *not* a woman." Clearly, the right thing to do at this point is withhold judgment entirely regarding the sex of the caller: you shouldn't believe that it was a woman and you shouldn't believe that it wasn't a woman. Now that E_B has neutralized E_A there is a 50/50 chance it was a woman and a 50/50 chance it was a man (setting aside the small number of people who are borderline male/female!). The fact that your roommate came along with some evidence E_B that undermined E_A did *not* mean you should go from believing "The 6pm caller was a woman" to believing "The 6pm caller was not a woman." It did *not* mean that he has given you even the slightest bit of evidence in favor of "The 6pm caller was not a woman." E_B doesn't show, at all, that "The 6pm caller was a woman" is false. All your roommate has done is *demonstrate the inadequacy of* the evidence you had in favor of "The 6pm caller was a woman"; he has not supplied any evidence that justifies your concluding "The 6pm caller was not a woman." All of that is fairly obvious, but I state it repeatedly and emphatically because it'll be important below.

Fortunately, your roommate next informs you that he spoke with your friend Fred early this afternoon and Fred said that he will be trying to call you *right at 6pm*, a few minutes after he gets off work. This is yet another piece of evidence, E_C. And of course E_C is good evidence for the belief "The 6pm caller was not a woman" (at least, it is good evidence when we couple it with your previous knowledge that Fred is male, he has promised to call at a certain time on many occasions in the past, and he always comes through exactly as he promises).

So, being the reasonable person you are, you now come to believe that the 6pm caller was not a woman, as it was your male friend Fred.

This story illustrates one very reasonable way to go from having an evidence-based belief "Claim C is true" to having an evidenced-based belief "Claim C is *not* true" (in our story C was "The 6pm caller was a woman"):

1. You start out with good evidence E_A in favor of "Claim C is true."
2. You then acquire good evidence E_B that shows the inadequacy of E_A so that E_A no longer provides significant support for "Claim C is true."
3. Finally, you acquire good evidence E_C in favor of "Claim C is false."

The advocate of the **Skeptical Approach** to the Problem of Gratuitous Suffering, which I'll describe in detail below, tackles the Gratuitous Premise with the same pattern, (1)–(3). Claim C in this case is the Gratuitous Premise. So the advocate of the Skeptical Approach admits that *initially* the thing to believe, before you think about it really carefully, is that there are gratuitous sufferings, as there is decent evidence for that view (so that is (1)), but under reflection that initial evidence for the Gratuitous Premise is ruined by additional evidence (and that's (2)), *and* then yet other evidence strongly suggests that there are no gratuitous sufferings (and that's (3)). So it's just like the phone call story.[39]

Here is a fictional but nevertheless realistic analogy that nicely illustrates what an advocate of the Skeptical Approach person is proposing.

Suppose it's 1960 and we are astronomers. We can of course see zillions of stars with our powerful telescopes. Let's pretend that there are just a dozen stars within ten billion miles of earth, and for each of those dozen stars we have been able to see planets orbiting them. So we have seen that all the "close" stars have planets. But all the other stars are at least a hundred times as far away (at least a trillion miles); call them "distant stars." Suppose further that for each of the distant stars we look at with those telescopes—and there are zillions of these distant stars—we don't see *any* planets around *any* of them.

One might initially think that that's excellent evidence that there are at least some stars without planets orbiting them—in fact, it is good evidence that there *lots* of stars without planets, the distant ones. But once I tell you a little more about the story you'll see that it's actually no evidence at all! The amazing reason is this: we know perfectly well that the telescopes we are using are not anywhere near powerful enough to detect any planets around distant stars. We have *no chance whatsoever* at spotting distant planets with those telescopes. Seeing distant stars isn't hard because they are so bright; distant planets, however, would be much, much darker and thus much, much harder to see (or to detect through other means). So just because we tried hard to see distant planets and completely failed to find any gave us *no reason at all* to think that there are stars without orbiting planets. For all we knew, every single distant star has orbiting planets—just as every close star has planets. Our methods of looking at distant stars weren't anywhere good enough to give us any decent evidence, pro or con, regarding the question of whether there are stars that don't have planets orbiting them. In sum (the reason for the italics will become plain in a moment):

> The fact that we see lots of *distant stars* and almost none of them are observed to have *planets* gives us no reason at all to think that there really are *distant stars* with no corresponding *planets*. The reason: the methods we have for seeing whether *distant stars* are coupled with *planets* are really inadequate.

Analogously, the advocate of the Skeptical Approach is saying this (notice the similarity indicated with italics):

> The fact that we see lots of *instances of suffering* and almost none of them are observed to have *outweighing goods* gives us no reason at all to think that there really are *instances of suffering* with no corresponding *outweighing goods*. The reason: the methods we have for seeing whether *instances of suffering* are coupled with *outweighing goods* are really inadequate.

So the comparison is this: our methods for discovering planets around distant stars are very unreliable; analogously, our methods for discovering outweighing goods are very unreliable. That's the end of the analogy. Now I'll present the aspects of the Skeptical Approach, which are analogous to E_A–E_C.

In the phone call story we started out with some decent although not strong evidence for "The 6pm caller was a woman." Analogously, the Skeptical Approach advocate says that we start out with some decent evidence for the Gratuitous Premise. It should strike you as somewhat odd that we are all the way into chapter 7 and have yet to encounter an official-looking argument on behalf of the Gratuitous Premise! (At the end of chapter 5 I gave the official-looking argument for the Consequence Premise.) The reason I haven't articulated one, as you might guess, is that it just seems pretty obvious to most people that the Gratuitous Premise is true, and theists generally agree that that's exactly how things *seem*. In a nutshell, the reason most of us think that it certainly looks as though there are gratuitous sufferings has two parts:

(a) We think we haven't even come close to finding goods that justify all suffering (this remark is contrary to the PHOG Approach).

(b) We think we are smart enough that if those outweighing goods existed we would have found a decent portion of them by now, given how hard we have looked for them, how smart we are, and how we are already pretty good at discovering in everyday life when bad things are worthwhile because they're coupled with good things. No doubt, we would miss *some* of the outweighing goods, maybe even quite a few, but surely we wouldn't be *really bad* at finding the outweighing goods.

Please notice that the argument doesn't include anything silly like "We seem to have not found the outweighing goods; so, the goods probably aren't there to be found." Instead, it includes something plausible: a *very large* group of many of the *smartest* humans in history have looked *incredibly hard*, over many *centuries*, to find the goods and have utterly failed; so, the goods probably aren't there to be found. There's nothing stupid or obviously fallacious about that idea.

The basic argument for the Gratuitous Premise utilizes those two ideas, (a) and (b), as follows.

1. There is a large group P of people who are *very intelligent*, who have spent a *great deal* of time (centuries) thinking *very hard* about the relation between suffering and various conceptions of God, and who have undertaken a very long (again, centuries), intelligent, heartfelt, and otherwise serious search for goods that justify suffering. These are the many intelligent folks who have thought long and hard about suffering. They include people from all walks of life, but they are mainly philosophers and theologians.

2. We in group P are *very* good at spotting outweighing goods for all sorts of things we do or experience that we would rather not do or experience. There are literally millions of examples from everyday life: doing unpleasant things at work, going to the dentist, making investments (thereby not enjoying the money now), being nice to unpleasant people, waiting at traffic lights, doing laundry, sifting the cat's litter box, etc. We can very often figure out when enduring something unpleasant is "worth it." More specifically, we are very good at two separate things:

    (a) When upon the intelligent reflection mentioned in (1) we come to think that doing X is worth it because X is coupled with some outweighing good G, it's often the case that we are right in that judgment: X really is coupled with G and G really does make X worthwhile (so X is worth it; X might be getting a shot at the doctor's office).

    (b) When upon the intelligent reflection mentioned in (1) we come to think that doing X is *not* worth it because X is *not* coupled with any outweighing good, it's often the case that we're right in that judgment: there is no outweighing good for X (so it's not worth it; X might be buying some expensive trinket for a four-year-old child—who we can tell will be just mildly pleased and then forget all about it in about five minutes).

    And the combination of (2a) and (2b) means we are quite good at spotting outweighing goods for all sorts of instances of *non-human* suffering, since large amounts of non-human suffering are just like human suffering (e.g., burning pains, stabbing pains, throbbing pains, chronic pains, primal fears, etc.).

3. If a large group of people fits the description in (1) and (2) and if goods existed that justified even *most* suffering (and keep in mind that most

suffering is had by non-human animals), the people in that group very probably would have noticed the outweighing goods for a considerable percentage of the instances of suffering. After all, there are lots of them and they've tried very hard and with great intelligence (as per (1)), and (2) implies that they are pretty good at this task. They would no doubt miss out on some, perhaps even a great many, of the connections among goods and instances of suffering, but they would surely discover a quite large percentage of them.

4. Thus, by (1)–(3) if goods existed that justified even *most* suffering, then people in P very probably would have noticed the outweighing goods for a considerable percentage of the instances of suffering.

5. However, the people in P have *not* noticed the outweighing goods for a considerable percentage of the instances of suffering. We have failed to discover goods–sufferings connections for most instances of suffering. (This is the denial of the PHOG Approach; so the Skeptical Approach is definitely different from the PHOG Approach.)

6. Thus, by (4) and (5) it's highly probable that there aren't goods that justify even most suffering. Of course, this would mean there is gratuitous suffering.

In brief: if the zillions of cases of appalling suffering were justified by being paired with goods that made them worth it, then we surely would have discovered a large part of that fact by now, given our impressive brains and literally centuries-long devotion to the issue. But we haven't. Thus, it definitely looks as though many of those instances of suffering are not paired with outweighing goods; they are gratuitous.

Notice that the argument does not proceed this way: here is *a particular case* of really horrific suffering; it is highly unlikely that there is any outweighing good for *it*; so, it's highly likely that it is gratuitous; thus, there is gratuitous suffering. The argument for the Gratuitous Premise is non-specific in that it doesn't purport to identify a particular instance or even class of sufferings as gratuitous. This kind of non-specific argument is obviously legitimate. For instance, I can't identify any planets outside of our solar system that have water on them, but given the overwhelming number of stars and planets just in our one galaxy (several hundred billion stars in our galaxy alone; and there are billions of galaxies in the universe), I have excellent reason for thinking that there are such planets. Another example: I can't identify any missing socks in my house (after all, they are *missing*), but I have excellent reasons to think they exist. Similarly, although I may or may not feel confident that I can identify a particular gratuitous suffering, I may have excellent reason for thinking that there are such things; that's what the advocate of (1)–(6) is saying.

The argument for the Gratuitous Premise has four premises: (1), (2), (3), and (5) (claim (4) is a subsidiary or "half way" conclusion; (6) is the main conclusion). The advocate of the Skeptical Approach is willing to accept the premises with one exception: she says that (2b) is false. By admitting the truth of the rest of the argument's premises she has admitted that there is *some* good reason to believe the Gratuitous Premise. I think this is an admirable position to take: as I said above it's obvious that it *seems* as though there is a great deal of gratuitous suffering—and this "seeming" holds up even after tons of competent, intelligent reflection—and any theist worth her salt has to admit that fact about how things seem, even if her ultimate view is that things are not as they appear! The combination of (1), (2a), (3), and (5) is what I'll call the "initial evidence" in favor of the Gratuitous Premise, the initial considerations that the theist is happy to admit give us some reason to think there is gratuitous suffering.

In sum, this theist is willing to admit the truth of this generalization, (2a):

- If after careful thought (by lots of really intelligent folks, over many centuries, etc.) we tend to agree that such-and-such instances of suffering were worth it because they were appropriately coupled with such-and-such outweighing goods, then we are usually or at least quite often right in that judgment.

But she says that this other generalization, the closely analogous (2b), is crucially different and we have serious reason to doubt it:

- If after careful thought (by lots of really intelligent folks, over many centuries, etc.) we tend to agree that such-and-such instances of suffering were *not* worth it because they were *not* appropriately coupled with any outweighing goods, then we are usually or at least quite often right in that judgment.

Premise (2a) says: when we work really hard and *do* find something we think is a good that outweighs some suffering, then we're usually right in that judgment; (2b) says: when we work really hard and *don't* find a good that we think outweighs some suffering, then we're usually right in that judgment. So characterized, the difference in the two premises is plain.

> Q65: Explain in your own words the difference between (2a) and (2b) in the argument for the Gratuitous Premise.

More carefully, the Skeptical Approach advocate says two things: first, there are compelling considerations that should make us doubt (2b); second, there are further considerations, separate from the first set, that should make us think (2b) is actually false. We already saw, with the phone call story, that these two things are different. When the roommate told us that the voicemail message was not from 6pm but from earlier in the day, that gave us good reason to doubt "The 6pm caller was a woman" but it gave us no reason to assert it was actually false (that is, it gave us no reason to conclude that the caller was a man). But then new considerations came to light to show us that "The 6pm caller was a woman" was really false (the new considerations: we learned that our reliable male friend Fred had said he would call at 6pm).

> Q66: I invented the argument for the Gratuitous Premise. Usually, in books and articles on the problem of evil it is not set out in any detail. Did I miss out on a better argument for that premise, a more convincing one? If so, what is it? Be creative.

> Q67: The argument for the Gratuitous Premise explicitly rejects the PHOG Approach in one premise; which one?

> Q68: Premise (2b) in the argument for the Gratuitous Premise is the key: if it's true, there probably is gratuitous suffering and the 4-Part God probably doesn't exist. Do two things with respect to (2b): think of some good reasons to think it's true, and think of some good reasons to think it's false.

Here is the first set of considerations the skeptical theist wants us to focus on, the ones that are supposed to make us think the odds that the Gratuitous Premise is true are only around 50/50 at best:

(A) Each of us from our own personal experiences has seen how surprisingly often a really bad thing actually led to outweighing goods—even though at the time the bad thing was happening there were *no* signs that everything would turn out all right. (I gave an example of this from my own life: some experience with near poverty when I was a child and teen.)

(B) We have learned how tricky it is to judge when some instance of suffering is outweighed by some good. People have extraordinarily different conceptions of what counts as suffering, what things are good, how good some things are compared to other things, etc. Furthermore, the whole field of ethics is a nightmare, with little agreement on philosophical matters or on relatively general non-philosophical matters (e.g., there are many people who think that almost all moral truths are relative to so many different factors that it is hard to say anything true about morality that is general yet substantive).

(C) We have seen with our discussion of the PHOG Approach that there are several important yet often overlooked goods that are paired with a significant amount of suffering (even if they don't show that *virtually all* suffering isn't gratuitous, as the PHOG Approach advocate thought).

What these three observations are supposed to show, according to the advocate of the Skeptical Approach, is that *there is an excellent chance that we are actually highly unreliable when we say that some suffering is not worth it.* (The name "Skeptical Approach" is intended to reflect the idea that we should be skeptical of our ability to spot outweighing goods linked with suffering.) More exactly, the claim is this: there is an excellent chance that we *always* make bad mistakes when we think that an instance of suffering fails to be linked with an outweighing good (our mistake is this: contrary to what we thought there is an outweighing good linked with the suffering), and this liability shows us that we are in no position to think that we are actually quite good at spotting outweighing goods for suffering, as (2b) insists.

At this point in the argument, according to the advocate of the Skeptical Approach, we should think that there's roughly a 50/50 chance there is gratuitous suffering. We have some reason to think there is such suffering, but we also have strong reason to think we aren't at all trustworthy in making that kind of judgment; these two reasons more or less cancel each other out. Our attitude towards the Gratuitous Premise should be akin to our attitude towards the idea that the number of pennies in our house is an even number: our evidence doesn't suggest it's true but it doesn't suggest it's false either. At this point the reasonable thing to do with respect to "There is gratuitous suffering" is the same thing we should do with respect to "There are an even number of pennies in my house": we should withhold judgment on it, neither believing it's true nor believing it's false.

The next thing that happens according to the advocate of the Skeptical Approach is that additional evidence kicks in with the purpose of giving us evidence that there actually is no gratuitous suffering whatsoever:

(D) There is strong if inconclusive evidence that the 4-Part God exists. (Recall that the Confident Approach required there to be *conclusive* evidence, even if it can't be articulated; the Skeptical Approach is more modest, and thus more plausible, than the Confident Approach on this matter.)

(E) And this book has articulated the excellent evidence for the Consequence Premise, which says that if the 4-Part God exists, then there is no gratuitous suffering.

Anyone can see what those two pieces of information (D) and (E) lead to: if they are true then there is strong if inconclusive evidence that there is no gratuitous suffering. We were already at the 50/50 point with respect to the Gratuitous

Premise (that's supposed to be the upshot of (A)–(C)). And (D) and (E) are strong enough that they should tilt us towards thinking that the premise is false.[40]

The evidence mentioned in (E) was articulated in chapters 2 and 5. That's real evidence, so (E) is pretty solid. But you will also have no doubt noticed that (D) presents *no evidence whatsoever* that the 4-Part God exists: it's a *mere assertion* that there is evidence for the 4-Part God! Well, anyone can assert anything; mere assertions don't amount to evidence. So the obvious question is this: is there any *real* evidence for the 4-Part God—apart from the not insignificant fact that many, many smart people who have great respect for reason and evidence believe, after years of thinking about it at a high level of expertise, that the 4-Part God exists?

That's a key question to ask when evaluating the Skeptical Approach. But it's not the only key question. In order to have some precision when evaluating the Skeptical Approach, which is what our task is in the rest of this chapter, we should note exactly what the approach says. It makes seven claims: (A)–(E) from before and then two more:

(F) If (A)–(C) are true, then we have no good reason to accept (2b). And that means we have no good reason to accept the reasoning behind the Gratuitous Premise, since (2b) is an essential premise of that reasoning.

(G) If (D) and (E) are true, then there is strong evidence against the Gratuitous Premise.

In the evaluation below I will focus on (A)–(D) while ignoring (E)–(G). I will also consider slightly modifying the idea in order to generate an alternative and perhaps better version of the Skeptical Approach.

As I mentioned above, (D), which says that there is *strong if inconclusive* evidence that the 4-Part God exists, is more modest than the corresponding claim of the Confident Approach, which said that our knowledge of the existence of the 4-Part God is so secure that we can simply dismiss the Problem of Gratuitous Suffering as resting on some false premise (either the Gratuitous Premise or the Consequence Premise) even if we haven't the faintest idea what justifies God in permitting so much suffering, if anything. But just because (D) is more modest doesn't mean it's true or even that there is good reason to think it's true.

As I mentioned in chapters 2 and 4, most philosophers think the *public*, non-testimonial evidence for the 4-Part God is poor—where the "public" evidence excludes private spiritual experience. Philosophers who think otherwise often accuse the first group of philosophers of avoiding the good versions of the arguments in favor of the existence of the 4-Part God, and basing their skeptical attitude on weak versions of those arguments. My own view, for what it's worth, is that no version, however sophisticated, of any argument for the existence of the 4-Part God is free of significant and fatal flaws—with the possible exception of the highly unsatisfying (because uninformative) but I think intriguing Social Argument given in chapter 4 that can be summed up with "Since so many truly excellent philosophers and other intelligent folks think the 4-Part God exists, and they do this after much truly expert reflection, there must be *some* decent evidence backing up their view, since if there wasn't there would not be so many philosophers and others who remain theists." Be careful: that's a *summation* of an argument; it's not the full argument itself!

In any case, the only way to evaluate (D) is to embark on a long discussion of the arguments and other potential sources of evidence for the 4-Part God's existence—including private spiritual experiences. This cannot be done here, although the project was started in chapter 4. It will have to suffice to note, as we did when discussing the Confident Approach, that the thorough evaluation of the Problem of Gratuitous Suffering requires a thorough evaluation of the potential sources of evidence for the existence of the 4-Part God.

On the other hand, we don't need a million pages of philosophy in order to say some useful things about (A)–(C).

As you have no doubt noticed, matters are getting complicated, with the argument (1)–(6) *for* the Gratuitous Premise plus the claims (A)–(G) *against* the Gratuitous Premise. Before we begin figuring out whether the Skeptical Approach has a good chance at success we need to make sure we *understand* it, which might be harder than you think. I'll now make some remarks meant to clarify the approach.

Q69: What are the best reasons *that don't merely assume theism is true* for us to think that we are really lousy at spotting outweighing goods— so lousy that we shouldn't trust our judgment that many instances of suffering have no such goods?

First clarification. We should make sure we understand how the PHOG and Skeptical approaches differ. Their advocates both endorse the existence of the 4-Part God. They both think there is no gratuitous suffering. So, they both reject the Gratuitous Premise, as they hold that all suffering has outweighing goods. They disagree, however, on whether we have the ability to discern the outweighing goods. The Skeptical Approach advocate says we just don't have the smarts to do this: in fact, she thinks it's hopeless for most cases of suffering. The PHOG Approach person says the opposite: she says that we have successfully discovered the bulk of the outweighing goods.

Second clarification. There is an easy conflation to make here, one that would ruin our evaluation of the Skeptical Approach. So we must avoid it. Here is one argument that demonstrates the conflation:

We should be highly skeptical of our ability to spot outweighing goods, precisely as the Skeptical Approach advocate says. After all, if the 4-Part

God exists then it stands to reason that he has arranged things so that all the suffering is outweighed by goods connected to those sufferings. God is omniscient and we are, compared to him, complete morons. So when we observe that we have been unable to see the outweighing goods hardly means we should conclude that the goods aren't there at all! Why on earth should we assume that we can understand God's plan? That's pure folly.

This argument strikes me as a reasonable one (or at least the beginning of a reasonable one). In fact, it is a brief argument for the Consequence Premise: *if* the 4-Part God exists, *then* he has arranged things so there is no gratuitous suffering—even if the outweighing goods are forever beyond our understanding. But this is *not* what the Skeptical Approach advocate is arguing; in fact, it is completely irrelevant to the approach.

The advocate of the Skeptical Approach says that, *setting aside the assumption that the 4-Part God exists*, we still should be skeptical of our ability to spot outweighing goods. As I am characterizing her, she is a fairly *ambitious* theist: although she is modest when she says that she doesn't know what the outweighing goods are, she is not modest when she claims that we have good *non-theistic evidence* that undermines the support for the Gratuitous Premise. That is, she wants to appeal to facts, with which even an atheist would agree, that make us very skeptical of (2b). In order to do this she needs to give us evidence that doesn't rely on the assumption that God exists. And that's precisely what (A)–(C) attempt to do. The Skeptical Approach person is saying this:

> Even atheists should admit that judging outweighing goods is *so* hard that we should have little or no confidence that there are any gratuitous sufferings—even though we have to admit that there are trillions of cases of atrocious suffering that don't appear to be linked with any outweighing goods. We can't assume that the *reality* of the situation is at all like how it *appears* to us, as we already know, on theism-neutral grounds, that we have good reason to think we are not at all trustworthy about these matters.

Notice that (A)–(C) nowhere assume that God exists. That's how the Skeptical Approach advocate attempts to win over the atheists (and agnostics).

Third clarification. Just because we *sometimes* make mistakes is no reason to be skeptical of our abilities. For instance, just because people sometimes hallucinate things or don't see things that are right in front of them is no worthwhile reason for me to be skeptical of my ability to determine if there is an alligator in my kitchen right now, as I'm in the kitchen, I'm perfectly sober and healthy, the lights are all on, and there are no distractions. Even though sense perception (visual, auditory, tactile, gustatory, olfactory) isn't *perfect*, we know that we are incredibly good at perceiving many things. Since we're so good at perceiving big, interesting, scary things like alligators in our kitchens when we're healthy and sober, and we're in the kitchen with the lights on, if we don't perceive an alligator there that's a truly excellent reason for concluding that there's no alligator there. We still might be wrong of course: it's at least minutely *possible* that some crazy person brought an alligator to my house, knocked down the inside walls between the cabinets on one side of the kitchen, and chained the peculiarly quiet alligator inside those cabinets! But it's silly to think that such a possibility has actually come to be or is even remotely likely.

What this all means is that the advocate of the Skeptical Approach can't be saying that our ability to spot outweighing goods is *merely imperfect*. Just because we aren't perfect at spotting alligators in kitchens doesn't mean we should say "Well, I don't see any signs at all that there is an alligator here but there's a real chance there's one here anyway, around a 50/50 chance." Similarly, just because we aren't perfect at spotting outweighing goods doesn't mean we should say "Well, I don't see any outweighing goods for those trillions of cases of horrific suffering but there's a real chance there are some anyway, maybe a 50/50 chance." Instead, the advocate of the Skeptical Approach has to say that our ability to spot outweighing goods is not just imperfect but actually quite untrustworthy: (2b) has to be completely off the mark. Being imperfect is one thing; being untrustworthy is something else entirely (e.g., Einstein was imperfect but extremely good at advanced physics; I am not just imperfect but utterly untrustworthy at advanced physics). She has to show us that we have some cognitive "block" that prevents us from spotting outweighing goods even when they are there (or, that we have a block that prevents us from seeing the links connecting the goods and the sufferings).

Fourth clarification. It isn't enough, in defending the Skeptical Approach, to point out that we may well miss *a lot* of outweighing goods. The advocate of the Gratuitous Premise (as well as the crucial premise (2b)) will be happy to admit that! (She will *also* probably insist that we may well miss a lot of outweighing evils, which some philosophers think is a crucial issue but one we won't pursue in this book.) Recall that the Gratuitous Premise says only that *some* pain and suffering lacks outweighing goods. It doesn't say anything like "*Almost every time* we don't see an outweighing good, there isn't one there to be seen." As I mentioned earlier, in order to deny the Gratuitous Premise you have to argue that it's plausible that *absolutely all* suffering has outweighing goods. The person who thinks the Gratuitous Premise (and (2b)) is true isn't saying that we're really good at spotting outweighing goods; she's saying that even though we might miss a lot of outweighing goods, it's highly unlikely that those hidden outweighing goods justify *all the many trillions of cases* of apparently unjustified suffering. To defend the Skeptical Approach one has to argue that not only have we missed some or even a lot of outweighing goods, but we have missed outweighing goods that are incredibly common throughout nature, as they are doing their hidden justifying work right under our noses! So the advocate of the Skeptical Approach is saying that we have missed something *really enormous* about how goods and suffering are related (that is, she isn't saying that we've missed just a few things here and there; she's saying we've missed almost everything).

Q70: "We should be highly skeptical of our ability to spot outweighing goods, precisely as the Skeptical Approach advocate says. After all, if the 4-Part God exists then it stands to reason that he has arranged things so that all the suffering is outweighed by goods connected to those sufferings. God is omniscient and we are, compared to him, complete morons. So when we observe that we have been unable to find the outweighing goods, we should not conclude that the goods aren't there at all! Why on earth should we assume that we can understand God's plan?" Tell us why that argument is bad.

Fifth clarification. As I have repeatedly said, the Skeptical Approach advocate says that we are really awful at spotting outweighing goods. But there are many ways we could be lousy at spotting outweighing goods, and they can be very different from one another. *This is crucial for understanding the approach.* So I want to give you a brief taste of some of these ways, as one of them seems (to me anyway) particularly supportive of the Skeptical Approach.

For the sake of numerical simplicity let's assume that there are exactly 1000 particular instances of suffering and all them are paired with outweighing goods (so we are supposing for a moment that the Gratuitous Premise is false, as the Skeptical Approach advocate says). Here are just two ways we could be lousy at spotting outweighing goods:

- Scenario A: We know the outweighing goods for just 100 of those 1000 cases. All told, there are 75 different goods that justify those 100 cases (so some goods justify more than one case of suffering). We don't know the outweighing goods for the remaining 900 of the 1000 cases. All told, there are 750 different goods that justify those 900 cases (although, again, we are unaware of this fact). So, there are a total of 825 goods that justify the 1000 cases of suffering, and we have spotted 75 of those 825. Thus, we have spotted a measly 9 percent (that's 75 out of 825) of the total outweighing goods.
- Scenario B: We know the outweighing goods for just 100 of those 1000 cases. All told, there are 75 different goods that justify those 100 cases. We don't know the outweighing goods for the remaining 900 of the 1000 cases. All told, there are just three different goods that justify those 900 cases (so these three goods are doing a *lot* of work). So, there are a total of 78 goods that justify the 1000 cases of suffering, and we have spotted 75 of those 78. Thus, we have spotted a whopping 96 percent (that's 75 out of 78) of the total outweighing goods.

In each scenario we are "lousy at spotting outweighing goods" in this exact sense: we have failed to spot the goods that justify 900 out of the 1000 cases of suffering. But the two scenarios are very different too: in scenario B we have an *excellent track record* in spotting outweighing goods—96 percent—whereas in the other scenario A we have an *awful track record* (only 9 percent). In scenario A we have missed out on a *lot* of the outweighing goods; in scenario B we have missed out on only a tiny number of outweighing goods but those very few goods are doing a tremendous amount of justifying of cases of suffering. The lesson from scenario B is weird: you can be lousy at spotting something in one sense (you've missed the outweighing goods for 900 out of 1000 cases of suffering) even though you have an excellent track record at spotting it in another sense (you've spotted 75 out of the 78 outweighing goods; so you've just missed out on the most important of them).

Now we can apply the lesson to the Problem of Gratuitous Suffering: it's possible that all the many trillions of cases of horrific suffering (that we have a hard time finding outweighing goods for) are outweighed by a *very small number of profoundly hidden goods*. That is, even if we have successfully spotted 99.3486766 percent of the goods that justify any suffering at all (so we are excellent at the task of spotting outweighing goods), if we miss just a few *and* those few are coupled with virtually all cases of suffering, as they are the most important outweighing goods, then the Gratuitous Premise is false even though we are quite expert at spotting outweighing goods. (So here we're saying that scenario B might be the right way to think about sufferings.) Hence, the Skeptical Approach advocate need not insist that we are "really terrible" at spotting outweighing goods. Instead, she has to insist only that we can't *trust* ourselves to make inferences like "We have tried our absolute best, over many centuries and using the considerable talents of a great many philosophers and theologians, and we still can't find outweighing goods for such-and-such instances of suffering; so, they are probably not there to be found."

Even so, we shouldn't overstate the odds of this scenario B possibility. If we are aware of many, many goods—and we are indeed aware of many, many goods that outweigh many instances of suffering—and none of those goods does much work in outweighing the many trillions of cases of horrific suffering left over, then what are the odds that the small number of goods that we've missed are so colossally wonderful *and* ubiquitous that they justify those trillions of cases of suffering? And if they are virtually ubiquitous, then why on earth do we keep missing them when they are coupled with virtually all cases of suffering?

Q71: The Skeptical Approach could posit Scenario A or Scenario B (from the fifth "clarification" of the approach). If you were a 4-Part theist who accepted the Skeptical Approach, which scenario would you think is more likely to be the true one? Why?

The advocate of the Skeptical Approach needs to argue that it would be utterly unsurprising to learn that not only have we failed to notice some outweighing goods but we have failed to notice the goods that are doing *almost all* of the "clean up work," the work of justifying the trillions of cases of horrific suffering. Allow me to once again engage in some pretend numbers for a moment, just to make sure we understand what's going on here. Suppose that we know of exactly 1000 cases of horrific suffering. Let us also suppose that we are confident that 14 of those 1000 instances are justified in that we have identified the goods they are coupled with that are so good that their goodness outweighs the badness of those 14 sufferings. As for the remaining 986 cases of suffering? We don't know what goods, if any, outweigh them. And now if the Skeptical Approach advocate says: "Well, look, since we're not total experts in spotting outweighing goods, maybe we've missed some that justify the remaining 986," then we will be very dissatisfied. That doesn't look like a plausible thing to say unless we admit that we not only fail to be "total experts" but we are completely untrustworthy at spotting outweighing goods, as we have missed out on the goods that justify 98.6 percent of suffering.

Everyone will be happy to admit that there simply must be a number of goods that justify suffering but we don't know about them. We all agree about *that*, as we are just agreeing that we aren't perfect at figuring things out. What the Skeptical Approach advocate needs to argue is that these hidden goods *justify virtually all suffering*. So she's not just saying we have missed a few goods here and there; she's saying we have missed the most important goods, by far. That's a much more significant and controversial claim.

Hence, what the advocate of the Skeptical Approach needs to do is make it reasonable to think that there are goods linked with our suffering *that are incredibly wonderful and almost ubiquitous*. Otherwise, if they are not so wonderful and common, then they can't serve as outweighing goods for the trillions of cases of horrific suffering. Thus, the crucial question isn't "Are there goods we don't know about?" or "Are there goods we don't know about that are linked with our suffering?" or even "Are there goods we don't know about that are linked with our suffering and are virtually ubiquitous?" Instead, the question is "Are there goods we don't know about that are linked with our suffering, that are virtually omnipresent, and that are incredibly wonderful?"[41]

Someone might come to the defense of the Skeptical Approach by pointing out that for all we know for sure many of the outweighing goods are located thousands of years in the future, or the distant past, or something similar. Moreover, she might continue, many of the other outweighing goods may be right under our noses, but currently inaccessible to us because of our cognitive limitations (e.g., we're not smart enough to see the coupling connections). My response: that's all perfectly true, but we aren't focusing on mere possibility or fantasy. The Skeptical Approach advocate is looking for *real reasons* why even after centuries of investigation we have failed to come up with solid reasons why God allows vast amounts of certain kinds of suffering. Engaging in "Yes, but what if?"

lines of thought is to fail to take suffering with sufficient *seriousness*. The Problem of Gratuitous Suffering is an extremely serious problem for theism, not to be taken lightly. The Skeptical Approach advocate, as I have described her, is to be commended for looking for real evidence that we are awful at spotting outweighing goods, and cheap talk about "Well, there *could* be outweighing goods that we have a very hard time discovering" is, well, *cheap* and does not address the issue with the gravity it merits.

Q72: "If there were outweighing goods that we could understand, then given how hard and long people have looked for them, we would have discovered them by now. And we haven't. To that extent, the thoughts behind the Gratuitous Premise are utterly reasonable. But we aren't looking for goods that would justify *humans* in allowing suffering to happen right under their noses. No, we are trying to see into the mind of God. We are trying to think of goods that would justify *God* in allowing suffering to happen right under his nose. But why on earth would anyone think that we are in a position to figure that out? That's nuts." Assess that line of thought.

Criticisms of the Approach

I'm finished with the clarifications. Now that we *understand* what the Skeptical Approach is supposed to accomplish, we can go on to *evaluate* it. That is, we are now in a decent position to see whether we have any good reason to believe that (A)–(D) are really true, as the Skeptical Approach advocate claims.

Most philosophers will say that the task of showing that (A)–(D) are true, cannot be pulled off successfully. First, consider (A) again:

> (A) Each of us from our own personal experiences has seen how surprisingly often a really bad thing actually led to outweighing goods even though at the time the bad thing was happening there were *no* signs that everything would turn out all right.

The critics say that this is an exaggeration at best: although it shows that we are *fallible* in making judgments of the form "This bit of suffering has no outweighing good," as we do indeed make mistakes in interesting real-life cases, it does nothing whatsoever to suggest that we are utterly untrustworthy on such judgments. Similarly, although *parts of* (B) are true,

> (B) We have learned how tricky it is to judge when some instance of suffering is outweighed by some good. People have extraordinarily different

conceptions of what counts as suffering, what things are good, how good some things are compared to other things, etc. Furthermore, the whole field of ethics is a nightmare, with little agreement on philosophical matters or on relatively general non-philosophical matters (e.g., there are many people who think that almost all moral truths are relative to so many different factors that it is hard to say anything general yet substantive).

as morality can indeed be quite tricky, there is no evidence that this shows that *in ordinary and relatively simple cases* judgments of the form "This bit of suffering has no outweighing good" are unreliable. For one thing, we usually make these judgments in our own communities and cultures, and so the culture-relativity of morality, if it exists at all, is usually not relevant. For another thing, although there is indeed significant disagreement among philosophers and other intellectuals regarding the fundamental principles and other philosophical issues of ethics, there is no such significant disagreement regarding simple, everyday judgments regarding when a bit of suffering is coupled with some good that makes it worth it. An analogy: there is profound uncertainty and disagreement among physicists regarding the fundamental truths regarding gravity, mass, spacetime, and the origin of the universe, but anyone can with almost no effort make millions of highly warranted ordinary physical judgments such as "X is bigger than Y," "X weighs four pounds," etc.

Q73: Moral judgment is a nightmare. It's a nightmare because it's so hard to list some substantive moral judgments that are actually true across the board—for all people in all cultures. No matter how innocent a judgment you come up with, of the form "You can't do X," it's usually not that hard to imagine a society in which X is not only permitted by the people in that society but they seem right to do so, as their society is so different from ours (so, yes, sometimes it's perfectly appropriate to eat cute kittens).

Notice that this doesn't apply to science. Jupiter has more than 20 moons, and no one cares what your society is like: it's just a brute fact about Jupiter. But whether or not it's morally okay to eat cute kittens ... well, it seems that *that* might depend on the society.

Assuming these remarks are roughly true, don't they mean that it's extremely hard to make moral judgments? And doesn't that give good credence to the Skeptical Approach—which says we can't be trusted to make moral judgments of the form "That bit of suffering wasn't coupled with an outweighing good"?

Furthermore, if (B) were true, then how could (2a) be true? Remember (2a):

> If after careful thought (e.g., by lots of really intelligent folks, over many centuries, etc.) we tend to agree that such-and-such instances of suffering were worth it because they were appropriately coupled with such-and-such outweighing goods, then we are usually or at least quite often right in that judgment.

If morality is so damn tricky, then how is it that we are so good at making *those* judgments—as the Skeptical Approach admitted when she said that (2a) was true? The advocate of the Skeptical Approach can't have it both ways: if she wants (B) to count as good evidence against (2b), then it's also going to count as good evidence against (2a). However, (2a) is exceedingly reasonable; so this point goes against the idea that (B) amounts to good evidence against (2b).

One shouldn't think that on *any* topic at all we should be skeptical about our abilities just because we know we are fallible while God is not. You can't just say "Well, God is supposed to be supremely knowledgeable, we're obviously not even close to being like that, so it should not come as a surprise that our confident judgments might be overturned by God." Partly for fun, and to refute that attitude, compare Dave Kingman with Babe Ruth. You've probably never even heard of the baseball player Dave Kingman. Some comparative career statistics:

In some ways, Kingman was an excellent player. He was a good home run hitter in particular. I had tremendous fun as a kid watching him play for the hapless Chicago Cubs during the 1978–1980 baseball seasons. But compared to Ruth? Please. I am glad that no one is bothering to compare my accomplishments to any of the philosophical giants.

Career Statistic	Ruth	Kingman
Batting Average	.342	.236
Home Runs	714	442
Runs Batted In	2213	1210
Runs Scored	2174	901
Hits	2873	1575
Strikeouts	1330	1816
Total Bases	5793	3191
Walks	2062	608
On-Base Percentage	.474	.302
Slugging Average	.690	.478
Won–Loss Record as a Pitcher	94–46	0–0
Earned Run Average as a Pitcher	2.28	9.00
Years Played	22	16

Now if God exists, are you going to take seriously the idea that his perfect knowledge of baseball might make it plausible that you could be wrong in your judgment "Ruth was a better baseball player than Kingman"? Nope. I happen to think Ruth was the best baseball player ever (mainly because in addition to being a great hitter he was an excellent pitcher, which makes him utterly unique), but I am modest enough to take seriously the idea that maybe Willie Mays, for instance, was the best ever. I know perfectly well that I'm fallible on these baseball judgments. But I'm not wrong about the Ruth–Kingman judgment. If I went to heaven and God said to me "Well, actually Kingman was a better baseball player than Ruth," then I would know that God was trying, unsuccessfully, to pull my leg (which of course would be funny, so I guess he *would* be pulling my leg in some weird sense).

How is morality different from baseball? Well, I suppose it might be difficult to think of two things more unalike. But my point here was a simple one: *your not coming even remotely close to knowing everything about T doesn't give you any good reason to think your confident judgments about T might be wrong*. In order for you to take seriously the idea that you're wrong in your judgment "On the whole, the Holocaust has no group of outweighing goods" you need some truly excellent evidence that you're really untrustworthy when it comes to judging outweighing goods. As we saw earlier in the chapter, general remarks about your fallibility are not going to suffice. What we're seeing now is that remarks such as "But God knows about morality much more than you do" won't help the advocate of the Skeptical Approach either. And yet, people who advocate the Skeptical Approach are constantly saying things like "given the huge gulf between God's knowledge and our knowledge, we should not find it at all odd or surprising that we don't find the reasons that justify God's permission of suffering."

I often encounter the response "But who knows about morality, really? And who knows what goods God might have set up?" These are empty words. The baseball example shows that we need decent evidence *specific to morality* that we are awfully untrustworthy regarding judgments about outweighing goods— even though (2a) is true. It is no good to just go on asserting that there are all sorts of goods or good-suffering connections we know nothing about. We need real evidence that our fallibility is so extreme that we can't trust our judgments about outweighing goods; and even if we admitted that someone knew infinitely more about morality than we did, we would *still* have no reason to think we were untrustworthy when judging the presence of outweighing goods. Again, just keep in mind the Kingman–Ruth case, which shows that even if we admit that God knows infinitely more about baseball than we do, we have no reason to think we are untrustworthy when judging matters like "Who was the better player: Ruth or Kingman?"

Thus, the advocate of the Skeptical Approach has to have a good answer to the question of why we should think we are very untrustworthy when it comes to judgments like "There is no *group of hidden goods* that shows that the Holocaust was justified" but not when it comes to judgments like "There is no *group of hidden baseball qualities* that shows that Kingman was better than Ruth." The advocate then attempts, with (A)–(E), to meet that challenge, explaining why our moral judgment is much less trustworthy than our baseball judgment. What we saw above were reasons to think that although our ability to make correct judgments about outweighing goods should be expected to be fallible—we are human, we're going to make lots of mistakes—there are no good non-theistic reasons for thinking that we are terrible at making such judgments.

Q74: What's the point of the Dave Kingman story?

Now consider (C):

> (C) Finally, we have seen with our discussion of the PHOG Approach that there are several important yet often overlooked goods that are paired with a significant amount of suffering (even if they don't show that virtually all suffering isn't gratuitous, as the PHOG Approach advocate thought).

The critics say that we have "seen" no such thing; (C) is just plain false. According to the critics none of the arguments of the PHOG Approach advocate (in chapter 6) were terribly impressive. The critic need not be extreme, however. She can admit that the PHOG Approach advocate was successful in showing that notions like free will, soul development, and knowledge, among other goods, might justify a lot more suffering than one might have expected, before one thought much about the issues. All by itself, that fact should perhaps make us *less confident* that there is gratuitous suffering. But the Skeptical Approach goal is to tell us that we should think that we are *quite untrustworthy* at spotting outweighing goods, and, the critics continue, the partial success of the PHOG Approach isn't up to that ambitious task (all the PHOG Approach advocate did was successfully argue that we might get some important things wrong about outweighing goods).

Now you might think that the Skeptical Approach advocate has an easy response to this criticism. She can point out that God is supposed to be the *perfectly* good, powerful, and knowledgeable creator. So, it would be utterly unsurprising if there were PHOGs outweighing all the hidden and unhidden evils! Given how good God is supposed to be, it simply stands to reason that there will be lots of good things coupled with all the bad things; and given how knowledgeable God is compared to us, it's entirely to be expected that many of those goods will be invisible to us, as we just aren't that perceptive compared to God and we know that morality is a very tricky thing. In fact, it's just plain *silly* to think that we are in any position to judge whether there are gratuitous sufferings! We aren't anywhere near omniscient in general or omniscient about good and evil. But God is, and we should not suppose that we can understand his ways. Moreover, if there are any hidden evils, God, because he is perfectly good, will have arranged things so that they are coupled with outweighing goods just like the evils we already know about.

But it should be clear at this point in our discussion that this response won't work at all: the response is yet another version of the argument for the Consequence Premise that if God exists and fits the 4-Part conception, then of course there are no gratuitous sufferings, as he has arranged PHOGs that justify everything—and we are just not wise enough to see it, so (2b) is false. That's a fine argument, but as we mentioned earlier the advocate of the Skeptical Approach had to come up with evidence *independent of theism* for her claim that we are so untrustworthy at spotting outweighing goods that (2b) is undermined.

(The formula for coming up with evidence *not* independent of theism for our untrustworthiness regarding moral judgment is easy. First, collect evidence for "The 4-Part God exists"—which will be the evidence not independent of theism—and evidence for the Consequence Premise. Assuming you've succeeded, you automatically have evidence that there is no gratuitous suffering. Then add in your evidence that we have failed to find the outweighing goods for most instances of suffering (this can be criticisms of the PHOG Approach). Then you can easily conclude that we are untrustworthy at finding outweighing goods—that is, that (2b) is false. The whole problem with this approach is the first step: finding good overall evidence for 4-Part theism.)

Q75: "The person who puts forward the Problem of Gratuitous Suffering has no proof of her key idea: premise (2b). I admit that (2b) isn't obviously stupid or false or irrational. But until she can provide us with some kind of decent evidence for it, the theist is entirely within her rights to not be bothered by it." Assess this line of reasoning.

I suspect the above criticisms of the Skeptical Approach show that the ambitious version of that approach is a failure: *there is no serious non-theistic evidence that we are lousy at spotting outweighing goods.* (A)–(C) aren't up to the job. Let me be perfectly honest: as far as I have been able to determine, there is no such non-theistic evidence. (The article by William Alston I mentioned in chapter 1 attempts to provide evidence, but most of it relies on theistic assumptions.) What truth is embodied in (A)–(C) is only weak evidence against premise (2b) in the basic argument for the Gratuitous Premise.

Q76: "Most theists think there is no gratuitous suffering. But if you are a theist who is convinced that there is no gratuitous suffering, then of course you think that all suffering is worth it—even the suffering you happen to inflict on others. So ... why be moral in your life? After all, by your own admission whatever suffering you inflict on people—yourself or others—will be worth it: according to you there will *always* be an outweighing good. For instance, perhaps you'd really like to kill some jerk. And you know how to get away with it. Well, why not do it? After all, you're already convinced that whatever suffering he experiences will have an outweighing good. And even if you get caught and go to prison, so what? All that suffering will be worth it too!" Assess this line of reasoning, which applies to *all* theists who are convinced that there is no gratuitous suffering (so it applies to both PHOG Approach and Skeptical Approach advocates).

Modifying the Approach

But that doesn't necessarily mean that the Skeptical Approach is a failure! Its advocate could shift gears and say this in response to the first criticism:

> In my view, the odds are very much in favor of God's existence. But let's set aside my arguments for theism, as I realize that many people disagree with me regarding the strength of that evidence. They think that if you look at the evidence, pro and con, regarding the 4-Part God's existence, no one clearly wins. They think that, very roughly, there is a 50/50 chance that the 4-Part God exists. Maybe it's 60/40 or 40/60, but the point is that it's very roughly split. For the sake of argument, I'll go along with their view. Now, if the 4-Part God doesn't exist, then there probably are zillions of instances of suffering that aren't coupled with outweighing goods, as that's certainly how things appear from a non-theistic perspective. But if he does exist, then given that he is supremely morally good, knowledgeable, and powerful, it stands to reason that there are outweighing goods for *all* suffering. Here we are just admitting that the odds are very much in favor of the Consequence Premise: if God exists, then there are outweighing goods for all suffering. So there are two possibilities, (a) and (b), and as we just admitted they are about equal in likelihood: (a) God doesn't exist and there are lots of instances of gratuitous suffering, and (b) God does exist and there is no such suffering. Hence, very roughly the odds are about 50/50 (or maybe 60/40, 40/60) that there is gratuitous suffering. So unless you have already made up your mind that God doesn't exist—so you think the odds that God exists are

something small, like only 1 out of 10—you should realize that the odds the Gratuitous Premise is true are somewhere around 50/50. Thus, you can't accept that premise! You have to withhold judgment on it. (It's like a flip of the coin: since you know the odds are only 50/50 it will land heads up, you'd be foolish to be confident that it will land heads up.) So, we shouldn't be at all confident in either (2b) or the Gratuitous Premise. Thus, the Problem of Gratuitous Suffering rests on a premise that the evidence just doesn't support enough. Only the foolishly overconfident will accept that premise, just like only the foolishly overconfident will be sure that a coin will land "heads."

If the relevant evidence shows that the odds are really somewhere around 50/50 that the 4-Part God exists, then it seems to me that the conclusion in the next to last sentence is probably true as well. So the speech has that positive feature. I also think that if you personally are *rationally* convinced that the odds are 50/50, and you go through something like the reasoning summarized above, and you don't read anything in the text below, then you're rational in concluding that the evidence doesn't support the Gratuitous Premise or (2b). But is it really *true* that the odds that the 4-Part God exists are very roughly 50/50?

Well, that depends on the strength of the evidence for and against the existence of the 4-Part God. And as I mentioned earlier, the clear majority of philosophers think the odds are pretty low. I have little reliable data to support a conjecture, but my years in philosophy lead me to guess that most philosophers think the odds are *very roughly* 1 in 10—although as I have insisted over and over again in this book, a not insignificant portion of competent philosophers (including some of the most accomplished ones) are 4-Part theists and it's not as though the non-theistic consensus is based on some knockdown proof or experiment. The upshots of these reflections are as follows:

- If the overall evidence regarding the existence of the 4-Part God is really good enough so that there is about a 50 percent chance he exists, then our *overall* evidence—theistic and non-theistic—doesn't support the Gratuitous Premise or the denial of that premise.
- If the overall evidence regarding the existence of the 4-Part God is so poor that there is only about a mere 10 percent chance he exists, then our overall evidence does support the Gratuitous Premise. So the PHOG and Skeptical approaches are ruled out.
- If the overall evidence regarding the existence of the 4-Part God is so good that there is about a 90 percent chance he exists, then our overall evidence goes strongly against the Gratuitous Premise.

So once again, the viability of a theistic response to the Problem of Gratuitous Suffering succeeds or fails on the question of the strength of our overall evidence for the existence of the 4-Part God. We have seen this for both (D) and the speech above that was meant to replace (A)–(C). And we also saw it when evaluating the Confident Approach. Assessing the Problem of Gratuitous Suffering simply cannot be done well without thoroughly assessing the strength of the evidence for the 4-Part God.

Q77: A lot of intelligent, fair-minded, and informed people say that there is no real good evidence *for or against* the existence of God (or even the 4-Part God). For them, the so-called arguments for God's existence suck, as do the so-called arguments against God's existence. (I write "so-called" in order to convey the derision these people have for the pro and con arguments.) Presumably, this means that they are agnostics: they think there is little reason to embrace theism (be a theist) or reject theism (be an atheist). So, they think the odds on "God exists" are roughly 50/50 and they are never going to get any better or worse.

Assume, in this question, that they are right about all that. Now, if you agree with them, what will your response be to the Problem of Gratuitous Suffering? In particular, what will your position be on the Gratuitous Premise? Will you think it's true, will you think it's false, or will you say "I just don't know"? Defend your answer.

Lessons

That last sentence brings up a tricky problem. In light of what has been said above it might be thought that we should proceed this way when trying to figure out how the 4-Part theist should respond to the Problem of Gratuitous Suffering:

1st: Figure out if there is good overall evidence for the 4-Part God.

2nd: If the evidence is really good, then perhaps we can avail ourselves of the Confident Approach or Skeptical Approach to the Problem of Gratuitous Suffering (or even the PHOG Approach, although that's a harder road to take).

3rd: But if the evidence is poor, then the Skeptical Approach is probably a failure (as is the PHOG Approach; and the Confident Approach will be as well for most people).

This makes it look as though we have two *separate* projects: figure out the worth of the alleged evidence for the existence of God—*before* thinking about the Problem of Gratuitous Suffering—and *then*, after that first project is completed, figure out the best theistic response to the Problem of Gratuitous Suffering using the information gathered in the prior project of examining the evidence for the 4-Part God. But philosophers think this is a mistake: the first project can't be competently carried out, even in part, before the second one is taken up in a thorough way. The reason: part of the perfectly standard evidence against the 4-Part God lies in three generally accepted facts: (a) there is a colossal amount of suffering that we haven't found the outweighing goods for, (b) we tend to *think* we are more or less trustworthy when looking for outweighing goods (especially when a huge portion of us have spent a long time searching and have come up empty), and (c) if there is gratuitous suffering, then the 4-Part God probably doesn't exist. The two projects—assess the evidence for and against the 4-Part God, figure out the best theistic response to the Problem of Gratuitous Suffering—overlap considerably. So you can't do the first before the second.

This makes matters messy. You have Fred the theist yelling in your ear that he's got excellent evidence that the 4-Part God exists, and since the Consequence Premise is true, that means that there is no gratuitous suffering despite the appearances. Then you have George the atheist yelling in your other ear that the evidence for gratuitous suffering is so powerful that it shows that the 4-Part God doesn't exist. Despite all the yelling, they both are intelligent, well-informed people.

Q78: Lots of people think we have two separate projects: figure out the worth of the alleged evidence for the existence of God—before thinking about the Problem of Gratuitous Suffering—and then, after that first project is completed, figure out the best theistic response to the Problem of Gratuitous Suffering using the information gathered in the prior project of examining the evidence for the 4-Part God. Tell us what's wrong with this approach.

I suspect that the best we can do is the following, although I won't defend the suspicion here:

1st: Figure out if there is excellent overall evidence for the 4-Part God *ignoring anything having to do with suffering*.

2nd: If the evidence is strongly in favor of the existence of the 4-Part God, then perhaps we can avail ourselves of the Confident Approach or

Skeptical Approach to the Problem of Gratuitous Suffering. Whether the "perhaps" will work out depends on the strength of the competing bodies of evidence: the evidence for God's existence vs. the evidence for our trustworthiness in finding outweighing goods (in particular, the evidence for (2b)).

3rd: But if the evidence is only weakly in favor of the existence of the 4-Part God, then the Confident, PHOG, and Skeptical approaches are probably failures for almost all of us.

A couple more points before I wrap up this chapter. To a certain extent, the Confident Approach and the Skeptical Approach have converged. The advocates of the former, you'll recall, start out very confident in the 4-Part God's existence and then conclude that at least one of the Gratuitous Premise and the Consequence Premise must be false. However, you'll also recall that most theists accept the Consequence Premise. So, those who take the Confident Approach quite often end up denying the Gratuitous Premise. When challenged with the vast amounts of suffering that *seems* gratuitous, they will have to conclude that humans just aren't trustworthy when trying to find outweighing goods. And they will conclude this even if they don't have theism-neutral evidence that we aren't trustworthy in that task. On the other hand, the Skeptical Approach advocates, assuming they have admitted failure in finding theism-neutral evidence that we are untrustworthy when trying to find outweighing goods, will end up in the very same boat: high confidence in the 4-Part God's existence, which is their basis for rejection of the Gratuitous Premise, but no significant theism-neutral evidence that we are untrustworthy at finding outweighing goods.

Thus far I have been considering the possible *evidence* in support of the Skeptical Approach. But as we have noted a couple of times previously in this book, there is a notion of evidential reasonableness and there is a notion of non-evidential reasonableness. The former requires genuine evidence; the latter (illustrated by the story involving Fred and Dr. Quack) does not. A few paragraphs back I said that the Skeptical Approach is a failure for a person if she doesn't already know that the 4-Part God exists (and even if she does have that knowledge, if the evidence for the Gratuitous Premise is strong enough, it could take away her knowledge and thus the viability of the Skeptical Approach as a response for her to adopt). That's right: it will be a failure in the evidential sense. But if a person adopts the Skeptical Approach she could do so reasonably even without the requisite theistic knowledge: we saw this with the Confident and PHOG approaches. This would be a very watered down kind of success but that doesn't mean it's nothing at all.

Q79: Some people think the PHOGS comes down to just two ideas that have a decent chance of being true:

a. Premise (2b), in the argument for the Gratuitous Premise, is very likely true. When it comes to judging outweighing goods, we aren't stupid—especially given that we've worked incredibly hard on the judging for literally centuries. So, given that the other premises are just as or even more likely to be true, it's highly likely that the Gratuitous Premise is true. And there is simply no good reason for denying the Consequence Premise. So, it's highly likely that the conclusion of the two premises is true: there is no 4-Part God.

b. It is highly likely that the 4-Part God exists. Theists aren't stupid; some of the greatest geniuses of all time have been theists. In fact, *most* of them have been theists. Are we supposed to believe that their brains turn to mush when it comes to religion? Please. Moreover, lots of people insist that they have actually *perceived* God; and we have no independent reason to think they're insane. And it's highly likely that the Consequence Premise is true. Thus, it's highly likely that the Gratuitous Premise is false. And that means that it's highly likely that (2b) is false.

As you can see, (a) reasons from "we aren't stupid about (2b)" to the denial of 4-Part theism whereas (b) reasons from "we aren't stupid about 4-Part theism" to the denial of (2b). In that sense, the two positions are opposites. Is there a way of seeing who is right on this crucial matter? Defend your opinion.

Let me sum up the main results of this chapter:

i)   The Skeptical Approach advocate claims that there is good albeit not overwhelming evidence for the 4-Part God's existence. But the clear majority of philosophers who have looked at the alleged sources of *public* evidence for the 4-Part God's existence have concluded that the public evidence is quite weak. Whether private evidence is up to the task is another matter, one discussed in chapter 4 (e.g., in the Social Argument).

ii) She also says that we are so incredibly awful at spotting outweighing goods that we should have no confidence that "There are no gratuitous sufferings" is true—despite the fact that we are aware of trillions of cases of ghastly pain and suffering that we don't see any justification for even after looking for justifications for many centuries. Her assertion is not merely that we are less than perfect in spotting when an instance of suffering is outweighed by some good. Instead, her idea is that we are *incredibly awful* at it.

iii) There are various ways we could be "incredibly awful" at spotting outweighing goods. At one end of the spectrum we have missed just a very small number of goods that are doing a phenomenal amount of justifying; at the other end of the spectrum we have missed a great number of different goods that collectively do all that justifying. (Alternatively, we haven't missed out on goods but linkages.)

iv) There doesn't seem to be much significant non-theistic evidence that we are awful at judging when there is no outweighing good coupled with an instance of suffering. There are considerations that show we are prone to some significant errors, but that's about it.

v) If our overall evidence for the existence of the 4-Part God makes it roughly 50/50 that he exists, then we should probably not be confident that there are any gratuitous sufferings: we should withhold judgment on the Gratuitous Premise. But as mentioned in (i) most people who have looked at the alleged public evidence for the 4-Part God think that it isn't nearly that good.

vi) The advocates of the Confident and Skeptical responses to the Problem of Gratuitous Suffering typically converge in their views.

vii) Just like with the Confident and PHOG approaches, even if the evidence isn't on someone's side when she adopts the Skeptical Approach, her adoption could be reasonable in the watered down sense illustrated by the Fred and Dr. Quack story.

Q80: Construct a list of bullet points, each stating a part or crucial fact about the Skeptical Approach. Go through the entire chapter.

8

GOD IS NOT WHAT YOU THINK HE IS

What the Approach Says

Now we introduce the last remaining potentially rational and informative option for the theist, the **Non-4-Part Approach** to the Problem of Gratuitous Suffering:

> The theist accepts the conclusion that the 4-Part God doesn't exist but explains how that conclusion is consistent with her theistic beliefs. Here is what this theist might say: "I *agree* that there is no supremely morally good, knowledgeable, and powerful creator of the universe. That is, I agree that the conclusion of the two premises (Gratuitous and Consequence) is true. But my version of theism is consistent with that result, so I'm not troubled by it."

In one sense, there are exactly four ways to fill out the Non-4-Part Approach, corresponding to the four parts of the 4-Part conception of God: (i) deny that God is creator, (ii) deny that God is supremely morally good, (iii) deny that God is supremely knowing, and (iv) deny that God is supremely powerful. A theist who takes any of these approaches is free to just accept the Gratuitous Premise, the Consequence Premise, and their conclusion that the 4-Part God doesn't exist. But each of (i)–(iv) is still pretty open-ended: two theists could approach (ii), for instance, in very different ways. For example, as we will see below one person could say that God is just like us in being morally good sometimes and morally bad sometimes; while another person could say that God is not a moral agent at all and his actions simply don't have any moral status whatsoever (good, bad, or something in between). Both people are saying that God isn't supremely morally good but they are doing so in completely different ways.[42]

There's a mistake that's really easy to make when considering the Non-4-Part Approach. Some people are tempted to respond to the Problem of Gratuitous Suffering by just altering the 4-Part conception more or less at random, picking some modification to it just because the modification "seems a bit reasonable and can do the job of getting around the Problem of Gratuitous Suffering." That's a bad way to respond to the Problem of Gratuitous Suffering. You shouldn't say to yourself anything like "Well, heck: maybe God isn't as powerful as some theologians say. If he isn't, then the problem of suffering goes away. So, let's just say that his power is limited. That'll do the trick in dealing with the Problem of Gratuitous Suffering! Problem solved!" Instead, you need *real evidence* that the modification is actually correct, that the new conception of God is *accurate* in the sense that it fits the way God really is. There are many, many ways to alter the 4-Part conception so that the Problem of Gratuitous Suffering goes away; in order to have a *rational and informed* theistic response to the problem you have to have *good reasons* for thinking that your alterative conception of God is the *true* one—the one that correctly characterizes God. Of course, the advocate of the 4-Part conception also needs good reasons for thinking that her conception is the true one! It's not as though the 4-Part conception is obviously superior to every other conception of God.

How *should* one conceive of God anyway? I have found that people have remarkably diverse conceptions of God—usually more diverse than that portrayed by philosophers who write about God. Presumably, we should conceive of him based on our *evidence* for him. If our evidence comes solely from spiritual experience, for instance, then we should form our conception of him based on the details of those experiences. If our evidence primarily comes from a certain abstract philosophical argument, then we should let the details of that argument dictate our conception. If our evidence has multiple sources, then we will have to pool them and weigh their details to come up with our picture of what God is supposed to be. In any case, the key point is that we let the *evidence* do the talking when thinking of what God is supposed to be; we do *not* just stick with what we've been taught or what strikes us as a conception of God we can "live with" or are "comfortable with" (unless, of course, the evidence just happens to happily secure the conception we have been taught or find comfortable).

Q81: Most theists endorse, or are disposed to accept if they think about it, all four parts of the 4-Part conception. But why? Suppose you were convinced that something created and designed the universe. Since "design" implies "intelligence," you're saying that there is an intelligent creator of the universe. Why might you also think that the creator is supremely good, knowledgeable, or powerful? What evidence could you point to in order to justify your commitment to the latter three characteristics?

One final point before I get started. Strictly speaking, a Non-4-Part theist is simply someone who is a theist but who thinks at least one of the four parts of the 4-Part conception fails to be true of God (that's the definition of "Non-4-Part theist"). She need not accept the two premises, Consequence and Gratuitous. However, for the most part in the arguments that follow I assume I am dealing with a Non-4-Part theist *who accepts the truth of the Gratuitous Premise*. That is, most often I will restrict my attention to the Non-4-Part theist who says that the 4-Part conception is inaccurate *and* there are gratuitous sufferings (I don't make any assumption regarding what she might say about the Consequence Premise, but in virtually all real cases a theist accepts that premise). If she rejects the Gratuitous Premise, then of course her approach to the Problem of Gratuitous Suffering must be similar to those already considered above that reject that premise: Skeptical, PHOG, and (depending on the details) Confident.

Here I list and offer just a few comments on seven ways of filling out the Non-4-Part Approach.[43] While you read them please keep in mind the disclaimer that I've stated before: what appears in this book isn't meant to finally *settle* the matter but instead start you off on thinking about the options in a fruitful and advanced way.

Conception of God as Unconscious

God is **Unconscious**. The advocate of this conception rejects every part of the common idea that God loves, cares, desires, thinks, has plans, etc. Instead, he is akin to an unconscious "force." He is some kind of impersonal yet immeasurably powerful non-physical force or presence or whatever with no mind at all—or at least a mind extremely unlike ours in that it has nothing even remotely close to emotions, desires, thoughts, beliefs, or reasons.

For instance, someone might take the common saying "God is love" completely literally: God really is just a certain kind of emotion, one experienced by humans and some other animals. Well, then God is nothing like a person or other conscious entity. Under this idea God doesn't love us; God just is love itself. But this doesn't mean that love is really a conscious entity of some kind. Love is no more a conscious agent than fear or any other emotion.

If this conception of God is accurate, then it seems to follow that the various religions are virtually completely false, as they certainly take God to have either those psychological characteristics or other psychological characteristics importantly similar to those. In addition, if God fails to have those characteristics then there seems to be no reason at all to *worship* him: why should we worship a powerful yet unconscious something-or-other that creates the universe without anything like knowledge or awareness or thought? Sure, the unconscious God created the universe, but that hardly makes "it" worthy of worship. For instance, if it had created a universe of constant, unimaginably horrible suffering for all creatures, it would certainly not be worthy of worship! *All by itself*, being creator of the universe definitely does not mean being worthy of worship, trust, love, or devotion. This issue, captured with the question "Is this Non-4-Part God worthy of worship or love or devotion?", will show up several times below, as it is crucial. I call it the **Problem of Religious Attitudes**: if our overall evidence says that God doesn't fit the 4-Part conception, then we lose good reason to have most of the usual religious attitudes towards God, such as worship, trust, devotion, and love.

It's worth noting that the Unconscious God view isn't being criticized based on how it deals with allegedly gratuitous sufferings. If God is an unconscious force, as the view says, then it hardly seems reasonable to criticize such a God for allowing gratuitous sufferings: we can rightly criticize it about as much as we can rightly criticize gravity. *So the view does indeed get around the Problem of Gratuitous Suffering entirely.* The problem is the price of the solution: such a God does nothing whatsoever to deserve worship, love, adoration, respect, etc. The whole idea of salvation or anything similar goes out the window. And if that's right, then religion is a complete joke.

Conception of God as Morally Bad

> God is **Morally Bad**, at least in part. The advocate of this conception holds that God loves, cares, desires, has plans, and thinks (and therefore the various popular religions are right to that extent) but is morally flawed. Just like us, sometimes he allows bad things to happen to people even when he can easily prevent them and knows the bad things are going to happen and won't lead to any good. He is not significantly morally superior to us.

It won't do to just say that God is a *tiny bit* short of moral perfection, since that won't help the theist avoid the challenge of the Problem of Gratuitous Suffering. *That problem nowhere says God has to be completely morally perfect.* Even if he's a shade below perfection, it still seems that with his great knowledge and power he should have created a universe with no gratuitous suffering. If the advocate of the Morally Bad God proposal wants to admit that God exists but there are trillions of cases of gratuitous suffering, then she is going to have to say that God is *very* far from moral goodness.

However, if we accept the idea that God is morally bad a lot—if he *knowingly* allows many trillions of cases of horrific suffering that he *knows* lead to no good (here we're assuming not merely the truth of the Gratuitous Premise but the idea that there is a *great deal* of gratuitous suffering) and he *knows* he could prevent with his tremendous power and he knows make him morally bad—then why on earth would we feel any compulsion to worship or love him? He doesn't seem to be that great anymore, or deserving of our moral admiration, respect, or love. I may fear him and I might be tempted to go through the motions of worshiping him in order to gain his favor, but I'll know that he won't be worthy of it. In fact, he is a complete jerk and deserves our contempt, not worship or respect or love, even if we might try to fake worshipping him. Religious activity becomes, at best, something one fakes in hopes that the tyrant won't notice one's insincerity; religion as usually conceived is utterly destroyed. The Morally Bad God proposal gets around the Problem of Gratuitous Suffering but only by succumbing to the Problem of Religious Attitudes.

> Q82: If you're a theist who thinks the Old Testament is even roughly accurate in its portrayal of God, then doesn't it seem that God is definitely not supremely morally good? After all, he looks like he approves of things like murder, vengeance, revenge, and even genocide. How can a theist consistently uphold the accuracy of the Old Testament and the 4-Part conception?

Conception of God as Morally Unassessable

God is *Morally Unassessable*. The advocate of this conception holds that he loves, cares, desires, has plans, and thinks, but for some reason morality doesn't apply to him at all, so neither he nor his actions are morally good *or* bad *or* anything in between. He is no more a moral being than a rock or tree is—although the rock and tree aren't conscious and don't love us while God is conscious and does love us.

There are three problems with this proposal. The *first* is the difficulty in seeing how he could love and care for us; know so much about good, evil, salvation, and suffering; have lots of power over what happens to his creatures; and yet not be a moral agent. One would think that when a being with that awareness, emotion, knowledge, power, and ability *acts* (i.e., does something, makes something happen, allows something to happen), her actions are morally evaluable/assessable as morally good, bad, or somewhere in between. Suppose there is a large robot that has no more awareness than a calculator, and the robot blindly runs over people thereby injuring them. It avoids the charge of being morally bad because it has no idea what it's doing. The same result holds if the robot is programmed to help people: if the robot has no awareness whatsoever of what it is doing—no more awareness than a calculator—then it doesn't deserve moral praise anymore than your calculator deserves moral praise for giving you the right answer to "$78 \times 854 =?$". But unlike the robot God knows *exactly* what he's doing, knows *exactly* what is going to result, knows *exactly* what it means to the people or other creatures involved, and he loves and cares deeply about us. So how can what he does to us not be assessed on a moral scale?

One can try to justify the Morally Unassessable God view with arguments like "Well, God is the author, in some sense, of all morality; so morality doesn't apply to him." Let's assume for a moment that that's right: he sets the moral rules (somehow) and as a consequence he is somehow "prior to" those rules. So his nature, his inner essence, somehow lies beyond or prior to morality altogether. But it's not at all clear that this claim, even if true, shows that morality doesn't apply to God's *actions*, the things he does or knowingly allows to happen that affect his creatures. (Note that one can "do something" morally bad just by doing *nothing*, as when one sits idly by and watches something awful transpire without trying to stop it even though one knew it was going to happen and knew that one could easily prevent it without significant cost.) If I'm the guy who invents a game (e.g., baseball), then *when I play the game* the rules apply to me just as much as they apply to anyone else playing the game. Since God knows that he is acting in the universe—at the least, he knowingly creates it, knows what is going on in it, and has the ability to continually modify it—he knows he is "playing the game" of morally evaluable behavior, as he is acting in such a way that obviously affects us and other animals. By creating or sustaining our environment he is responsible for much of our lot. It simply doesn't matter whether God is beyond comprehension or the designer of morality or utterly unique or non-temporal or without parts or otherwise radically different from us and other creatures (as many theologians say he is): the fact that he has all that power and knows all about our pain and suffering means that his "actions" of creation (both in the beginning of the universe, if the universe had a beginning, and in the sustaining of the universe from moment to moment) have *moral weight*, they are the type of things that can be morally good or bad. Now if he didn't know what was going on, or never had anything to do with our creation, or was unable to do anything about anything, or was under some similar restriction (like the robot), then his actions might not be morally evaluable; but none of that is true under the proposal we're considering.

Notice that I have yet to assume that this allegedly morally unassessable Non-4-Part God allows gratuitous sufferings. All I've done is suggest that it is hard to see how the *actions* of a being with the knowledge, awareness, and power that the Morally Unassessable God view says God has, could fail to be morally assessable—even if his *inner nature* or being isn't morally assessable. It is hard to see how the Morally Unassessable conception is coherent, independently of any issue regarding suffering.

An advocate of the Morally Unassessable God view might reply to my criticism by noting that since God is the author of morality, he sets up the moral rules in such a way that all his actions are *guaranteed* to be morally good. This idea won't work as a reply to the criticism, for two reasons. First and most important, it is straightforwardly admitting that God's actions are *morally assessable*! So really, it is in direct contradiction to the *Morally Unassessable* view we are considering. Second, it is not very helpful, when discussing the Problem of Gratuitous Suffering, to just announce "Well, according to my theory everything God does is automatically morally acceptable." The person worried about the Problem of Gratuitous Suffering says that God's actions are morally assessable and yet God seems to be knowingly allowing us to suffer horribly even when he knows perfectly well that nothing good is connected to it and he could easily have made a universe without gratuitous suffering. To reply with "Well, there may or may not be such gratuitous sufferings, but in any case God's actions are always and necessarily morally perfect" is to *run away* from the problem altogether, not respond to it in a rational and informative manner. In fact, it looks like a retreat to the Confident Approach, as it is saying that since we *already know for sure* that God's actions are perfectly moral, we can conclude that either there are no gratuitous sufferings or that such sufferings exist but are somehow morally just fine.

So, in sum, the first problem with the Morally Unassessable God view is that the view seems false: if God has all the knowledge, awareness, power, and mental characteristics people say he has, including the power to prevent gratuitous sufferings, then contrary to the proposal his actions and inactions lie within the moral sphere even if his "inner nature" is somehow outside of the reach of morality. At least, I have yet to hear any reason to think that God can have all that knowledge, love, and awareness and yet his actions have no moral status at all. (This first criticism isn't saying that God is a *person*, whatever that comes to; it's just saying that his actions (and failures to act) are morally evaluable even if he or his nature isn't.)

Now here is the *second* problem with the Morally Unassessable God view: if morality doesn't apply at all to God *or* his actions—as the current proposal says—then it's not clear why we should *worship* or be otherwise devoted to him, and if that's the case then religion is a complete waste of time even if theism is true. Just because God is very impressive (e.g., the all knowing, all powerful creator) hardly means that we should worship him. I might admire his knowledge and power, and be thankful that he created the universe and me (provided I'm living a happy life), but admiration is very far from worship (e.g., I also admire the power of a hurricane and the knowledge had by an evil character, but this has squat to do with worship) and I would have thought that the only thing worth *worshipping* would have to be *morally* pretty awesome. This is the *Problem of Religious Attitudes* again: we escape the Problem of Gratuitous Suffering but the cost is too high.

But that's not a great criticism, at least by my lights. The *third* problem with the Morally Unassessable God view is a related but much better criticism: if morality doesn't apply to God's actions *and he allows gratuitous sufferings*, there is no good reason to worship or trust or be devoted to him (the italicized bit signifies the difference between the assumptions of the second and third criticisms). Of course, all the good things in the universe and in my life come from God (either directly or indirectly), as he's the creator, but that's clearly a bad reason to worship him: he also knew quite well that he was causing or permitting many trillions of cases of horrific suffering that have no outweighing good, as they were definitely not worth it. If he gets any credit for being the ultimate supplier of the good, then he also gets credit for being the ultimate supplier of the bad. It's also hard to see how he really loves or cares for his creatures when he often *knowingly allows them to suffer without reason* and his actions are neither good nor bad (again, we're assuming at this point that the advocate of the Morally Unassessable God view admits that there is gratuitous suffering). It may be perfectly reasonable for me to go through the motions of worshipping him, if I think one simply must do so in order to get some benefit, but such worship is a mere pale echo of genuine devotion. So when all is said and done *I don't really care* whether he or his actions are morally assessable: any creator that knowingly allows zillions of cases of gratuitous suffering is nowhere near worthy of worship or trust or love or devotion or anything similar, and it hardly matters whether he is morally assessable. Thus, even if the Morally Unassessable God view were *entirely right*, it still wouldn't address the concerns of the person worried about suffering.

One might reply that the basis for our worshipping God is that he has provided us with the path to salvation. That seems like a pretty praiseworthy thing for him to provide. But if the path is available through his means, then are we saying that he is *good* because of his providing the path? If so, then he (or his action) is morally assessable after all. So this line of reasoning can hardly support the advocate of the Morally Unassessable God view. Furthermore, he can hardly be congratulated or praised merely because he provides some great things for us: he is also knowingly providing us with tremendous suffering even though he could have arranged things so that that suffering either didn't happen or wasn't gratuitous.

In sum, the third problem with the Morally Unassessable God view is that *if it is correct* and, on top of that, there are gratuitous sufferings, then it's not clear that there is good reason to worship or trust or love or be devoted to God, and that undermines religion. Thus, if you endorse this particular Non-4-Part Approach, then it appears that you should renounce all traditional theistic religion even if you stick with theism.

Q83: As we just saw, one way of filling out the Non-4-Part Approach is to deny that God is supremely moral. There are two ways to do this: (a) he might be somewhat like us, in that he has good and evil in him; alternatively, (b) he has no good or evil whatsoever in him. If a person accepts either one of these ideas, the Problem of Gratuitous Suffering just plain evaporates: there is no problem for her anymore than there is for the atheist.

First, explain why the previous sentence is true.

Second, explain why even though the Problem of Gratuitous Suffering is not a problem for the advocates of either (a) or (b), a *new* problem comes in its wake, one that hinges on one's religious attitudes and behavior.

Conception of God as Epistemically Deficient

God is *Epistemically Deficient* (as mentioned previously, the term "epistemic" picks out a closely-knit set of concepts such as knowledge, evidence, reason, understanding, and wisdom). The advocate of this conception holds that God isn't supremely knowledgeable. As we have noted a couple times in this book, the notion of being "supremely" knowledgeable is pretty unclear. This theist says that God had no way of knowing that his creation would lead to gratuitous suffering. And he isn't aware of it *now* either, so he doesn't act to prevent it (or maybe he can't act in the universe, which looks like a severe limitation on his power). So no matter how one spells out "supremely knowledgeable," God fails to meet that condition.

  In order for God to be excused from gratuitous suffering it's not sufficient to say "Well, he lacks infallible, perfect knowledge of the future": if he has imperfect, probabilistic, fallible knowledge—or even mere reasonable true belief—of immediate future suffering, then his goodness and power has to make him arrange things so the suffering either doesn't happen or isn't gratuitous. In addition, if he is all powerful, then presumably he can use his power to know about his suffering creatures. So really, this proposal has to say that he knows next to nothing about us (so he's extremely far from omniscient) and doesn't have the power to know about us either (so he's far from omnipotent as well).

  It is indeed hard to see how God is supposed to know everything. In fact, it's awfully hard to see how he knows much of anything at all. Does God know what it's like to smell freshly ground coffee beans? I don't see how: he has no nose. Does he know how to throw a curve ball in baseball? How could he, given that he has no arms and has never even tried to throw a ball? It's easy to say in response "Well, God knows stuff through some other way," but saying it doesn't make it true or reasonable to believe. And here's another problem with the whole "omniscient" idea: does he know exactly what the future holds? Does he know what people with free will are going to do when they make free decisions? In fact, how does he know *anything at all* about the physical universe, the actions of humans or just gusts of wind, given that he lacks not just sense organs but a physical body? *Any* knowledge he has looks like a complete miracle to me. (Some Christians say that God was once a human being, Jesus, and he at least had the ability to know all those things; but it is not plain how that helps, as God is usually supposed to be supremely knowing well *before*, and independently of, Jesus' arrival on the scene.) On occasion, people will offer ways of thinking of God's knowledge that seem odd, at least to me. For instance, perhaps God "knows" all about the physical world to the extent that he knows what he is doing, and of course the thing he is doing is creating the world every single moment. To my mind, doing something and knowing perfectly the result of that action have little to do with each other; I just don't see any real connection. Sometimes it's said that God's "knowing" things is just identical to his creating them. Again, this just looks like a use of "knowing" that has almost no relation to how we ordinarily use "knowing." To that extent, I'm at least a little sympathetic with the Epistemically Deficient God proposal. I would prefer to stay away from the contemplation of such mysteries about God's epistemic characteristics, since I see no fruitful way to probe them: they all seem like miracles.

But note that it's not enough to say that God doesn't know everything: that alone doesn't get God off the hook. I don't know everything but I know quite well that lots of people are going to suffer terribly from hunger and war over the next year in many places around the world—in fact, with just a few minutes of research I could tell pretty accurately *which* particular groups of people will be starving. If I had a decent amount of power, then this *highly limited* knowledge would make me able to do something significant about that suffering—especially if I was *very* powerful. It is often said, in support of the Epistemically Deficient God idea, that if God lacks foreknowledge of the free choices of any beings with free will, then he would not know how the history of our world will unfold. But so what? My puny knowledge of the world allows me to know just fine about the vast sufferings of humans and non-humans—even suffering that hasn't happened yet. So the proposal really has to be that God doesn't merely fail to be all knowing but has *very little knowledge at all*—certainly a lot less than most of us have. Any adult human knows that there is going to be a colossal amount of apparently gratuitous suffering for the foreseeable future—and, again, it's awfully easy to pinpoint it (just look at countries where we know perfectly well that people are starving and will continue to starve). But then why worship or be at all devoted to the epistemically deficient God? If he doesn't know about the colossal amount of suffering going on all over our planet, then what makes you think he knows you even exist? The guy is utterly clueless about his own creation![44] Again, the price of solving the Problem of Gratuitous Suffering is falling to the Problem of Religious Attitudes.

Q84: Suppose the 4-Part God exists. How does he know that the New York Yankees were the best team in baseball in the 1950s? Did he read it in a book? Watch the games? Was he there on the playing field? Did he read the minds of people who read about it in the paper?

Now, there is a tricky issue here with all this worthy-of-worship talk that I've been engaging in: what is it about God or anything else that allegedly makes him or it worthy of worship or devotion? As we already saw above, it can't be the (alleged) fact that he is the creator: if he had created a universe of endless suffering he would hardly be worthy of worship or devotion. Same for the idea that he *commands* worship or other activities or attitudes from us: if he commanded it but created a universe of nothing but suffering even though he knew he could create a universe with no gratuitous suffering, then once again he would fail to be worthy of worship or any similar extremely positive attitude. Similarly for being supremely knowledgeable or powerful: an evil entity could have those qualities, for all we can tell. My best guess is that if God is worthy of worship or devotion, then it's either because of his moral perfection or because of something he's purposively done that is morally perfect and momentous. If God is truly morally perfect, then I suppose we should worship him, provided we know this fact about him and are capable of worship. But if God knowingly allows heaps of gratuitous suffering, then of course it is hard to see how he is morally perfect. Even if God has given us a path to salvation, and salvation is the highest conceivable good thing, if he has *also* knowingly allowed for trillions of cases of gratuitous suffering, then I don't see how he is worthy of worship, devotion, trust, or admiration. As I said, this whole "worthy of worship/devotion" issue is a tricky one, and I have to rest content with merely raising it to our attention.

Conception of God as Weak

> God is **Weak**. The advocate of this conception says that God is not supremely powerful no matter how you fill out that notion (although using the word "weak" here is a bit over the top since we are still saying he is the creator of the universe!). In fact, he did his absolute *best* when making this universe, and he could not have made it even one bit better. So he can be morally perfect while making a universe with lots of gratuitous suffering because he couldn't get rid of it, since he lacked the power.

There are some pretty simple questions that put into doubt the common assumption among philosophers that God is supposed to be "all powerful." As I said above, I don't see how God has the power to smell freshly ground coffee beans or throw a curve ball (philosophers have responses to these doubts, some of which are intelligent). But setting those questions aside is the right thing to do here, as they don't matter to the issues we have before us.

The Weak God proposal is similar to the proposal we encountered when evaluating the (fifth way of filling out the) Compatibilist Approach. In that chapter, one idea we looked at said that God does indeed have all possible power, and he used that power to the maximum, but even with such power our universe is the best that could be made by him. Now the theist who endorses the Weak God conception is saying that God does *not* have all possible power (so this is a different idea!) but even so he did his absolute best in creating the universe. What the two proposals have in common is the thought that God did his absolute best when creating this universe.

Unfortunately, I know of no good reason to think that the Weak God proposal has merit. Why think the actual universe is the very best God could manage with his limited power? How on earth would one have the slightest idea that this is true?

Here's one answer to that question: Satan. Suppose that Satan exists and through his enormous power is thwarting the all good God at every turn. God is doing his best in creating and maintaining the universe but he's not all powerful because there is another comparably powerful entity. We had a brief look at this idea when discussing the PHOG Approach in chapter 6.

The problem with this idea is whether to believe that there is this extremely powerful and evil being. Of course, there is significant evil in the world, but that doesn't mean that there is some incredibly powerful being behind it. Even so, some people think Satan really exists. For my part, I don't know of any evidence for Satan's existence (I think many theistic philosophers agree on this point). Moreover, most people who believe in Satan also think that God is much more powerful and must have some good reason for allowing Satan to do incredible harm. These people are often PHOG Approach advocates: God allows Satan to have free will, and Satan uses it to ruin things. As we saw in chapter 6, the problem with this alleged PHOG is pretty obvious: the value of Satan's free will hardly seems high enough to justify untold billions of cases of suffering; so it's hardly clear that the Strength Requirement is met. Moreover, it's not clear that the Existence Requirement is met, as we have little evidence that (a) Satan exists, (b) Satan has free will, and (c) Satan's misuse of his free will is generating most apparently gratuitous suffering. (It doesn't help to say that God allows Satan to inflict suffering so that we can be driven to God; we already dealt with various "communion with God" ideas in the PHOG chapter.) Many of us heard all or some of these things about Satan as children when learning about our religion, but that hardly means they're true! If we just accepted what we were told as children, we sure wouldn't be reading a book like this now, would we?

Is there another way to reasonably embrace the Weak God proposal? Well, here is one way: *if* you were already convinced that there were gratuitous sufferings, *and* that God fit the "morally perfect," "knows everything," and "creator" parts of the 4-Part conception, *and* you were convinced of the Consequence Premise, *then* you would be thinking that God fits three out of the four parts of the 4-Part conception and if he had also fit the last part then there would have to be no gratuitous suffering, which you take to be false. So, it will be quite logical for you to conclude that he must not fit the "all powerful" idea.

This is an entirely reasonable inference to make for those who meet the three conditions described above:

- You are convinced that God exists and fits the "morally perfect," "knows everything," and "creator" parts of the 4-Part conception, but you are not convinced of the "all powerful" part.
- You are convinced of the truth of the Consequence Premise, which says that if God fits the 4-Part conception then there is no gratuitous suffering.
- But you are also convinced that there are gratuitous sufferings.

If that's you, then at this point you haven't the slightest idea *how* it is that God's power limited him in creating a universe only as good as ours, but your beliefs have forced you to such a conclusion. But now you have some tough questions to answer.

First, why are you convinced of "all knowing" and "morally perfect" but not "all powerful"? On what grounds are you confident with "all knowing" but are doubtful about "all powerful"? I don't know how someone could answer that question in a plausible way backed up by evidence (that was the problem with the Satan idea).

Second, the Weak God proposal inherits a version of the primary problem with the Confident Approach: we need to presuppose that you are justifiably supremely confident in the *3-Part* God.

Third, how is God's power limited? How did it come to be that his power is limited at all? Imagine that the universe has a beginning in time. God is about to make the beginning of the universe. What could possibly be limiting him? What could be holding him back from doing whatever is possible? When we think of things with limited power we imagine physical beings who are limited by the limitations of their bodies or minds. But none of that applies to God, who has no body and whose mental capacity has no limit. It is hard to imagine how his power could be limited in any way at all. Indeed, some people think that all God has to do to create something is to *will* that it exist. Of course, it's also hard to see how he could have *any* power at all given that he doesn't have a body; any creative activity at all looks like a complete miracle. But if you're willing to grant him the miracle of having *some* creative power, then given that he is the non-physical creator of the universe it is hard to see how there is anything to stop him from having *unlimited* creative power (with the exception that he can't do anything that's logically impossible, such as make twice two equal to seven). You might object: but how could God have the power to know all about our future if we have free will? Good question! But that just shows, once again, how utterly mysterious it is that God could know anything at all about the physical world given that he has no sense organs and isn't physical at all.

In any case, most of the theists I know find it vaguely repugnant to think of God *striving*, doing his damndest when creating the universe. We get a picture in our minds of God sweating and huffing and puffing while he creates. Presumably, such a picture is ridiculously inaccurate, since God has no body at all. But the idea that this was the very best God could do strikes most philosophical theists as alien to their conception of God.

However, this much can be said for the Weak God proposal: if we had good overall evidence that God existed and fit that conception, then we would have solutions to both the Problem of Gratuitous Suffering *and* the Problem of Religious Attitudes, at least in part. After all, it still seems reasonable to worship and love a being that created the universe, knows everything, and is morally perfect. But given that he can't *do* much of anything about suffering, he can't be *trusted* about much of anything that happens in the physical universe. And there is still the mystery of how he could be powerful enough to create the universe but unable to do anything about suffering.

Q85: At least some versions of the Non-4-Part approach seem to have a huge advantage over the 4-Part approaches: the latter have to come up with good evidence that something fits the entire 4-Part conception, while the former have to come up with good evidence that something fits less than the 4-Part conception. Explain why this is true (e.g., you could talk about the Cosmological, Fine-Tuning, and Social arguments).

Conception of God as Non-Individual

God is **Non-Individual**, as he is not an individual being at all. Instead, God is the "ground of being." Alternatively, God is not the "ground of being" but being itself: God is pure existence. Either way, God has none of the qualities mentioned in the 4–Part conception, as only an individual thing could have those qualities.

If this is meant as poetry or something else inspirational, then I suppose it might be coherent, valuable, insightful, and even profound for all I know. But if it's meant literally, then I think it's just plain incoherent. I understand that God might be unique in the sense that he fails to fall into any standard category and in that sense then he fails to be an individual like the rest of us. I fall into many categories: conscious being, living being, mammal, human, male, middle aged, philosopher, father, and *Harry Potter* fan. Every reader of this book will also fall into the first four categories. Even something abstract like a number falls into lots of categories: the number 28 falls into the categories whole number, composite number, even number, divisible by 7, and perfect number (i.e., it is equal to the sum of its divisors). Perhaps God is so mysterious that he doesn't fall into any substantive category we can think of, so strictly speaking he's not the creator, a person, good, powerful, knowledgeable, etc. By these lights, the 4–Part conception is way off.

Nevertheless, I can think of one category he has to fall into in order to exist at all: individual thing. Even something like a principle or idea is an individual thing (an individual principle, an individual idea). So I don't see how the Non-Individual proposal is supposed to be plausible. And even if I'm wrong and God somehow exists but not as an individual thing with any of the four qualities mentioned in the 4–Part conception, then God is so utterly mysterious that I don't see any reason to love, trust, respect, or worship him. Practicing religion looks ridiculous.

The next idea might be an improvement.

Conception of God Involving Analogy

> God has qualities such as goodness, power, and knowledge only *analogically*, not literally. Although he is not knowledgeable, literally speaking, he has something analogous to knowledge; the same holds for other central qualities of God. Taken literally, the 4-Part God doesn't exist; taken analogically, the 4-Part God does exist.

For centuries many astute theologians and philosophers have claimed that our categories such as knowledge, power, love, and goodness don't really apply to God in a literal fashion.[45] Instead, they say, God's knowledge is merely *analogous* to ordinary instances of knowledge. A key question here is this: how similar is God's power (or knowledge, or goodness, or love, or whatever) to ordinary power (knowledge, goodness, love, etc.)? For instance, if you are convinced that there are gratuitous sufferings, and you're also convinced that if God is *awfully close to being* literally supremely morally good, powerful, and knowledgeable, then there would be no gratuitous suffering, then you will have to conclude that God, if he exists, is a *huge distance* from supremely good, powerful, and knowledgeable. But then we have our familiar problem from this chapter: if God's qualities are so different from ours, if they are only very distantly analogous to knowledge, power, or goodness, then although we have avoided the problems associated with the 4-Part conception, have we not lost any basis for loving, trusting, adoring, respecting, or worshipping him? You might say "But he loves us," but that's true of your mom too, and you don't worship her (I hope). Furthermore, if the notions of knowledge, power, and goodness that apply to God are so different from the notions that apply to us, then why think that his love is anything similar to the love we are accustomed to? If his knowledge is only distantly analogous, then won't his love be too? What basis is there for loving or trusting or worshipping something whose characteristics are only very faintly related to goodness, love, knowledge, etc.?

In short, there are two ways to go with the Analogy proposal and neither looks like it solves our worries about suffering adequately:

- God's knowledge, goodness, and power are only distantly related to human knowledge, goodness, and power; so the 4-Part conception is a gross exaggeration at best. But then what is it about God that makes him worthy of worship or admiration or respect or love? The Problem of Gratuitous Suffering is solved but the Problem of Religious Attitudes is not.
- God's knowledge, goodness, and power are very closely related to human knowledge, goodness, and power; so the 4-Part conception is almost literally true. But if his knowledge, goodness, and power aren't mysterious because they are closely analogous to ours, then it remains a mystery how he can allow

gratuitous suffering. In effect, by keeping close to the 4–Part conception the Problem of Gratuitous Suffering is not avoided.

Q86: There are several ways of filling out the Non-4-Part Approach. Some of them easily handle the Problem of Gratuitous Suffering. However, they subsequently encounter a problem having to do with our attitudes towards God. Explain what the problem is *and* how it differs in strength for different ways of filling out the Non-4-Part Approach.

9

WARRANTED AND UNWARRANTED CONCLUSIONS

We have reached the end of our meditations on suffering. I started this book with a very simple two-premise argument which served as our focus:

1. Consequence Premise: if the universe has been created by a supremely morally good, knowledgeable, and powerful being, then that being arranged things so that there is no gratuitous suffering.
2. Gratuitous Premise: but there is gratuitous suffering.
3. Thus, the 4-Part God doesn't exist.

But that was just a summary of the argument. The full "official" argument consists of seven premises, the premises we encountered in the chapters 5 and 7 arguments for the Consequence Premise and Gratuitous Premise (or eight premises, if you count separately (2a) and (2b) from the argument for the Gratuitous Premise).

I don't think we can be confident that all those premises are true; we don't have enough evidence for them (especially the pivotal premise (2b)). But that doesn't mean we have failed to make any important philosophical discoveries. Here are some big-picture conclusions that I think are warranted by the arguments in this book (some of these come from the summaries at the ends of chapters 4, 5, and 7).

A. ***Compatibilist Approach:*** There isn't much to say on behalf of the Compatibilist Approach. The theist should probably look elsewhere for an adequate response to the Problem of Gratuitous Suffering.
B. ***Confident Approach:*** If a person already *knows for certain* (and not merely feels abundantly confident, which is a merely subjective matter) that the

4-Part God exists, then she can rationally if not informatively deduce that one of the two premises simply must be false even if she has no idea which is false. Thus, the Confident Approach could succeed, *provided* the initial impressive theistic knowledge is already securely present. But such certain knowledge is probably rare if it exists at all, so this won't help most people respond to the Problem of Gratuitous Suffering. If a person *thinks* she knows for sure that the 4-Part God exists, but she actually has no such knowledge, then she won't have evidence on her side when she concludes that at least one of the premises is false. So it looks as though the approach is practically irrelevant (in the goal of generating an evidentially rational response to the problem that applies to *many* theists) even if it succeeds in a select few cases.

C. **PHOG Approach:** If a person already has detailed and impressive knowledge of God *and other crucial divine matters*, then she may have a rational and informative response to the Problem of Gratuitous Suffering along the lines of the PHOG Approach. She could use her detailed knowledge of the afterlife or the state of communion with God or original sin to pull off the PHOG Approach, thereby proving, at least to herself and other similarly informed individuals, that her overall evidence goes solidly against the Gratuitous Premise. Thus, the PHOG Approach could succeed, *provided* the initial detailed theistic knowledge is already securely present. However, since the detailed knowledge would have to be incredible, as it would require knowledge of all sorts of linking facts and good–suffering strength comparisons that just don't end up in any standard theistic doctrines, this response to the Problem of Gratuitous Suffering is probably available to *at most* a very tiny fraction of people. To that extent it is practically irrelevant (in the goal of generating an evidentially rational response to the problem) even if it succeeds once in a while. Furthermore, there are loads of good reasons to doubt that much of that detailed theistic "knowledge" is even true.

D. **Skeptical Approach I:** If a person already had secure knowledge of the 4-Part God's existence, then she could take her secure belief in the Consequence Premise and competently deduce that the Gratuitous Premise is false; she could also infer from her secure belief that we have failed to find the outweighing goods (so now she is relying on knowledge of the failure of the PHOG Approach) that we are quite untrustworthy when attempting to find outweighing goods. Thus, a certain way of filling out the Skeptical Approach could succeed, *provided* the initial theistic knowledge is already present and we knew of the failure of the PHOG Approach. This option is not much different from (B) above (which is why I said the Confident and Skeptical Approaches often end up converging).

E. **Skeptical Approach II:** The ambitious way of filling out the approach attempts to find *theistically neutral* evidence that shows that we are exceedingly untrustworthy when making judgments about outweighing goods. Unfortunately, there appears to be little such evidence.

F. **Skeptical Approach III:** If the overall evidence one has concerning the 4-Part God's existence is good enough that the odds are roughly 50/50 he exists, then one could use one's knowledge of the Consequence Premise to justifiably infer that for all we know we are untrustworthy in making judgments about outweighing goods, so we should no longer be confident in the Gratuitous Premise. But it is very controversial that the overall evidence typical people have is so favorable to theism.

G. If we know the Consequence Premise is true, and our reasons for the Gratuitous Premise—in particular, the evidence for the crucial premise (2b)—are strong enough, then they may be stronger than the reasons to believe that the 4-Part God exists. And if that's the way things are, then the previous three options will be rational responses for even fewer people than indicated above.

H. **Non-4-Part Approach:** When it comes to the Non-4-Part Approach we have a mixed bag. Some of the various proposals under that banner might succeed in rationally and informatively responding to the Problem of Gratuitous Suffering, but the costs will strike many as prohibitive, as they leave us with little or no basis for religious practice and attitudes.

I. In (A)–(H) I was looking at the possibility of someone having good overall *evidence* in her adoption of various theistic responses to the Problem of Gratuitous Suffering. The doubts regarding those possibilities leave open the possibility that a person could be reasonable in a non-evidential sense in adopting those responses (as in the Fred–Dr. Quack story).

What would be ideal in a theistic response to the outrage of suffering would be this: a response that doesn't presuppose secure knowledge in theism *and* doesn't require us to abandon religion. (It would be even better if it defused the worry in (G) and it were informative in the sense of giving us at least a rough idea of the goods that outweigh suffering, but that's asking for a great deal.) In this book I have argued that if we base our view on the evidence currently available to us, then we have no such response. So maybe the ideal response is unavailable (life is rarely ideal). Moreover, if we want a response that is open to a significant number of people, then the PHOG Approach is most likely ruled out; if we want a response that doesn't rule out religious practices and attitudes, then most versions of the Non-4-Part Approach are probably ruled out. That would leave us with the Confident and Skeptical responses, but they face two main hurdles: *if only a few people have certain knowledge in the 4-Part God's existence,* then it looks as though those responses won't be open to a significant number of people; *if the evidence for (2b) is pretty strong,* then even if people knew that the 4-Part God exists, if they also digested the evidence for (2b) then they could lose their knowledge of God as well as a rational response to the Problem of Gratuitous Suffering.

Q87: This book investigates the question of how the theist might attempt to respond to the Problem of Gratuitous Suffering in a *reasonable and informative manner*. But aren't there alternatives? Suppose that you're a theist—not necessarily a 4-Part theist but definitely a theist. Suppose further that you are well aware of the Problem of Gratuitous Suffering (although you haven't read a whole book on it). Is there anything terribly wrong with just throwing up one's hands and admitting that one has no real idea what to say about the Problem of Gratuitous Suffering—even though one sticks to one's theism? Tell us what, if anything, is wrong with doing so. Try and think of real people you know who do just this (there are millions of them; surely you know some personally.)

Does any of this mean we should become atheists or agnostics, or reject the idea that we should worship or love God, or adopt some other anti-religious conclusion?

Surprisingly, no. Even if (A)–(I) were completely true, it would not mean that there are no rational and informative theistic responses; that should be clear from the conclusions in (A)–(I) themselves (e.g., the Non-4-Part Approach often solves the Problem of Gratuitous Suffering even if it falls prey to the Problem of Religious Attitudes). In addition, if we drop the "informative" condition on theistic responses to the Problem of Gratuitous Suffering, then as we have noted a few times in this book the Confident and Skeptical responses might be rational without being informative. Finally, notice that the conclusions are peppered with phrases such as "most likely" and "probably." They are meant to remind us that the arguments were not conclusive. Whether the defects I have found in the five theistic approaches to the Problem of Gratuitous Suffering can be repaired or otherwise dealt with in such a way that any of the theistic responses is reasonably seen to be successful is a matter for investigation beyond the arguments of this book. By saying that (A)–(I) are "conclusions" all I really mean is that they are claims in the direction suggested by the arguments in this book: it doesn't mean that the arguments have firmly established those theses with the "probably" and "most likely" clauses removed. Philosophy is hard, even if rewarding, and it's usually difficult, to put it mildly, to establish any profound conclusion once and for all. I view the progress that this book makes in this way: I identified most (but not all) of the main obstacles standing in the way of each potentially reasonable and informative theistic approach to the Problem of Gratuitous Suffering, and then the next moves (which aren't in my book) are those of the advocates of those approaches. They have to respond to my objections, showing how each one can be answered. The dialogue continues beyond the considerations of this book: *there is no knockdown argument here that theism is incorrect or otherwise undermined.*

This little book is a good beginning; there are plenty of other works on the relation of God to suffering that you could fruitfully explore. All we have shown here is that the Problem of Gratuitous Suffering is a formidable one for the theist who aims to provide a rational and informative response to it—even if that theist is super smart.

I also think that if you *admit* to yourself that you cannot think of any satisfactory theistic response to the Problem of Gratuitous Suffering (or the combination of that problem and the Problem of Religious Attitudes), even after working on it for awhile—and I think that is the position most intelligent, self-aware, reflective theists find themselves in—then it's highly likely (although not guaranteed) that you should be *wary* in your theism. You should think "Wait a minute; there is a real, serious chance that I'm wrong about God really existing—or at least fitting the 4-Part conception." You should probably *significantly lower your confidence* in theism even if you need not lower it so much that you entirely give up being a theist. But what does that mean?

I think that the reflective theist who lives her life far from the stratosphere of philosophical thought approaches the problem of suffering from a perspective quite different from that of the philosophy professor—yet it's philosophical and profound. She reflects on the nature of suffering. She sees the pain, cruelty, and injustice in our world. As a decent, thinking person she finds this deeply troubling. Then she realizes that she has no real idea why all this suffering happens. She can't console herself with happy, hopeful thoughts like "Well, God is mysterious" or "God must have some master plan that makes it all fit together" or "Well, there must be some explanation of it." She knows that other people say these things and then move on with their lives, but she realizes that at the end of the day she has no real reason to rely on such thoughts. She looks askance at the smiling, happy, confident members of her religious organization and says to herself "*I can't be like that.*"

It's not clear to me what this conclusion amounts to, although I think it's a wise conclusion to draw. She is now distrustful of theism. She need not conclude that God doesn't exist, or that God isn't good, or that God isn't powerful or loving or wise. For all she knows, he could be all those things even with all that horrific suffering. Neither will she necessarily think that she should abandon all religion, or even that she should give up worshipping God. But *if* she is going to continue with those beliefs and way of life, then she knows it's going to have to be subtly different all the way through, in every detail. She has to give up being a *confident* theist, like the smiling, happy friends of hers in her house of worship. Perhaps this is the argument that best captures what reflective non-philosophical theists justifiably experience when ruminating over the existence of horrific suffering:

1. There is a great deal of truly horrific suffering.
2. As far as I can tell, even with the help of others, a frighteningly large portion of that suffering happens without reason. I can no longer pacify myself with comforting thoughts such as "Well, God must have his reasons."
3. Thus, I just can't be a confident theist anymore.

This strikes me as a good argument: the premises are true (i.e., the second one is true for many of us while the first is just plain obviously true), and they seem to offer some serious support for the conclusion. The latter is vague, to be sure, but I hope it's not so much as to be useless.

On that matter, this endorsement of what might be called *Wary Theism* has practical consequences. I'll point out just one.

Most theists put a lot of stock in certain religious texts. Jews and Christians tend to think the Bible, or at least large portions of it, is inspired by God and when correctly interpreted is infallible. Naturally, there is quite a bit of disagreement on how to interpret it, but most Christians and Jews think that large portions if not all of the Bible are flawless properly understood. People of other faiths have analogous beliefs regarding other religious texts.

But what we have learned here should lead us to reject this optimism regarding the Bible's accuracy—or the accuracy of any other religious text whose central claims aren't backed up by a decent amount of theism-neutral evidence.[46] If you are a Wary theist, you know that if God exists then he has seen fit to permit trillions of cases of horrific suffering, most of it seemingly senseless even though people have fought extremely hard to discover outweighing goods. Now here is the key point: if God is willing to screw us over when it comes to pain and suffering, then why think he won't do the same with religious texts? If you were tempted to endorse the thought that goes "God would not permit our central religious text to be inaccurate, as that would just ruin religion and surely God would not want that," think about the analogous idea that "God would not permit trillions of people and animals to suffer horribly; surely he would not want that." This is not to suggest that we should think the Bible or other religious texts are inaccurate. Instead, the idea is that we should no longer have much if any confidence that they are accurate (absent straightforward theism-neutral evidence in favor of certain central claims of those texts). One thing we learn from the Problem of Gratuitous Suffering is that *God, if he exists, has created a world that in some tremendously important respects is utterly unlike what we would expect a loving, knowledgeable, good, and powerful being to make.* When put to heart, that should make us wary of theistic claims and practices in general.[47]

NOTES

1. "The Inductive Argument from Evil and the Human Cognitive Condition," in James Tomberlin (ed.), *Philosophical Perspectives, 5: Philosophy of Religion* (Atascadero, CA: Ridgeview Publishing Press, 1991).
2. The issue isn't whether Alston agreed with the sentence as misquoted by Keller. He very well might have. In fact, Alston thought (at one time anyway) that upon extended expert reflection (that Alston helpfully tried to supply us with) one can see that the inductive argument is not significantly better than the logical argument— although I'm sure that Alston knew very well that most philosophers who have investigated the matter strongly disagree with him there even though they agree with him regarding the status of the logical argument. We are in the midst of seeing that the issue here is twofold: Keller got the quote wrong in a telling way, and (more seriously) the explanation of the misquote reveals that Keller is either untrustworthy or incompetent (or both) regarding the topic.
3. Richard Dawkins, *The God Delusion*, London: Bantam Press, 2006, 78.
4. I know this from observation: observation of scientists trying to do philosophy. But I also know it from experience: before earning my PhD in philosophy I acquired a BS and an MA in physics.
5. The name "Consequence Premise" was chosen because it is a premise that draws out an alleged *consequence* of the 4-Part God's existence (where "4-Part" will be defined in the text above): the consequence that there is no gratuitous suffering.
6. There are other philosophical problems that fall under the banner "problem of evil," although they aren't nearly as close to real-world concerns as the Problem of Gratuitous Suffering is. Near the end of this chapter I will articulate the two most familiar ones and explain how they are different from and less worrisome than the one this book is about.
7. In addition to the one discussed in the text above, the speech stands as an *accusation of pigheadedness* on the part of the person who thinks all suffering has outweighing goods. The idea is that no matter what happened (on Earth, in the afterlife) these deniers of gratuitous suffering would never give up their view, even if the evidence of gratuitousness just kept on piling up forever. No doubt, this is true of *some* deniers of gratuitous suffering—every large group of people has members with significant cognitive weaknesses—but I doubt whether it applies to all of them. In this book

I don't comment on the *motives* of theists; instead, I evaluate their *reasons* behind their responses to the Problem of Gratuitous Suffering.

8. Just because it's a "simpler" challenge doesn't mean it's simple. For one thing, the whole notion of an instance of suffering being "coupled with" a good can be a very tricky affair, one that we will not probe in depth in this book.

9. To say that it's an "accurate" conception of God is *not* to say that the conception describes *all* the important aspects of God. All it means is that everything the conception attributes to God is correct; so it can leave things out too.

10. Some philosophers claim that there is *no reason at all* for thinking there are gratuitous sufferings. (That probably sounds strange to you.) However, in my judgment they are employing an alternative notion of reason. In the sense of "reason" I am using, they would be happy to admit that there is plenty of reason to accept both premises. I discuss this issue a bit more near the end of chapter 4.

11. There are several versions of "the" Logical Problem of Suffering, and they can be quite different (e.g., usually the argument attempts to derive a contradiction from the claim "Suffering and the 4-Part God exist"). In the text above I articulate just one of them, and I do so with minimal accuracy. The term "logical" in the title is a little misleading, but we need not explore why.

12. You might object: infinity (symbolized with "∞") is a number, and no number is greater than it; so there is a single greatest number. Ahh, but did you know that there are actually *infinitely many* infinite numbers? Weird but true! There is a proof, called "Cantor's Diagonal Proof," that proves this. Most philosophers, and virtually all mathematicians, should be able to explain it to you even if you have very little background in mathematics (e.g., you don't need to know calculus, or geometry, or algebra, or anything like that in order to understand the proof). Aside from that proof, some philosophers (such as myself) doubt that infinite "numbers" are actually numbers at all, even though they are mathematical objects of a different kind and Cantor's proof demonstrates their infinite multiplicity.

13. If in the universe there is suffering but never any gratuitous suffering, then the badness of each bit of suffering is outweighed by the goodness of some good that is linked with that instance of suffering. One might think that means that the *total* amount of goodness in the whole universe is greater than the total amount of badness: for every bit of suffering, there is a *greater* good, so the sum of the goodness of the goods has to be greater than the sum of the badness of the sufferings. (This isn't clear though: perhaps one bit of goodness can outweigh two independent sufferings even though the sum of the badness of the sufferings is greater than the goodness of the good. Whether this makes sense depends on how we weigh goodness and badness and how we understand the links between them, which I'm not going to discuss in any precise way here but is relevant when assessing the Strength Requirement of chapter 6; in a more sophisticated treatment of the Problem of Gratuitous Suffering these intricacies would have to be addressed.) But presumably there are many possible universes God could have made that fit that description (the description: no gratuitous sufferings plus more good than evil), some better than others. So even if he creates a universe that has no gratuitous sufferings (in which case the Problem of Gratuitous Suffering goes away), that doesn't mean he has created the best universe he could (which would make the Problem of the Inferior Universe go away). Hence, the Problem of Gratuitous Suffering is different from the Problem of the Inferior Universe. I should remind you, however, that other contemporary philosophers offer definitions of "gratuitous suffering" different from mine that make the two problems of evil much more closely related. I think this is unfortunate, as I hold that there are two interesting philosophical problems of evil (setting aside the Logical one), with importantly different virtues and vices, and we should keep them distinct.

14. Keep in mind what I mean by "informative": the response has to tell us which premise it thinks is false and it has to offer an explanation of why it is false. Later, in chapter 7, we will see how a theistic response might be less informative than this but not utterly uninformative.

15. Did you see the funny bit there? The PHOG advocate is saying that the outweighing goods are hard to discover—as if they are wrapped in a deep fog.

16. For the many notions of faith see John Bishop, "Faith," *The Stanford Encyclopedia of Philosophy (Fall 2010 Edition)*, Edward N. Zalta (ed.) http://plato.stanford.edu/archives/fall2010/entries/faith/.

17. Suppose that there really are people who know for certain that God exists and fits the 4-Part conception—and they know this *on their own*, either through some fancy piece of reasoning, from either philosophy or science, or through some special personal experience (and never mind how this could happen). Suppose further that this person is your mom. And your mom assures you that God exists and fits the 4-Part conception (although of course she doesn't use the term "4-Part conception," which is an invention of this book). So now you believe in the 4-Part God because a *legitimate* expert informed you that the 4-Part God exists. If those are the circumstances of your life, wouldn't you be completely reasonable in responding to the Problem of Gratuitous Suffering by adopting the Confident Approach—as long as you had no good reason to doubt her? That's a good question, but I won't explore it in this book since it's premised on an idea I criticize: the idea that your mom has that super-duper knowledge.

18. More accurately, the approach can be and often is uninformative in three respects: first, it need not tell us which of the two premises is false; second, the advocate of the approach might not have anything impressive to say in defense of her certainty of the 4-Part God's existence (despite *knowing* that the 4-Part God exists); and third, if it says the Gratuitous Premise is probably the false one, it may not say anything regarding the goods that outweigh all instances of suffering.

19. There are several other famous arguments for God's existence, but in the interests of brevity I will treat just the three articulated above. For instance, some people think that miracles happen and make the existence of God highly likely. Like most philosophers, I think the evidence for miracles is shabby. I realize that some people *say*, in written and oral forms, that they have witnessed such-and-such miracle, but without a great deal of independent evidence there is little reason to believe them even when it's plain that they are being perfectly sincere, honest, and intelligent (other times it's clear that the alleged "miracle" definitely did happen, but there is little reason for thinking that it indicates anything supernatural). I can confidently say that philosophers generally think the arguments for God's existence that I'm leaving out of this book aren't any better than the ones I'm including.

20. Notice that the conclusion is modest in the sense that it doesn't say anything as strong as "God exists" or even "It is highly likely that God exists." I will comment on this feature later.

21. Here I take some liberties in omitting all sorts of technical qualifications that won't matter to our investigation.

22. One reason I can't fully explain why is that "the" Fine-Tuning Argument actually comes in a variety of different forms, and it would take a lot of words and complex argumentation to go over them all in a fully responsible manner.

23. I am here ignoring dark matter and energy, which are called "dark" because so little is known about them.

24. As we'll see below, some physicists insist that the Big Bang is not an "event," considered as something that happens at a certain time.

25. Years earlier Einstein came up with the "Special Theory of Relativity." GTR is a significant improvement on it.

26. This premise is not saying that there was a beginning but infinitely many years have passed since then. Instead, it's saying that there was no beginning at all and for any finite number of years you can imagine, the universe's past is older than that.

27. The next few paragraphs are based on parts of my essay "Spirituality, Expertise, and Philosophers," in Jon Kvanvig (ed.) *Oxford Studies in Philosophy of Religion*, v. 1, Oxford: Oxford University Press 2008, 44–81.

28. The qualifier "serious" is crucial. As I noted earlier in this chapter, there is no "serious" scientific controversy regarding the very high evidential status of the theory of evolution, but this doesn't mean that you can't find people who dispute that theory. And a final remark on the Social Argument: what do you think of its chances to show that the thing being perceived (in meditation) is the creator of the universe, or all powerful, or all knowing, or perfectly morally good? Could a perception of God show the perceiver any of those (alleged) facts? Usually, the "spiritual experience" part of the Social Argument is not intended to justify those ideas, which are supposed to get their support from other sources of evidence.

29. Let me engage your imagination in order to clarify the key premises. First, imagine that there are exactly 1000 possible universes that God has the ability to make real. There are probably infinitely many, but to illustrate my points it's fine to use a finite number we have a good handle on, such as 1000. God is choosing which of the possible universes to make; he's choosing which one to make real. Imagine that the possible universes are like little marbles on a table and God is choosing which of them to make real. Here is a thought: about 100 of the possible universes have consciousness, love, and happiness in them while the other 900 fail to have all three of those. That is, in 100 of those universes there would be beings who are conscious and who sometimes experience love and happiness. Now, in some of those 100 universes there are beings who experience gratuitous suffering, but in some others the beings never experience any gratuitous suffering even if they experience some non-gratuitous suffering. Let's suppose that there are 20 universes in which conscious beings experience love and happiness but no gratuitous suffering. So, we are saying that it's possible for God to make a universe with consciousness, love, happiness but without gratuitous suffering—that's exactly what premise (b) is saying. 80 of the universes are consciousness-love-happiness-gratuitous-suffering universes while 20 of the universes are consciousness-love-happiness-no-gratuitous-suffering universes.

    Now suppose that God has decided to make a universe with consciousness, love, and happiness. That is, he has decided to choose among the 100 universes mentioned above. Thus, he has set aside 900 of the possible universes. Which one of the 100 will he choose? Will he choose one from the group of 80 or one from the group of 20?

    Premise (d) says that since God is supremely good and knowledgeable, he will choose one of the 20 universes with no gratuitous suffering. That is, since he knows exactly what he is doing, and he's perfectly good, he won't choose one of the 80 consciousness-love-happiness-gratuitous-suffering universes that he can make over one of the 20 consciousness-love-happiness-no-gratuitous-suffering universes that he can make. He will prefer to make one of the 20, since they don't have gratuitous suffering while the 80 do.

    So there were two key claims: 4-Part God has the ability to make at least some universes with consciousness-love-happiness-no gratuitous suffering; and the 4-Part God will not choose one of the consciousness-love-happiness-gratuitous-suffering universes over the consciousness-love-happiness-no-gratuitous-suffering universes that he can make. Premise (b) is the first claim; premise (d) is the second claim.

30. As we will see below, the advocate of the PHOG Approach occasionally claims that there is not a hidden outweighing *good* but a hidden *linkage* between a familiar good and many instances of suffering.

31. The importance of the qualifier "group" will become apparent later in the chapter.

32. Another bit of repetition: criticisms of one PHOG often apply to a second PHOG, so I restate them each time. I do this so that the reader can judge the different PHOGs independently of one another.

33. Recall the two notions of "gratuitous suffering" noted in chapter 2. On mine, all it takes for the badness of suffering S to be outweighed is for S to be appropriately coupled with some good G whose goodness outweighs the badness of S (e.g., S led to G). On the alternative notion of gratuitous suffering, for suffering S to be outweighed it has to meet my condition plus another: although it seems as though God could have created a universe without suffering S but with good G, the only ways he could have done so would have involved the universe containing some alternative bad thing that's at least as bad as S (or it would have lost a really good thing other than G). When evaluating the PHOG Approach, the two different notions force different evaluations. I treat just the first notion here, although much of what I say holds for the alternative notion.

34. I am not taking "soul" to mean the same as anything like "the non-physical part of a person that is somehow linked with the brain" (in other parts of philosophy it has that meaning). I want to interpret it so that a *physicalist* about humans and animals—that is, someone who thinks that humans and animals are entirely physical beings—can accept the existence of souls by saying that they are physical. If "soul" is taken to indicate something non-physical, then of course the Existence Requirement is very much in doubt, as there is little evidence that we have non-physical souls.

35. These points hold for related "punishment" ideas. For instance, one might think that all those many trillions of cases of horrific suffering are coupled with, and are thus justified by, the fact we are all guilty of not loving God, and God is now showing us what it's like to exist without communion with him. Same three problems arise.

36. It sounds odd to say God ever "intervenes" in nature because, after all, he is supposed to be the creator of nature. How can he intervene in his own creation? Usually one "intervenes" in something that is at least partially initially independent of one; but the whole universe is God's creation, even every second, according to some versions of theism anyway. So, in the above sentences "intervene" may have to be used in a special sense. In the official statement of the idea, with (a) and (b) above in the text, I have intentionally omitted the use of "intervene" entirely in order to sidestep the issue.

37. I won't broach the issue of whether Jesus really was the "Son of God" (nor will I address the issue of what that phrase is supposed to mean).

38. There are many other alleged PHOGs that won't do the trick—at least, I know of no reason to think they are promising. For instance, one might say that God himself is the PHOG that justifies all suffering, as he is appropriately linked to absolutely everything (since he's the creator of the universe) and he's perfectly and infinitely good (so his goodness outweighs any suffering). But this proposal is a failure; I'll give just three reasons why. First, it's a retreat to the Confident Approach, as it starts by assuming the 4-Part God exists; so it inherits the limitations of that idea. Second, it does nothing to show that the linkage is of the right type (and I doubt that it is the right type, although I won't argue the point here). Third and most important, if the idea were right then God could make a universe filled with virtually nothing but *unending horrific suffering for all creatures* and yet there would be no gratuitous suffering since he is an infinitely good thing appropriately linked to all that suffering. This strikes me as nuts, the kind of proposal that someone can take seriously only if she is deranged, is driven to irrationality via intellectual desperation, or has put almost no thought into the proposal.

39. Actually, the temporal order is not important. I keep it merely because it makes things simple and won't cause trouble with any subsequent arguments.

40. At the beginning of this chapter I mentioned that the Skeptical Approach combined elements of the PHOG and Confident Approaches. As promised: (C) comes from the former and (D) comes from the latter.

41. More precisely, the Skeptical Approach is saying this: there are some goods that (a) are unknown *or known* to us, (b) are unknowingly linked with many trillions of cases of suffering, and (c) are so wonderful that they outweigh the badness of the instances of horrific suffering they are linked with. That is, the goods that are doing the bulk of outweighing may well be familiar to us but what we've missed is that they are indirectly linked with our suffering: the goods aren't profoundly hidden but the links are. We saw this possibility in the PHOG Approach chapter with the idea that the laws of nature provide hidden links between our suffering and familiar goods like knowledge, happiness, etc.

42. Of course, a theist could reject more than one part of the 4-Part conception. Since I will be examining the rejection of each part in turn, my discussion will apply to those theists as well.

43. Over the centuries—and even today—some theists have characterized God in ways that might strike you as positively ridiculous, even insane. I won't be commenting on those approaches because they usually have problems not different from the ones I go over in this chapter.

44. You could say that God has all possible knowledge *for a non-physical being*, such knowledge is puny compared to ours, and this explains why he allows so much gratuitous suffering. Yes, you could say that, but how would that help at all with the Problem of Gratuitous Suffering?

45. Actually, the idea is usually that *many* of the qualities we attribute to God are held only analogically; but there are *central* qualities that he has literally.

46. Many people think that there is an enormous amount of theism-neutral evidence that proves that the Bible is flawless. I'm sorry to say that these people are usually brainwashed. They will not read this far into this book.

47. Acknowledgements on parts of rough drafts: Kyle Walton, Sean Landis, Stephen Grimm, Brian Davies, Mark Nelson, John Davenport, Margaret Frances, Allan Hazlett, Aaron Hanson, Keith Elmore, Richard Atkins, and Shannon O'Neill. Special thanks to Margaret Frances for editing the entire work.

INDEX